SCHAUM'S OUTLINE OF

THEORY AND PROBLEMS

of

DATA PROCESSING

•

by

MARTIN M. LIPSCHUTZ, Ph.D.

Professor of Mathematics
Hahnemann Medical College

and

SEYMOUR LIPSCHUTZ, Ph.D.

Professor of Mathematics
Temple University

SCHAUM'S OUTLINE SERIES

McGRAW-HILL BOOK COMPANY

New York   St. Louis   San Francisco   Auckland   Bogotá   Guatemala   Hamburg   Johannesburg
Lisbon   London   Madrid   Mexico   Montreal   New Delhi   Panama   Paris
San Juan   São Paulo   Singapore   Sydney   Tokyo   Toronto

To our children:
Saul and Karen
and
Marc, Erik, and Audrey

MARTIN LIPSCHUTZ is currently a professor of mathematics and director of a computer center at Hahnemann Medical College. He has previously taught at Fairleigh Dickinson University and at the University of Bridgeport, and was a Fulbright professor in Taiwan. He received his doctorate from the Courant Institute of Mathematical Sciences of New York University. Among other books, he has written *Schaum's Outline of Differential Geometry*.

SEYMOUR LIPSCHUTZ, who is presently on the mathematics faculty of Temple University, formerly taught at the Polytechnic Institute of Brooklyn and was a visiting professor in the Computer Science Department of Brooklyn College. He received his Ph.D. in 1960 at the Courant Institute of Mathematical Sciences of New York University. His other books in the Schaum's Outline Series include *Fortran* (with Arthur Poe), *Discrete Mathematics*, and *Probability*.

Schaum's Outline of Theory and Problems of
DATA PROCESSING

2 3 4 5 6 7 8 9 10 11 12 13 14 15 16 17 18 19 20 SH SH 8 6 5 4 3 2 1

Sponsoring Editor, David Beckwith
Production Manager, Nick Monti

Library of Congress Cataloging in Publication Data

Lipschutz, Martin.
  Schaum's outline of theory and problems of data processing.

  (Schaum's outline series)
  Includes index.
  1. Electronic data processing. 2. Electronic data
processing—Problems, exercises, etc. I. Lipschutz,
Seymour, joint author. II. Title. III. Title: Theory
and problems of data processing.
QA76.L53   001.64   80-15610
ISBN 0-07-037983-1

Preface

Data processing and data processing devices have been around almost since the beginnings of civilization. However, it was only with the introduction of the electronic computer in the latter half of the twentieth century that data processing emerged as a well-defined and important discipline. Today data processing courses are offered in almost all colleges and universities, in business and vocational schools, and even in some high schools.

This book presents the basic concepts of data processing, in particular, of electronic data processing. As a glance at the Table of Contents will show, all important topics in the subject are covered, and there are many accompanying examples and illustrations to clarify the material. Each chapter is followed by numerous solved problems, wherein the basic ideas are applied, and a set of review questions to help the reader test his or her understanding of the subject matter. The book is suitable as the text for a formal course in data processing or for an introduction to computer science, as a supplement to existing texts in these areas, or as a guide to home study. We note that no knowledge of mathematics beyond arithmetic, or of any business methods, is presupposed.

We wish to thank Lucia Carballo for her help in proofreading, and we also want to express our gratitude to the staff of the McGraw-Hill Schaum's Outline Series division, particularly David Beckwith, for their invaluable aid and cooperation.

MARTIN LIPSCHUTZ
SEYMOUR LIPSCHUTZ

Contents

CONTENTS

Chapter 1

Introduction

1.1 TWO CATEGORIES OF DATA PROCESSING

Modern data processing with machines falls into two broad categories, *punched-card data processing* and *electronic data processing.* Punched-card data processing systems consist of various electromechanical devices, such as sorters, collators, reproducers, calculators, and tabulators, which operate on punched cards. Electronic data processing systems consist of various input and output devices connected to an electronic computer. The latter systems can process very large amounts of data in very little time.

One major difference between the two categories is that the punched-card systems usually require manual intervention between the different data processing operations, whereas the electronic processing systems perform the different operations automatically.

Although the types of machines in both categories may vary from one institution to another, there are some general concepts in data processing which apply in all cases. In this chapter we introduce these basic concepts.

1.2 DATA PROCESSING DEFINED

Data are any collection of facts. Thus, sales reports, inventory figures, test scores, customers' names and addresses, and weather reports are all examples of data. Even photographs, drawings, and maps are considered data. Note that data may be numerical, e.g. inventory figures and test scores, or they may be nonnumerical, e.g. customers' names and addresses, drawings.

Data processing is the manipulation of data into a more useful form. Data processing includes not only numerical calculations but also operations such as the classification of data and the transmission of data from one place to another. In general, we assume that these operations are performed by some type of machine or computer, although some of them could also be carried out manually.

Some texts distinguish between the terms "data" and "information," defining information as processed data. We will use the two words interchangeably.

1.3 DATA PROCESSING CYCLE

Data processing consists of three basic steps, *input*, *processing*, and *output*. These three steps, related as in Fig. 1-1, constitute the *data processing cycle.*

Input. In this step the initial data, or *input data*, are prepared in some convenient form for processing. The form will depend on the processing machine. For example, when electromechanical devices are used, the input data are punched on cards; but if electronic computers are used, the input data could be recorded on any one of several types of input medium, such as cards, tapes, and so on. The various input media are discussed in detail in Chapter 3.

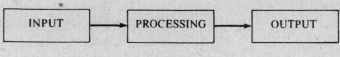

Fig. 1-1

1

Processing.   In this step the input data are changed, and usually combined with other information, to produce data in a more useful form.   Thus, paychecks may be calculated from the time cards, or a summary of sales for the month may be calculated from the sales orders.   The processing step usually involves a sequence of certain basic processing operations, which we discuss in more detail in Section 1.5.

Output.   Here the results of the preceding processing step are collected.   The particular form of the output data depends on the use of the data.   For example, output data may be paychecks for employees, a printed summary of monthly sales for management, or simply data to be stored for further processing at a later date.   The various output media are treated in Chapter 3.

EXAMPLE 1.1   During the semester a professor gives three tests and a final exam.   At the end of the semester the grades must be processed and a final grade sheet for the class submitted to the department.   The input data are the students' names and their four scores.   This input is usually recorded in the professor's roll book, with the names in alphabetical order.   The professor processes the input data by averaging the three tests and then counting the final exam as 50% of the final grade (see Problem 1.10).   A letter grade is then assigned to each student.   The output data will consist of the students' names and their letter grades, with the names in alphabetical order on the final grade sheet.

1.4   EXPANDED DATA PROCESSING CYCLE

Frequently, three more steps are added to the basic data processing cycle of Fig. 1-1 to obtain the expanded data processing cycle shown in Fig. 1-2.   We discuss the additional steps.

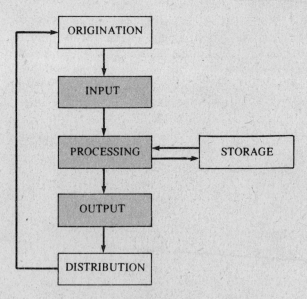

Fig. 1-2

Origination.   This step refers to the process of collecting the original data.   An original recording of the data is called a *source document.*   For example, the source documents of Example 1.1 are the graded test papers of the students.   Note that if there were any questions concerning a student's final letter grade, one could go back to the source documents, the student's test papers, to see if any error had been made during the processing step.

Distribution.   This step refers to the distribution of the output data.   Recordings of the output data are often called *report documents*.   For example, the report document of Example 1.1 is the class grade sheet which is forwarded to the registrar.   The arrow in Fig. 1-2 which goes from the Distribution box back to the Origination box indicates that report documents may become the source documents for further data processing.

Storage.   This step is crucial in many data processing procedures.   Data processing results are frequently placed in storage to be used as input data for further processing at a later date. The two arrows between the Processing box and the Storage box in Fig. 1-2 indicate the interaction of these two steps.   A unified set of data in storage is called a *file*.   Usually a file consists of a collection of records, where each record contains similar *data items*. In turn, a collection of related files is called a *data base*.

EXAMPLE 1.2   Most institutions keep a master payroll file containing employees' payroll records.   The data items on a record might include the employee's name, social security number, pay rate, earnings to date, and deductions to date.   The file is used together with the employees' time cards to process the weekly payroll checks (see Problem 1.11).   Figure 1-3 shows the processing cycle.

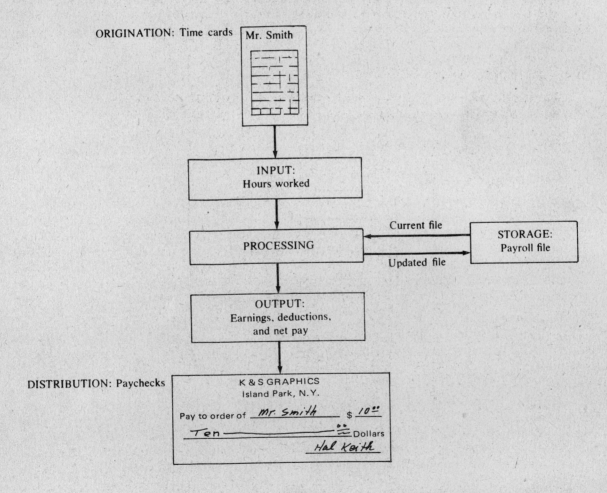

Fig. 1-3

The source documents are the time cards.   The input data consist of the number of hours worked, as shown on the time cards, together with the master payroll file.   The output, determined during the processing cycle, consists of the statement of earnings, deductions, and net pay, together with an updated payroll file. The report documents are the employees' paychecks, which are usually attached to individual updated statements of earnings and deductions.

1.5 DATA PROCESSING OPERATIONS

A data processing procedure normally consists of a number of basic processing operations performed in some order (not necessarily the order of their description below).

Recording. Recording refers to the transfer of data onto some form or document. It occurs not only during the origination step (on the source documents) and during the distribution step (on the report documents) but throughout the processing cycle.

EXAMPLE 1.3 A professor records the scores of his students in his roll book. At the end of the semester he calculates the final grades and records them in his roll book. He receives the grade sheet from the registrar and records the final grades on it. The registrar then records the grades on the students' master file. Each student's grades in the master file are recorded on a transcript which is then sent to the student.

Duplicating. This operation consists in reproducing the data onto many forms or documents. Duplicating may be done while the data are being recorded manually, or it may be done afterwards, by some machine. For example, one may record a report by typing it, at the same time duplicating it using carbon paper. On the other hand, one may record a sales transaction by punching the data onto a card, and may then duplicate the card using a duplicating machine.

Verifying. Since recording is usually a manual operation, it is important that recorded data be carefully checked for any errors. This operation is called *verifying*. For example, punched cards and typed reports are reread for correctness.

Classifying. This operation separates data into various categories. Classifying can usually be done in more than one way. For example, a set of student questionnaires may be classified according to the student's sex, or according to the student's year at school.

Sorting. Arranging data in a specific order is called *sorting*. This operation is familiar in everyday life. The names in a telephone book are sorted into alphabetical order, employee records may be sorted according to employee ID number. In these cases, unclassified data are sorted. Sorting may also take place after classifying. For example, a set of student questionnaires may first be classified according to student's year at school; then each classification may be sorted alphabetically according to student's (last) name. Records can often be sorted in more than one way (see Problem 1.19). The data item which determines the sorting is called the *key*.

EXAMPLE 1.4 Suppose that a file of employee records contains the data items: name, social security number, ID number, and work location. If the file is to be sorted according to the alphabetical order of the names, then the name field is the key; but if the file is to be sorted according to social security number, then the social security number is the key.

Merging. This operation takes two or more sets of data, all sets having been sorted by the same key, and puts them together to form a single sorted set of data. Figure 1-4 indicates the main algorithm (rule) for merging. Specifically, it shows two numerically sorted decks of cards being merged by filing at each step the lower of the two first cards into the combined deck. (If the two cards bear the same number, a subrule decides which card is filed.) When one deck is empty, the cards in the other deck are put at the end of the combined deck.

Calculating, or performing numerical calculations on the (numerical) data.

Table look-up, searching, retrieving. This operation refers to finding a specific data item in a sorted collection of data.

EXAMPLE 1.5 Figure 1-5 shows how certain calculations are performed in a customer's invoice. The number

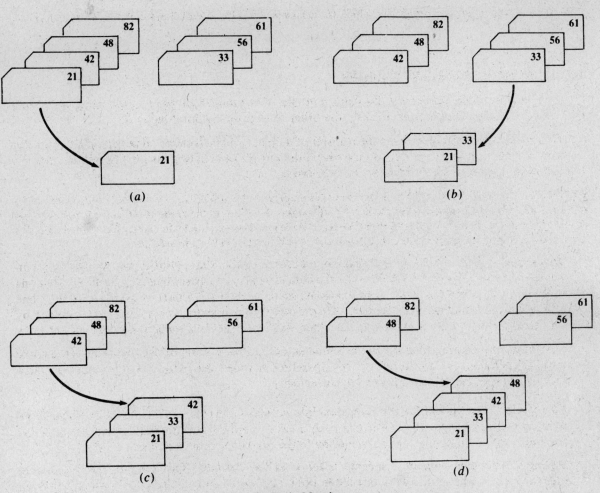

Fig. 1-4. Merging

of units and the unit price are multiplied to obtain the item amount.   The item amounts are then added to obtain the invoice subtotal.   The discount rate on $486 is found by searching in Table 1-1.   The computation is then completed as in Problem 1.12.

Table 1-1

Sales Amount	Discount
$50.00 or less	0%
$50.01 to $100.00	5%
$100.01 to $200.00	10%
$200.01 to $500.00	15%
More than $500.00	20%

Summarizing and report writing.   In this operation a collection of data is condensed and certain conclusions from the data are represented in simple, clear form.   For example, a salesman may write a monthly report summarizing the data on all his invoices.   The report may contain the total sales, distribution according to area, and recommendations for advertising of certain items.

SMITH'S CLOTHING STORE			
Sold to: a. Jones 14 Broadway Patterson, N.J.			Date: 9/8/x5
Number	Item	Unit Price	Amount
3	Coats	78 —	234 —
5	pants	22 —	110 —
8	shirts	11 —	88 —
3	sweaters	18 —	54 —
		Subtotal	486 —
		Discount 15%	72 90
		Total	413 10

Fig. 1.5

Solved Problems

DATA PROCESSING CONCEPTS

1.1   Identify one basic difference between punched-card data processing and electronic data processing.

Punched-card data processing commonly involves manual operations between the various machine operations, whereas in electronic data processing all operations are performed automatically.

1.2   Give examples of a type of data processing not mentioned in Problem 1.1.

There can also be manual data processing.   For example, a desk calculator may be used for arithmetic calculations; a credit-card machine may be used for recording a sale; names may be alphabetized by inspection.

1.3   Give examples of data processing which do not involve any numerical calculations.

There are usually no numerical calculations when the input data are names of people or products. For example, a hospital keeps an alphabetized list of its patients; an airline keeps a list of reservations for each flight; a professor keeps an alphabetized list of students in each of her classes.

1.4   Describe the relationship, if any, between records, files, data items, and data bases.

Data items are individual units of information, e.g. name, address, number of items in inventory, weekly sales total, grade in a course. A record normally consists of a set of related data items, e.g. an employee record would consist of various data items concerning a given employee. A file is a unified set of data which is usually in the form of a collection of records. (Not all files are subdivided into records, e.g. the government may keep a file consisting of all information on a particular airplane disaster. Such a file is, in effect, a single record.) A data base is a structured set of files.

DATA PROCESSING CYCLE

1.5   The basic data processing cycle contains three steps: (*a*) input, (*b*) processing, (*c*) output. Briefly describe each step and tell how the three steps are related.

(*a*)   The data are prepared for processing.

(*b*)   The data are changed into a more useful form.

(*c*)   The processed data are exhibited in some form.

As illustrated in Fig. 1-1, the flow of data is from Input to Processing to Output.

1.6   Which of the following are examples of the processing step: (*a*) calculating paychecks from time cards, (*b*) printing a summary of monthly sales, (*c*) punching data on cards, (*d*) alphabetizing a list of names?

Only (*a*) and (*d*) are processing steps. Clearly, (*b*) is an output step. On the other hand, (*c*) may be an input step (if the data are original), or it may be an output step (if the data have been processed).

1.7   The expanded data processing cycle contains three additional steps: (*a*) origination, (*b*) distribution, (*c*) storage. Briefly describe each step, and tell how they are related to the three basic steps and to one another.

(*a*)   Original data are recorded.

(*b*)   Output data are distributed to interested parties.

(*c*)   Data are filed away to be used at a later date, or previous data are retrieved for current processing.

Data flow from Origination to Input, and from Output to Distribution; and there is a two-way flow of data between Storage and Processing. In addition, data from Distribution may go back to Origination for further processing. These relationships are pictured in Fig. 1-2.

1.8   Define source documents and report documents, and give the relationship, if any, between them.

The documents on which original data are recorded are called source documents, and the documents on which final results are distributed are called report documents. Sometimes report documents become source documents for further data processing.

1.9   State the step of the expanded data processing cycle to which each of the following activities corresponds: (*a*) subtracting total deductions from gross earnings, (*b*) recording the data on a sales invoice into a journal, (*c*) writing a receipt for merchandise just sold to a customer,   (*d*) collecting sales invoices for a billing procedure,   (*e*) updating employees' earnings records,   (*f*) mailing a monthly bill to a customer.

(*a*) processing,   (*b*) storage,   (*c*) origination,   (*d*) input,   (*e*) storage,   (*f*) distribution.

1.10   Students Peter, Paul, and Mary received the following scores in three tests and the final exam:

Name	Test 1	Test 2	Test 3	Final Exam
(*a*) Peter	88	74	92	89
(*b*) Paul	73	68	84	81
(*c*) Mary	94	91	97	92

The professor averages the three test scores, and counts the final exam as 50% of the final grade.   Find the final grade for each student.

(*a*)   Add the three test scores and divide by three:

$$
\begin{array}{r}
88 \\
74 \\
\underline{92} \\
3)\overline{254} \\
85 \quad \text{(rounded to the nearest point)}
\end{array}
$$

Since the final exam and the average of the tests each count 50%, average those two numbers:

$$
\begin{array}{r}
85 \\
\underline{89} \\
2)\overline{174} \\
87
\end{array}
$$

Thus 87 is the final grade.

(*b*)

$$
\begin{array}{r}
73 \\
68 \\
\underline{84} \\
3)\overline{225} \\
75 \\
\underline{81} \\
2)\overline{156} \\
\text{Final Grade} \quad 78
\end{array}
$$

(*c*)

$$
\begin{array}{r}
94 \\
94 \\
\underline{97} \\
3)\overline{282} \\
94 \\
\underline{92} \\
2)\overline{186} \\
\text{Final Grade} \quad 93
\end{array}
$$

1.11   Figure 1-6 shows a weekly time card of employee Mr. Brown.   If there is a half hour for lunch, and if Mr. Brown's rate of pay is $5.80 per hour, find the gross pay for Mr. Brown.

Name: Mr. John Brown		
Day	In	Out
Monday	8:00 AM	4:30 PM
Tuesday	9:15 AM	4:30 PM
Wednesday	8:00 AM	4:00 PM
Thursday	8:15 AM	3:00 PM
Friday	8:00 AM	4:00 PM

Fig. 1-6

Calculate the number of hours worked each day:

Mon. 8,   Tue. $6\frac{3}{4}$,   Wed. $7\frac{1}{2}$,   Thur. $6\frac{1}{4}$,   Fri. $7\frac{1}{2}$

The sum is 36 hours for the week.   Multiplying by 5.80, we obtain:

$$
\begin{array}{r}
5.80 \\
36 \\
\hline
3480 \\
1740 \\
\hline
208.80
\end{array}
$$

Thus the gross pay is $208.80 for the week.

1.12   Using Table 1-1, find the net amount if the gross sales are: (*a*) $85.00,   (*b*) 620.00,   (*c*) $146.00.

First find the discount rate in the table.   Then multiply to obtain the amount to discount. Finally subtract to find the net amount.

(*a*)   The discount rate is 5%.

Multiply: 85.00   Subtract: $85.00
                   0.05   4.25
             ―――――   ――――――
             4.2500   NET $80.75

(*b*)   The discount rate is 20%.

Multiply: 620.00   Subtract: 620.00
                    0.20   124.00
             ――――――   ――――――
             124.0000   NET $496.00

(*c*)   The discount rate is 10%.

Multiply: 146.00   Subtract: 146.00
                    0.10   14.60
             ――――――   ――――――
             14.6000   NET $131.40

DATA PROCESSING OPERATIONS

1.13   Give a brief description of   (*a*) recording,   (*b*) verifying,   (*c*) duplicating.   What is the relationship, if any, between these data processing operations?

(*a*)   Transferring data onto a standardized form for processing.

(*b*)   Checking recorded data for error.

(*c*)   Reproducing recorded data onto many forms.

The operations normally will be performed in the given order.   First, data are recorded; next, the recording is verified; and then, if there are no errors, the data would be reproduced, if necessary.

1.14   Give a brief description of   (*a*) sorting   and   (*b*) merging,   and describe the relationship, if any, between these two operations.

(*a*)   Arranging data in some order.

(*b*)   Combining two or more sorted sets of data into one sorted set of data.

Clearly, merging must come after sorting, since merging involves sorted sets of data.

1.15   Give a brief description of   (*a*) retrieving,   (*b*) calculating,   (*c*) summarizing.   Is there a necessary order of performance of these three operations?

(*a*) Finding a particular item of data in a collection of data.

(*b*) Computing numerical results.

(*c*) Condensing output data to exhibit specific information.

   Data could be retrieved from storage before, during, or even after the performance of calculations; so there is no order relationship between these two operations. However, summarizing will normally come after retrieving and calculating.

1.16 Give a brief description and an example of the data processing operation of classifying.

   Classifying separates data into various categories. For example, students may be classified as male or female, or may be grouped by age. Observe that the categories in question need not have any order.

1.17 Below is a sequence of four steps in the billing procedure of a small department store. State two or more basic data processing operations which are performed in each step. (*a*) The sales clerk fills out the customer's sales invoice at the time of purchase. He gives one copy to the customer and keeps a copy for bookkeeping. (*b*) The next morning the invoices are collected, alphabetized, and recorded in a ledger arranged by customer's name. (*c*) At the end of the month, using the ledger, a clerk calculates and records the debit balance for each customer. (*d*) Wherever there is a nonzero balance he also prepares a bill, one copy of which is mailed to the customer and the other is kept on file for future reference.

(*a*) Data are recorded and duplicated at the same time.

(*b*) The data on the invoices are sorted alphabetically and then recorded.

(*c*) Data are calculated and then recorded.

(*d*) Customers are classified according to whether they have a zero or a nonzero balance. The unpaid balance is recorded and duplicated.

1.18 Suppose that a file of employee records contains the following data items: (*a*) name, (*b*) social security number, (*c*) marital status, (*d*) number of dependents, (*e*) annual salary. How might the file be sorted? classified?

   The file could be sorted according to either the employee's name or social security number, since either item would uniquely determine a particular employee. On the other hand, the file could be classified according to (*c*), (*d*), or (*e*). If most employees had different salaries, then classifying the file according to annual salary would not be very useful; instead, the file might be classified into ranges of annual salary.

1.19 Table 1-2 gives the names of four employees, their social security numbers, and their employee ID numbers. Sort the names (*a*) alphabetically, (*b*) numerically according to social security number, (*c*) numerically according to employee ID number.

Table 1-2

Name	Social Security Number	ID Number
Jones, A.	086-24-1111	235
Brown, D.	213-19-7777	187
Young, R.	176-18-5555	211
Grant, C.	101-29-6666	125

The key to each sorting is different.   The order of the names after the sorting follows:

(a)	(b)		(c)	
Brown, D.	Jones, A.:	086-24-1111	Grant, C.:	125
Grant, C.	Grant, C.:	101-29-6666	Brown, D.:	187
Jones, A.	Young, R.:	176-18-5555	Young, R.:	211
Young, R.	Brown, D.:	213-19-7777	Jones, A.:	235

Review Questions

DATA PROCESSING CONCEPTS

1.20   Data processing with machines falls into two broad categories.   What are these categories?

1.21   Which of the two categories of data processing can process a greater amount of data in a given time?

1.22   Which of the following are examples of nonnumerical data: (a) test scores,   (b) customers' names,   (c) bank balances,   (d) photographs?

1.23   Which of the following are examples of data processing: (a) numerical calculations,   (b) classification of data,   (c) transmission of data from one place to another?

1.24   There are general concepts in data processing which apply regardless of the type of data and processing device.   True or false?

1.25   Complete the following statements.
   (a)   A set of related data items is called a _____.
   (b)   A collection of files is called a _____.
   (c)   A set of similar records is called a _____.

DATA PROCESSING CYCLES

1.26   Name the three basic steps in the data processing cycle.

1.27   Name the three additional steps in the expanded data processing cycle.

1.28   Which boxes in the flow diagram of the expanded data processing cycle are connected by a double arrow, i.e. data flow in both directions?

1.29   What is the name given to the documents on which the original data are recorded?

1.30   What is the name given to the documents on which final results are distributed?

1.31   Students Marc, Erik, and Audrey receive the following scores in three tests and the final exam:

Name	Test 1	Test 2	Test 3	Final Exam
Marc	92	88	96	90
Erik	77	66	88	92
Audrey	83	75	92	88

Find the final grade for each student if the professor (a) averages the three test scores, and counts the final exam as 50% of the final grade; (b) averages the three test scores, and counts the final exam as 40% of the final grade; (c) drops the lowest test score, averages the other two test scores, and counts the final exam as 50% of the final grade.

1.32 Figure 1-7 shows weekly time cards for employees Saul and Karen. There is a half hour for lunch. Find the gross pay for each employee if the rate of pay is (a) $5.00 per hour; (b) $5.00 per hour, with time and a half for more than 40 hours in the week; (c) $5.00 per hour, with time and a half for more than 8 hours in any day.

Name: Saul		
Day	In	Out
Monday	8:00 AM	4:30 PM
Tuesday	8:15 AM	4:00 PM
Wednesday	8:00 AM	5:45 PM
Thursday	9:30 AM	4:00 PM
Friday	8:00 AM	4:30 PM

Name: Karen		
Day	In	Out
Monday	8:00 AM	5:00 PM
Tuesday	8:00 AM	4:30 PM
Wednesday	8:30 AM	5:45 PM
Thursday	8:00 AM	5:30 PM
Friday	9:00 AM	4:30 PM

Fig. 1-7

1.33 Which of the following are examples of source documents: (a) a time card, (b) the cost of a tube of toothpaste, (c) the amount of sales tax, (d) a waitress's check?

1.34 Which of the following are examples of report documents: (a) a customer's bill, (b) a monthly sales summary, (c) the ZIP code of Woodridge, N.Y., (d) the retail cost of a certain shirt?

1.35 Using Table 1-1, find the net amount if the gross sales are (a) $88.00, (b) $44.00, (c) $555.00, (d) $111.00, (e) $333.00.

DATA PROCESSING OPERATIONS

1.36 Match each of the data processing operations listed on the left with the phrase on the right which best describes it.

(1) Recording.   (a) Checking data for errors.
(2) Duplicating.   (b) Transferring data onto a standardized form.
(3) Verifying.   (c) Separating data into various categories.
(4) Classifying.   (d) Arranging data in a specific order.
(5) Sorting.   (e) Arranging two sorted sets of data into one sorted set of data.
(6) Merging.   (f) Reproducing data onto many forms.

(7) Calculating.   (g) Condensing output data to exhibit specific information.

(8) Retrieving.   (h) Computing numerical results.

(9) Summarizing.   (i) Finding a particular item of data in a collection of data.

1.37 Name the basic data processing operation which best describes each of the following: (a) separating a set of student questionnaires according to student's sex, (b) computing the amount of tax on a customer's invoice, (c) filling out a sales order, (d) alphabetizing a set of test papers, (e) preparing a list of recently hired employees for management, (f) putting together two sorted sets of invoices to form one sorted set of invoices.

1.38 What is the term used to describe the data item with respect to which a set of records is sorted?

1.39 Below is a list of ten students, their student ID numbers, and each student's letter grade in a computer course. (a) Sort the students alphabetically by name. (b) Sort the students numerically by ID number. (c) Classify the students according to sex. (d) Classify the students according to grade.

Name	Mary	Tom	Dick	Harry	John	Karen	Susan	Marc	Joyce	Bob
ID	333	321	576	158	244	678	123	502	439	283
Grade	C	A	B	F	C	A	B	D	B	C

1.40 Very often when a large number of test papers need to be alphabetized, a teacher will (a) separate the papers into three batches, depending upon whether the first letter of the student's name falls into the group A to F, G to N, or O to Z; (b) alphabetize each batch separately; (c) put the three batches together, one following the other.   State the basic data processing operation that is performed in each of the three steps.

Chapter 2

Developments in Data Processing

2.1 INTRODUCTION

From antiquity, man has invented devices to assist him in calculating and processing data. There are three types. A *manual-mechanical* device is a simple mechanism powered by hand. The abacus and slide rule are examples of this type. An *electromechanical* device is usually powered by an electric motor and uses switches and relays of the type found in household appliances. The desk calculator and punched-card data processing equipment are examples of this type. An *electronic* device, such as a modern computer, has as its principal components transistors, printed circuits, and the like.

In this chapter we outline the historical evolution of these machines, and conclude with a short discussion of careers in data processing.

2.2 THE DARK AGES (5000 B.C.–1890 A.D.)

The earliest data processing equipment were all manual-mechanical devices. We refer to the era when these machines were used exclusively as the Dark Ages of data processing.

Abacus (c. 5000 B.C.)

Probably developed in China, the abacus is a frame with beads strung on wires or rods (Fig. 2-1). Arithmetic calculations are performed by manipulating the beads. The abacus is still widely used in the Orient. An adept abacus operator can calculate faster than a clerk using a desk calculator.

Napier's Bones (1617)

John Napier, a Scottish mathematician, described this device in the year of his death. His "bones" are a set of eleven rods with numbers marked on them in such a way that by simply placing the rods side by side products and quotients of large numbers can be obtained. Napier is best known for the invention of logarithms, which in turn led to the slide rule.

Fig. 2-1

14

Oughtred's Slide Rule (c. 1632)

Although the slide rule appeared in various forms in Europe during the seventeenth century, its invention (and the invention of the sign × for multiplication) is attributed to the English mathematician William Oughtred. Basically a slide rule consists of two movable rulers placed side by side. Each ruler is marked off in such a way that the actual distances from the beginning of the ruler are proportional to the logarithms of the numbers printed on the ruler. By sliding the rulers one can quickly multiply and divide.

Pascal's Calculator (1642)

At age 19, Blaise Pascal, the great French mathematician, invented what may be considered the first adding machine. The device registered numbers by rotating a cogwheel gear by one to ten steps, with a carryover rachet to operate the next-higher-digit wheel when the given cogwheel exceeded ten units (see Fig. 2-2). The automobile odometer is an example of a device that still uses a series of cogwheels to calculate data. Pascal's machine was improved by the philosopher and mathematician Leibniz, whose "Wheel" (1673) could also perform multiplication and division.

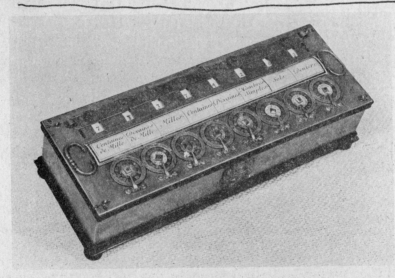

Fig. 2-2

Jacquard's Loom (1801)

Joseph Marie Jacquard, a French weaver, invented the first punched-card machine. The pattern woven by the loom was determined by the placement of holes in a control card: only those threads whose guiding hook encountered a hole in the card could enter the pattern.

Babbage's Difference Engine (1823)

Only part of this machine was ever constructed (see Fig. 2-3). It is based on the principle that, for certain formulas, the difference between certain values is constant. A machine of this type was later adopted by insurance companies for computing life tables.

EXAMPLE 2.1 We illustrate the principle behind the difference engine using the formula $y = x^2$. The first two columns of Table 2-1 give values for x and x^2. The third column gives the *first difference*, denoted by Δ, of consecutive values of x^2. The fourth column gives differences of consecutive numbers in the Δ-column; it is called the *second difference* of x^2, and is denoted by Δ^2. Observe that all second differences have the same value, 2. It follows that the square of any number can be calculated by repeated addition of 2's to the starting values, 1 and 3. Thus,

$$4^2 = 2 + 5 + 9 = 2 + (2 + 3) + (\overline{2 + 3} + 3 + 1)$$

Fig. 2-3

Table 2-1

x	x^2	Δ	Δ^2
1	1		
2	4	3	
3	9	5	2
4	16	7	2
5	25	9	2
6	36	11	2

Babbage's Analytical Engine

Charles Babbage followed the difference engine with a much deeper and more general conception (c. 1833). This machine, never realized owing to the limited technology of the time, would have contained many features of present-day computers, including punched-card input, storage unit, arithmetic unit, printing unit, and control by a sequential program.

2.3 THE MIDDLE AGES (1890–1944)

The Middle Ages of data processing are said to have begun when Dr. Herman Hollerith, a statistician with the U.S. Bureau of the Census, completed a set of machines to help process the results of the 1890 census. Using 3 by 5 inch punched cards to record the data, he constructed a box to sort the data and a manually fed, electromagnetic counting machine to tabulate the data. The 1890 census was processed in one-fourth the time needed for the 1880 census. Hollerith left the Census Bureau to build and sell his own tabulating machines. His company was the forerunner of IBM Corporation. His successor at the Census Bureau, Dr. James Powers, also left to form his own company, which ultimately became Sperry Rand Corporation.

In 1908, Powers patented a 20-column punching machine. In the same year Hollerith developed a vertical sorting machine which processed almost 200 cards per minute. In 1911, Hollerith developed a horizontal sorter whose rate was almost 275 cards per minute.

The speed and capabilities of punched-card machines continued to improve. Verifiers were invented to check that the right data were entered into the cards. Collators were invented to merge several sorted decks of cards into a single sorted deck. Electromechanical accounting machines were developed which could read cards containing both alphabetical and numerical data, perform simple arithmetic operations, and print the results.

2.4 THE MODERN AGE (SINCE 1944)

Mark I (1944)

Major innovation. The first computer capable of automatically performing a long sequence of arithmetical and logical operations.

The brainchild of Howard G. Aiken, a professor of applied mathematics at Harvard University, the Mark I was built by IBM Corporation. It was an electromechanical (relay) device, like the calculators which preceded it; subsequent computers were all electronic.

First-Generation Computers (1946–1959)

Major innovations. Vacuum tubes in place of relays; stored programs.

The first large-scale vacuum-tube computer, the ENIAC (Electronic Numerical Integrator and Calculator), was completed in 1946 by John Mauchly and Presper Eckert at the Moore School of Electrical Engineering at the University of Pennsylvania. It could accomplish in one day what the previous computers took 30 days to perform. In 1947 the ENIAC was moved to the Aberdeen Proving Grounds, a government research center, where it continued to operate until 1955.

Table 2-2

Manufacturer	Model
Moore School of Electrical Engineering	ENIAC; EDVAC
Cambridge University	EDSAC
Univac	UNIVAC I; UNIVAC II
Burroughs	E101; Burroughs 2202
Honeywell	Datamatic 1000
IBM	Mark II; Mark III; 604 Electronic Calculating Punch; IBM 650; 702; 704; 705; 709
National Cash Register	CRC; 102A; 102D
RCA	BIZMAC I; BIZMAC II

In the mid-1940s, the famous mathematician John von Neumann, together with H. H. Goldstine and A. W. Burks, developed the concept of the *stored* program: the list of instructions (program) which controls the operation of the computer, coded in the same way as the input data, is initially stored in the computer along with the data, and then this program is executed automatically. The first computer to use the stored program was the EDSAC (Electronic Delayed Storage Automatic Computer), completed in 1949 at Cambridge University in England. The first American computer to have the stored-program feature was the EDVAC (Electronic Discrete Variable Automatic Computer), which was also built at the Moore School; it was completed in 1952. In the EDVAC, the computer program was fed into the data storage unit by means of a punched paper tape.

In 1946, Eckert and Mauchly formed their own company, which in 1949 was incorporated as the Univac division of Remington Rand, Inc. In 1951, the UNIVAC I became operational at the Bureau of the Census. This computer was self-checking and used magnetic tape for data input and output. The UNIVAC I was run 24 hours a day until 1963; it is remembered for having predicted the election of Dwight D. Eisenhower in 1952.

Another UNIVAC I (this was the first computer to be produced in quantity) was put to business use (the first such application) by the General Electric Corporation in 1954. Other first-generation computers are listed in Table 2-2.

Second-Generation Computers (1959–1965)

Major innovations. Solid-state devices (transistors) in place of vacuum tubes; magnetic core storage.

In this period computers became much smaller in size, faster, more reliable, and much greater in processing capacity. Built-in error detecting devices were installed and more efficient means were developed to input and retrieve data from the computer. Also, more efficient programming methods became available.

Many companies manufactured second-generation computers, and many of these were used for business applications. See Table 2-3. The most popular second-generation computer was the IBM 1401, of which some 15 000 were manufactured.

Table 2-3

Manufacturer	Model
Burroughs	B5000; 200 series
Control Data	CDC 1604; 160A
General Electric	GE 635; 645; 200
Honeywell	400 series, 800 series
IBM	7070; 7080; 7090; 1400 series; 1600 series
RCA	501
Univac	UNIVAC III; SS80; SS90; 1107
Philco	2000
NCR	300

Third-Generation Computers (1965–1970)

Major innovations.   Integrated solid-state circuitry; improved secondary storage devices; new input/output devices (visual display terminals, magnetic-ink readers, high-speed printers).

The new solid-state circuitry increased the speed of the computer by a factor of 10 000 over the first-generation computers.   Arithmetic and logical operations were now being performed in microseconds (millionths of a second) or even nanoseconds (billionths of a second). In the third generation, the primary storage unit, or *memory*, of the computer was greatly augmented by *secondary* (or *mass*) *storage* devices located outside the computer proper.   All this, together with faster input and output devices, made possible *multiprocessing* and *multiprogramming*, whereby a number of data processing problems from different sources could be run virtually at the same time on a single centrally located computer.   (These important topics are discussed in Section 6.5.)   Table 2-4 lists some of the principal third-generation computers.

Table 2-4

Manufacturer	Model
Burroughs	5700; 6700; 7700
Control Data	3000 series; 6000 series; 7000 series
Digital Equipment	PDP-8 series; PDP-11 series
General Electric (division purchased by Honeywell)	GE 600 series; GE 235
Honeywell	200 series; 60 series
IBM	System/360 series; System/370 series
RCA (division purchased by Univac)	Spectra 70 series
Univac	1108; 9000 series
NCR	Century series

Fourth-Generation Computers (since 1970)

Major innovations.   Microprocessors; further improvement of mass storage and input/output devices.

A *microprocessor*, pictured in Fig. 2-4, is a tiny solid-state device, no bigger than a pea, which in itself is a small computer capable of performing arithmetic and logical operations.   Because of microprocessors, the fourth generation includes (1) large computers that are much faster, much less expensive, and of much greater data processing capacity than equivalent-sized third-generation computers; (2) a multitude of relatively inexpensive *minicomputers* (actually first introduced in the third generation); (3) even further miniaturized computers, called *microcomputers*.

Among the advanced input/output devices employed in fourth-generation computers are optical readers, by which whole documents can be fed into the computer; audio response terminals, by which an operator can vocally introduce data or instructions; and graphic display terminals, by which an operator can feed pictures into the computer.

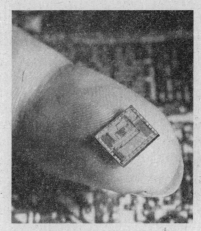

Fig. 2-4   (*Courtesy of Intel*)

2.5   DEVELOPMENT OF COMPUTER LANGUAGES AND SOFTWARE

The previous sections discussed the development of computer *hardware*, i.e. the physical equipment used to process data. Beginning with the Mark I there arose a need for computer *software*. In its broadest definition, software comprehends computer programming languages and translators, application programs, operating system programs, and documentation for the efficient use of the computer. Software will be discussed in detail in Chapter 6; here we simply give an historical sketch.

A *computer language* is the language which is used to write a program for the computer. When first-generation computers were introduced, programs were written in binary-based *machine language*, which is the only language actually understood by the computer. Unfortunately, machine language is very difficult (for humans) to use and varies from computer to computer. Second-generation computers saw the introduction of *assembly languages*, wherein symbolic codes were used instead of binary numbers. One then required an *assembler* program to translate assembly-language programs into machine language. Even so, assembly languages were still too complicated for general use.

The late 1950s saw the development of FORTRAN (FORmula TRANslation) and COBOL (COmmon Business Oriented Language). These are *high-level* languages, in that they use symbols and words similar to those of ordinary arithmetic and English and are independent of the computer on which the program is to be used. FORTRAN has become one of the most popular languages for general scientific applications, and COBOL the most popular language for general-purpose business applications. Such high-level languages require a *compiler* program which translates programs written in the high-level language into machine language. Among other high-level languages, some (e.g. PL/1, BASIC) are general-purpose languages, like FORTRAN and COBOL; others are special-purpose languages used for certain specific applications.

Computer programs are of two basic types. *Application programs* are the programs which are written to solve a particular data processing problem. They are usually written in a high-level language by the party who wishes the problem solved. *Operating system programs* are the programs needed to operate the computer; they are usually supplied by the manufacturer. In second-generation computers, operating system programs consisted mainly of assemblers and compilers. By the time third-generation computers appeared, there was a need for the manufacturer to provide the user with a variety of system programs. These included programs which provided for efficient allocation of computer memory, control of input and output operations, and supervision of the computer in a multiprogramming mode (Section 6.5).

A more recent development is *packaged programs*. These are collections of application programs provided by the manufacturer or some software company, for certain standard computer applications such as payroll, accounts receivable, and inventory control. The use of packaged programs allows the computer programmer to devote his energies to special applications unique to his company.

2.6   CAREERS IN DATA PROCESSING

Data processing has developed into one of the major industries in this country, offering employment in the following categories:

Computer operators handle the devices that feed data into and out of the computer. They are also responsible for keeping the logbooks and doing other paperwork related to these devices and for the supplies used with these devices. Computer operators usually study at vocational schools and then receive the rest of their training on the job.

Computer maintenance personnel are responsible for on-site servicing of computer hardware. They are much more highly trained than the computer operator, first at a trade school or an engineering college and then for at least a year by the manufacturer of the equipment.

Computer programmers are mainly responsible for writing programs for the computer. Contrary to common belief, programming is a very technical field, and programmers usually have a college degree in computer science or a related field. In addition, the programmer will need a year or two of on-the-job-training.

Systems analysts are responsible for the overall flow of information among the various departments of a large institution. Working directly under management, they organize the various data processing procedures throughout the institution and guide the programmers as to the type of programs to be written. A systems analyst usually has a graduate degree in either computer science or business management, in addition to several years of on-the-job training. Skilled analysts are in great demand and are highly paid.

Sales personnel. Since the modern computer is a highly technical machine and its applications are complex in nature, computer sales personnel will usually have a college degree in computer science, engineering, or business management. The ability to interact in a positive manner with people is an essential requirement for successful salesmanship. As always, there is a great demand for capable sales representatives.

Solved Problems

EARLY DATA PROCESSING (DARK AND MIDDLE AGES)

2.1   Briefly describe the three main types of data processing devices and give one or two examples of each type.

   Manual-mechanical devices are chiefly hand-operated, e.g. abacus, slide rule. *Electromechanical devices* are mostly powered by an electric motor and use switches and relays similar to those found in household appliances, e.g. card readers and card sorters (see Chapter 4). *Electronic devices* have such components as transistors and printed circuits, e.g. a modern computer.

2.2   Discuss the basis on which one divides the history of data processing into the Dark Ages, the Middle Ages, and the Modern Age.

   The Dark Ages refers to the period when only manual-mechanical devices were used; the Middle Ages refers to the period when punched-card data processing came into being; the Modern Age refers to the period when the electronic computer came into being.

2.3 Give the time period and some examples of devices of the Dark Ages of data processing.

The Dark Ages of data processing extend from approximately 5000 B.C. (the invention of the abacus) until about 1820 A.D. (Babbage's difference engine). Other important devices of this period are Oughtred's slide rule, Pascal's numerical cogwheels, Leibniz's calculator, and Jacquard's card-controlled loom. All these were manual-mechanical devices.

2.4 Why are (a) Pascal's calculator, (b) Jacquard's loom, important in the history of computing devices?

(a) It is considered to be the first adding machine. Specifically, the machine contains gears which enable certain carryover operations.

(b) It was the first machine that could be programmed to follow a set of instructions (recorded on punched cards).

2.5 Table 2-5 gives some differences for the formula $y = x^3 + 2$. The differences become constant after a certain order, and this is the principle on which Babbage's difference engine is based. Find the missing numbers a, b, c, and d in the table.

Table 2-5

x	$x^3 + 2$	Δ	Δ^2	Δ^3
1	3			
2	10	7		
3	29	a	12	
4	b	37	c	d
5	127	61	24	6

Each entry after the second column is the difference of the two numbers indicated in the table. Hence:

$$a = 29 - 10 = 19$$
$$b = 29 + 37 = 66$$
$$c = 37 - a = 37 - 19 = 18$$
$$d = c - 12 = 18 - 12 = 6$$

2.6 Why should Babbage's second machine, the "analytical engine," be of any importance, when it was never built?

In conception, the analytical machine was the prototype of the modern-day computer. It was to contain such things as a punched-card input, memory and arithmetic units, and a sequential program control for solving problems.

2.7 Sir Isaac Newton is reported to have said, "If I appear great, it is only because I stand on the shoulders of giants." On whose shoulders might Dr. Herman Hollerith, the father of punched-card data processing, have stood?

Joseph Jacquard's; the concept of storing data on a punched card (in this case, program data) is due to Jacquard.

2.8   Give the time period and the basic characteristic of the Middle Ages of data processing.

The Middle Ages of data processing began in 1890 with the use of punched cards for processing the census returns and extended to 1944, when the first computer was built. The distinguishing feature of this period is the use of electromechanical devices to process data recorded on punched cards.

2.9   Identify the two persons most associated with the Middle Ages of data processing, their contributions to data processing, and the companies they were instrumental in developing.

Herman Hollerith was the first person to build machines which processed data recorded on punched cards. He did this for the United States Bureau of the Census while tabulating the 1890 census. He later formed his own company, which was the ancestor of IBM.

James Powers followed Hollerith at the Census Bureau. His improved machines were used in the 1910 census. He later formed his own company, which evolved into Remington Rand Corporation and finally Sperry Rand Corporation.

MODERN DATA PROCESSING

2.10   Discuss the truth or falseness of the following statement: The Mark I initiated the Modern Age of data processing because it was the first electronic computer.

The first part of the statement is true. However, the second part is false. The Mark I was not an electronic computer; it was an electromechanical machine like those preceding it. It differed from the earlier machines in that it could carry out a long sequence of arithmetical and logical operations automatically, without manual intervention.

2.11   Give two major innovations in the first-generation computers.

(1) Computer programs were stored in the memory of the computer. (2) Vacuum tubes took the place of electromechanical devices.

2.12   Give three major innovations in the second-generation computers.

(1) Solid-state devices, such as transistors, replaced vacuum tubes. (2) Built-in error detecting devices were installed. (3) Magnetic cores were introduced as storage elements.

2.13   List three major advances of third-generation computers.

(1) Integrated circuitry was employed. (2) Secondary storage devices were greatly improved. (3) Faster input and output devices became available.

2.14   The *access time* is the average time needed to retrieve a data item from the unit. Since secondary storage devices typically have much longer access times than the computer's memory, why not eliminate secondary storage in favor of bigger memories?

Although the memory has faster access, secondary storage is cheaper (per unit of capacity) and more flexible (for instance, a secondary storage device can be shared by several computers).

2.15   The fourth generation of computers is characterized by microprocessors, minicomputers, and microcomputers. Distinguish among these.

A *microprocessor* is a single "chip" which by itself can perform the control, arithmetical, and logical functions of a computer. With the addition of some equally small memory chips and some input/output devices, it becomes a *microcomputer*; these should soon be pocket-sized. A *minicomputer* is a computer that is much larger in physical size and capability than a microcomputer, but is small, and very inexpensive, compared to the big machines listed in Table 2-4.

SOFTWARE, CAREERS

2.16 State which of the following are software: (*a*) transistor, (*b*) FORTRAN, (*c*) compiler, (*d*) integrated electronic circuit, (*e*) procedure for inputting data, (*f*) device which inputs data.

Software encompasses the programming languages and translators, programs, and procedures and codes devised for efficient use of the computer. (*a*), (*d*), and (*f*) are hardware. The others are software. FORTRAN is one of the high-level programming languages; a compiler is a program that translates a high-level language into machine language.

2.17 Describe, and name the originator of, the stored-program computer.

The earliest computers were adapted to a given problem by means of external wiring boards. In a stored-program computer, the step-by-step list of instructions for solving a particular problem is read into storage, just like input data. The computer then automatically carries out the sequence of instructions. The mathematician John von Neumann is credited with developing the concept of the stored program.

2.18 State two important properties of a high-level computer programming language.

The language is (1) independent of the particular model of computer, (2) similar to standard arithmetic and to the English (or French, Russian, etc.) language.

2.19 Briefly describe the work of (*a*) a computer operator, (*b*) a computer programmer, (*c*) a systems analyst.

(*a*) A computer operator handles the input and output devices of the computer.

(*b*) A computer programmer writes the lists of instructions required to solve particular problems.

(*c*) A systems analyst organizes and integrates the various data processing procedures throughout a large institution.

2.20 Which careers in data processing do not require a college degree?

The computer operator does not usually require a college degree. Most of the other careers, such as programmers, systems analysts, and sales personnel, do require a college degree. Maintenance personnel may or may not require a college degree, depending on the sophistication of the equipment.

Review Questions

EARLY DATA PROCESSING

2.21 The earliest calculating device that is still in use today is the (*a*) clock, (*b*) abacus, (*c*) difference engine, (*d*) sextant.

2.22 The first true adding machine was developed by (*a*) Euclid, (*b*) Oughtred, (*c*) Pascal, (*d*) Jacquard.

2.23   The invention of the slide rule is attributed to   (a) Babbage,   (b) Oughtred,   (c) Pascal,   (d) Napier.

2.24   The first machine which could be called the prototype of the modern computer was the   (a) weaving loom,   (b) difference engine,   (c) analytical engine,   (d) slide rule.

2.25   Table 2-6 gives differences for the formula $y = x^2 + x$.   Find a, b, and c.

Table 2-6

x	$x^2 + x$	Δ	Δ^2
1	2		
2	6	4	
3	a	6	2
4	20	b	2
5	30	10	c

2.26   The difference engine was based on the fact that successive differences for certain functions eventually become   (a) positive,   (b) negative,   (c) constant,   (d) small,   (e) large.

2.27   Punched cards are associated with the names   (a) Powers,   (b) Pascal,   (c) Jacquard,   (d) Leibniz,   (e) Hollerith.

2.28   Which of the following were developed by Charles Babbage;   (a) difference engine,   (b) calculating bones,   (c) numerical cogwheels,   (d) analytic engine?

2.29   To process the 1890 census, Hollerith developed   (a) the concept of punched cards,   (b) punched-card codes,   (c) punched-card processing devices,   (d) all of the above.

2.30   The devices that processed the punched cards for the 1890 census were   (a) manual,   (b) electromechanical,   (c) electronic.

MODERN DATA PROCESSING

2.31   The Modern Age of data processing began with the completion of the computer   (a) ENIAC,   (b) Mark I,   (c) UNIVAC I.

2.32   The Mark I was the first computer to: (a) use vacuum tubes,   (b) use transistors,   (c) use a built-in error detecting device,   (d) none of the above.

2.33   The ENIAC was the first computer to: (a) use vacuum tubes on a large scale,   (b) use a stored program,   (c) use paper tape as input medium,   (d) none of the above.

2.34   The EDSAC was the first computer to: (a) use vacuum tubes,   (b) use a stored program,   (c) use paper tape as input medium,   (d) all of the above.

2.35   The UNIVAC I was the first computer to: (a) use transistors,   (b) use a stored program,   (c) be used for business data processing,   (d) all of the above.

2.36   First-generation computers: (*a*) used vacuum tubes instead of switches and relays, (*b*) stored programs in the memory of the computer, (*c*) were built after 1945, (*d*) all of the above.

2.37   Second-generation computers used (*a*) vacuum tubes instead of electromechanical devices, (*b*) transistors instead of vacuum tubes, (*c*) integrated circuitry, (*d*) none of the above.

2.38   Third-generation computers: (*a*) were the first to use built-in error detecting devices, (*b*) used transistors instead of vacuum tubes, (*c*) were the first to use integrated circuitry, (*d*) none of the above.

2.39   Fourth-generation computers: (*a*) were the first to use microprocessors, (*b*) were built after 1970, (*c*) include microcomputers, (*d*) all of the above.

2.40   A microprocessor is (*a*) a solid-state device, (*b*) tiny as a pea, (*c*) capable of performing arithmetic operations, (*d*) capable of performing logical operations, (*e*) all of the above.

SOFTWARE DEVELOPMENTS, CAREERS

2.41   Machine language is the only language understood by the computer: True or false?

2.42   The compiler: (*a*) is a computer program, (*b*) translates a high-level language into machine language, (*c*) is part of software, (*d*) all of the above.

2.43   A high-level language: (*a*) uses symbols and words similar to those of ordinary arithmetic and English, (*b*) is independent of any particular computer, (*c*) requires a compiler to translate the language into machine language, (*d*) all of the above.

2.44   Consider the languages FORTRAN and COBOL.   Name the language which is used mainly for (*a*) scientific data processing, (*b*) business data processing.

2.45   Computer software includes (*a*) applications programs, (*b*) operating system programs, (*c*) packaged programs, (*d*) all of the above.

2.46   The stored-program concept was developed by (*a*) Hollerith, (*b*) Aiken, (*c*) von Neumann, (*d*) Eckert and Mauchly.

2.47   Computer operators: (*a*) normally require a college degree in computer science, (*b*) operate the devices which input and output data from the computer, (*c*) write computer programs for specific problems, (*d*) all of the above.

2.48   Computer maintenance personnel: (*a*) are responsible for the on-site service of computer hardware, (*b*) are usually more highly trained than computer operators, (*c*) require advanced training equivalent to at least one or two years of college, (*d*) all of the above.

2.49   The overall flow of information among the various departments of an institution is the responsibility of (*a*) computer operators, (*b*) systems analysts, (*c*) computer programmers, (*d*) the board of directors.

2.50   Computer sales personnel: (*a*) usually require a college degree, (*b*) normally are divided into hardware salesmen and software salesmen, (*c*) may be quite well paid, (*d*) all of the above.

Chapter 3

Storage Media

3.1 INTRODUCTION

Source documents come in all sizes and shapes; they may be handwritten sales receipts, typewritten monthly reports, tape recorded speeches, and so on. Usually the data on the source documents have to be put into some standard medium in order to be read into the computer. Also, data to be processed at some later time must be stored in such a way as to be readily accessible to the computer.

3.2 CHARACTERS

The smallest unit of information that is processed is a *character*. The 48 standard characters are as follows.

Alphabet: A B C D E F G H I J K L M N O P Q R S T U V W X Y Z

Digits: 0 1 2 3 4 5 6 7 8 9

Special characters: + − / * ( ) , . $ = '

The special characters (which vary somewhat from one data processing system to another) include a blank space. The alphabet and digits are sometimes called the *alphanumeric* or *alphameric* characters.

3.3 DATA ORGANIZATION

Characters are combined to form *data items*, such as names, addresses, ID numbers, and so on. A set of related data items treated as a unit is called a *record*, and a collection of similar, related records is called a *file*. Moreover, a structured set of files is called a *data base*.

EXAMPLE 3.1 (*a*) A record may contain a student's name, ID number, and final grades. The file would consist of the records of all the students. (*b*) A record may contain the information related to a single sales transaction, such as description of unit sold, inventory number, quantity, color, unit price, total cost, and date of transaction. The file would consist of all the sales transactions.

Types of Records

Records fall into the three broad categories discussed below.

Master records contain data that are relatively permanent. For example, the name, address, social security number, sex, and birthday of a student would appear on his master record. Similarly, name, address, and credit information would appear on the master record of a customer. A file of master records is a *master file*.

Detail records contain data corresponding to a single transaction or event. For example, the customer's name, his charge card number, the item purchased, and its price would appear on the detail record of a customer. Similarly, the name, student ID number, and grade in a particular course would appear on the detail record of a student.

Summary records are those that summarize a number of detail records; they are the records commonly used for reports. For example, one could have a summary record giving the total monthly sales for a given customer, or a summary (class) record giving the names, ID numbers, and grades of all the students in a given class.

Secondary Storage - recording memory is stored on tape-then brought into computer.

Types of Storage Media

Sequential-storage media. In these media the records composing a file are stored in linear fashion, one after another. One obtains information from a particular record by examining each record in the sequence until the desired record is reached. Accordingly, for efficient processing, a file should be sorted before being committed to the medium (see Problem 3.6). The principal sequential-storage media are punched cards, punched paper tapes, and magnetic tapes.

EXAMPLE 3.2 Sometimes a sequentially stored file contains a special record at the beginning and/or at the end of the file which contains information about the file itself. This record is called a *header record* if it occurs at the beginning of the file, or a *trailer record* if it occurs at the end of the file. Thus, a punched-card file may contain a header card which tells when the file was last updated, and also a trailer card which gives the number of cards (other than the header and trailer cards) in the file.

Random-access storage media. These media allow direct access to a particular record in a file without any examination of other records. The terms "direct access" and "random access" are used interchangeably in this context. The principal random-storage media are magnetic disks, magnetic drums, and the memory of the computer.

3.4   THE 80-COLUMN CARD

One of the first and still a popular input/output medium is the punched card shown in Fig. 3-1, the *80-column* or *IBM* card. It measures $7\frac{3}{8}$ inches long by $3\frac{1}{4}$ inches wide by 0.007 inches thick. The columns are numbered 1 to 80 from left to right.

Each column of the card contains 12 punching positions, which form 12 horizontal rows. The top row is called the *12-punch row* or *12-row*, the next row is called the *11-row*, and then they are numbered consecutively from *0-row* to *9-row*, as shown in Fig. 3-1. The top three rows are called the *zone-punch rows*, and the bottom ten rows are called the *digit-punch rows*. Thus the 0-row is both a zone-punch row and a digit-punch row. The top edge of the card is called the *12-edge* and the bottom edge is called the *9-edge*.

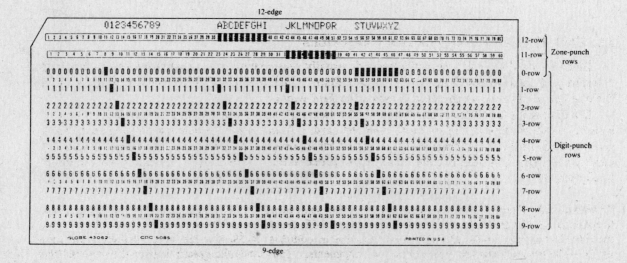

Fig. 3-1

Each column of the punched card can record a single character as a set of holes punched in the column. A digit is represented by a single hole punched in its corresponding row. Each alphabetic character is represented by two holes, one punched in a zone row and one punched in a digit row. The special characters are represented by other combinations. The specific code for the digits and alphabet appears in Table 3-1.

Table 3-1

Character	Rows Punched	Character	Rows Punched	Character	Rows Punched	Character	Rows Punched
0	0						
1	1	A	12, 1	J	11, 1		
2	2	B	12, 2	K	11, 2	S	0, 2
3	3	C	12, 3	L	11, 3	T	0, 3
4	4	D	12, 4	M	11, 4	U	0, 4
5	5	E	12, 5	N	11, 5	V	0, 5
6	6	F	12, 6	O	11, 6	W	0, 6
7	7	G	12, 7	P	11, 7	X	0, 7
8	8	H	12, 8	Q	11, 8	Y	0, 8
9	9	I	12, 9	R	11, 9	Z	0, 9

Finally, there is space at the top of the card, called the *graphic row*, where the characters which have been punched may be printed. These printed characters have no meaning to the computer and are there simply to make it easy for a person to read the data which are punched on the card. Similarly, some cards may be colored so that they are easily recognized by computer personnel.

A collection of cards is called a *deck*. The cards in a deck usually have some corner cut so that one can tell if all the cards in the deck are 12-edge up and facing the same way. The card pictured in Fig. 3-1 has the upper-left corner cut.

3.5   UNIT RECORD PRINCIPLE FOR CARD FILES

Since a data item, e.g. a person's name, is usually represented by several characters, a block of columns on a card is needed to record the data item. Such a block of columns is called a *field*, and the number of columns in the field is called the *field width*.

Depending on the number and kinds of data items in the record, a record can appear on part of a card, on one whole card, or on more than one card. A *unit record system* uses a single card for a given record, so that a file consists of a deck of cards, one record per card. The processing of the cards under such a system is called *unit record processing*. We will study this processing in detail in Chapter 4.

EXAMPLE 3.3 Figure 3-2 shows a card that records a sales order. The catalog number of the item appears in columns 1–6, the description of the item in columns 9–28, the number of these items sold in columns 31–34, the date in columns 36–42, the salesperson's name in columns 44–58, and the store number in columns 61–63. The last columns are reserved for any comments. Sometimes the descriptions of the data and the positions of the fields are printed on the data card, as in Fig. 3-2. (Again, this printing is for the people handling the card and is not read by the machines.) Note that such a record can be processed by a unit record system, since it occupies a single card.

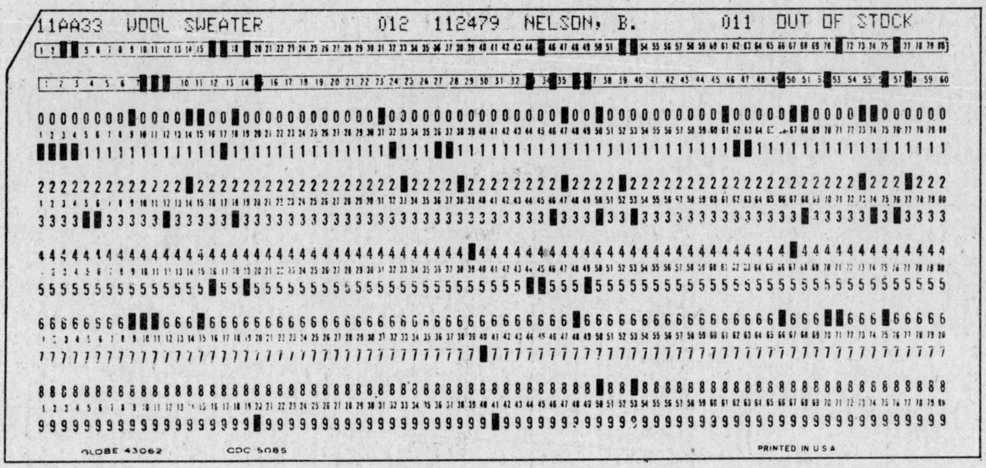

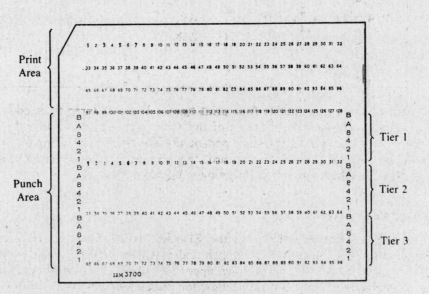

Fig. 3-2

3.6 THE 96-COLUMN CARD

A 96-column card, pictured in Fig. 3-3, was introduced by IBM in 1969. The card is smaller (2.63 by 3.25 inches) than the 80-column card, yet it can store 20% more information.

Fig. 3-3

A *print area* occupies approximately the upper 1/3 of the card and a *punch area* occupies the rest. The punch area is divided into three *tiers*, with 32 columns in each tier. Each column in a tier contains 6 punching positions, forming 6 rows across the card. The top two rows of each tier, called the *A-* and *B-rows*, are the zone-punch rows; the last four rows, called the *8-*, *4-*, *2-*, and *1-rows*, are the digit-punch rows.

Each column in a tier records a character by having various holes in the column punched. A digit is represented by punching the digit-punch row or rows whose digits add up to the desired digit (see Table 3-2). The alphabetic and special characters are recorded by holes in both zone and digit rows. Only a selection of the special characters is given in Table 3-2.

Table 3-2

Character	Rows Punched	Character	Rows Punched	Character	Rows Punched
0	A	J	B, 1	.	B, A, 8, 2, 1
1	1	K	B, 2	(	B, A, 8, 4, 1
2	2	L	B, 2, 1	+	B, A, 8, 4, 2
3	2, 1	M	B, 4	$	B, 8, 2, 1
4	4	N	B, 4, 1	)	B, 8, 4, 1
5	4, 1	O	B, 4, 2	;	B, 8, 4, 2
6	4, 2	P	B, 4, 2, 1	/	A, 1
7	4, 2, 1	Q	B, 8	,	A, 8, 2, 1
8	8	R	B, 8, 1	%	A, 8, 4
9	8, 1	S	A, 2	?	A, 8, 4, 2, 1
A	B, A, 1	T	A, 2, 1	:	8, 2
B	B, A, 2	U	A, 4	'	8, 4, 1
C	B, A, 2, 1	V	A, 4, 1	"	8, 4, 2, 1
D	B, A, 4	W	A, 4, 2	=	8, 4, 2
E	B, A, 4, 1	X	A, 4, 2, 1		
F	B, A, 4, 2	Y	A, 8		
G	B, A, 4, 2, 1	Z	A, 8, 1		
H	B, A, 8				
I	B, A, 8, 1				

The print area of the card contains four print lines. The first three lines correspond to the three punch tiers and accommodate printouts of the characters recorded in the three tiers. The fourth print line does not correspond to any part of the punch area, but it may also be used for printing. As in the case of the 80-column card, the printing is just to help a person read the information which is punched, and has no meaning to the computer.

3.7 PUNCHED PAPER TAPE

One of the oldest (Teletype equipment, the EDVAC) input/output media is punched paper tape—a continuous strip of paper about one inch wide. Characters are recorded on the tape by punching holes across its width. Depending upon its design, the tape has 5 or 8 punching positions, called *channels*. Figure 3-4 shows how the characters are coded on an 8-channel tape.

Paper tape has never been as popular an input/output medium as the 80-column IBM card. For one reason, the correction or insertion of a single character in the continuous strip is a time-consuming task. Also, paper tape lacks the durability and storage ease of the punched card. In fact, paper tape is being used less and less in data processing.

3.8 MAGNETIC TAPE

Magnetic tape is widely used when large amounts of data are to be stored sequentially. The magnetic tape used with computers is similar to that used in home tape recorders. Varying from $\frac{1}{2}$

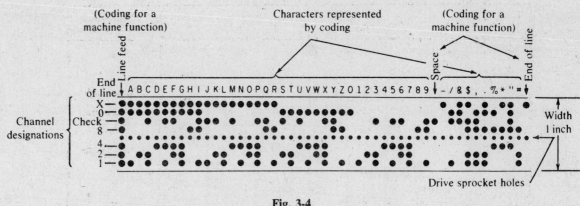

Fig. 3-4

600' - 2400'

inch to 1 inch in width, it is made of plastic that is coated on one side with a metallic oxide which may be locally magnetized. *EITHER ONE DIRECTION OR ANOTHER*

Data are usually recorded on the tape in either 7 or 9 parallel tracks (*channels*).   Figure 3-5 shows how the characters are coded on a 7-track tape; each bar stands for a small magnetized region.   This code uses four numeric channels, two zone channels, and a parity-check channel.

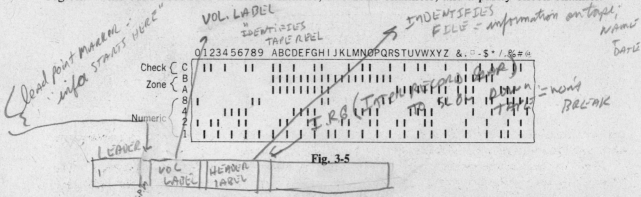

VOL. LABEL "IDENTIFIES TAPE REEL"   *IDENTIFIES FILE = information on tape; NAME + DATE*   *lead point marker "info starts here"*   *IRG (INTER RECORD GAP)*   *LEADER*   *VOL LABEL   HEADER LABEL*   *BLOCK = many rows   SLOW DOWN = non's BREAK*

Fig. 3-5

EXAMPLE 3.4   The C-channel in Fig. 3-5 gives an *even* parity check: a magnetic spot is added in this channel for all those characters where the number of spots in the other channels is odd.   Thus each character is coded in an even number of spots.   Now, suppose that after the data are recorded a magnetic spot is erased or obscured by dust.   Then the character from which the spot is missing will have an odd number of spots.   (It is highly unlikely that a character should lose *two* spots.)   By counting the number of spots for each character as the data are read back into the computer, one can detect where the error occurred.

Excluding the parity-check channel, the coding is the same' as on the 96-column punched card (see Fig. 3-3 and Table 3-2).   A detailed discussion of coding methods is given in Chapter 7.

Figure 3-6 shows how the alphameric characters are recorded on a 9-track tape, having four numeric channels, a parity-check channel (here an odd parity check), and four zone channels.   The two additional zone channels are used to record lowercase letters and additional special characters.   The channels are arranged differently on this tape, with the most often used channels in the center, where they are less susceptible to physical damage.

A magnetic tape alternates sections of data, called *blocks*, and sections of blank tape (about $\frac{3}{4}$ inch in length), called *interrecord gaps* (IRG), as pictured in Fig. 3-7(*a*).   Each block of data is transmitted to and from the computer at one time.   Recall from Section 3.3 that a file consists of logical units of data called *records*.   If there is to be a large number of characters in a record, then each block will correspond to a record.   In this case we say that the tape has been formatted into *single-record blocks*.   On the other hand, if the number of characters in a record is small, then several records will be stored in a block, as shown in Fig. 3-7(*b*).   In this case we say that the tape

(handwritten margin notes)
RT = READING TIME
GT = GAP TIME
TT = TOTAL TIME
TR = TRANSFER TIME
1 = ON; and 0 = OFF; EVEN
Parity = check on Bit amounts.

Track No.	0	1	2	3	4	A	B	C	D	.....	Z	Equivalent 7-track position
9											|	8
8			|	|			|	|				2
7	|	|	|	|	|	|	|	|	|		|	added zone
6	|	|	|	|	|	|	|	|	|		|	added zone
5	|	|	|	|	|						|	B
4	|							|				check (odd)
3	|	|	|	|	|							A
2		|		|			|		|		|	1
1					|			|				4

Fig. 3-6

(handwritten margin notes)
9 columns
8 bits = 1 byte = 1 CHARACTER
CHARACTER = ROW
200 to 1,600 BYTES per sq INCH
5000 to 404,000 BYTES / sec.
S/S = START/STOP TIME
INTER-RECORD GAP-TIME
TRANSFER RATE = speed at which info is taken from medium and put into main memory of computer.

(left margin handwritten)
END OF TAPE
END POINT MARKER = END OF INFO
TRAILER LABEL
SAME AS HEADER FILE
BLOCK COUNT

BLOCK OF DATA   BLOCK OF DATA   BLOCK OF DATA

(a)   Blocks with Interrecord Gaps

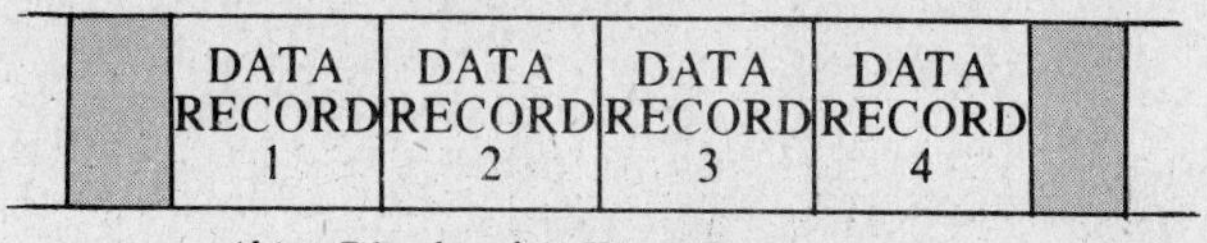

DATA RECORD 1   DATA RECORD 2   DATA RECORD 3   DATA RECORD 4

(b)   Block with Four Records

Fig. 3-7

has been formatted into *multirecord blocks*.   Multirecord blocking saves tape, and also speeds the input and output of data by minimizing the amount of tape motion.

The closeness of the characters recorded on the tape is called the *density* of the tape.   The density can vary from 200 characters per inch (low density) to 16 000 characters per inch (high density).   At high-density recording, a 10-inch reel of 2400 feet of tape can hold as much information as 500 000 punched cards.   As compared to punched cards, magnetic tape has certain *advantages*:

(1)   Data are stored much more compactly on magnetic tape, and the tape is much easier to handle than the equivalent deck of punched cards.

(2)   A reel of tape costs much less than the punched cards it replaces and is, in addition reusable.

and certain *disadvantages*:

(1)   A tape can be read only by a machine, whereas punched cards can be read visually by an operator.

(2)   When a tape tears, some data will always be lost.   On the other hand, a mutilated card can easily be replaced with no loss of information.

Because the above advantages outweigh the disadvantages, punched cards have been largely replaced by magnetic tape or some other mass storage mediums.

3.9   MAGNETIC DISK

Both punched cards and magnetic tape share a disadvantage in that they are sequential-storage media.   The records in a file have to be read one by one until a particular desired record is located;

the access time (Problem 2.14) for magnetic tape may be as much as 10 seconds. Magnetic disks, on the other hand, are a random-access medium; a particular record in a file can be found directly. The access time for a magnetic disk is less than 0.01 second.

A magnetic disk unit consists of 5 to 50 magnetic disks about $1\frac{1}{2}$ to 3 feet in diameter (similar to a stack of phonograph records) turned by a single drive shaft [Fig. 3-8(a)] at speeds of up to 2400 rpm. Both surfaces of each disk are coated with a compound similar to that on a magnetic tape, on which the data are recorded. In the most common design, for each side of each disk there is a reading and recording head that moves in and out between the disks to locate itself next to the spot on the disk where the data item is to be read or recorded, as illustrated in Fig. 3-8(b).

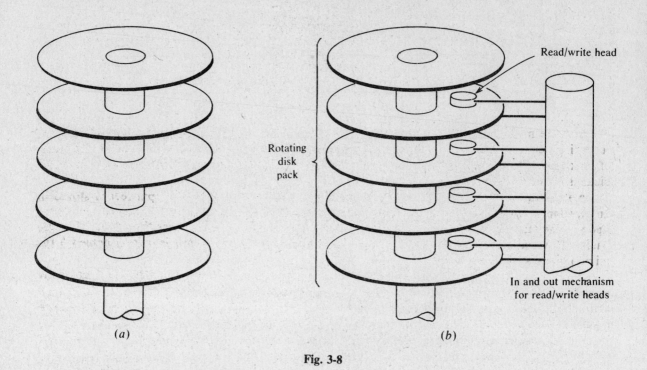

Fig. 3-8

A surface of a disk has from 50 to 100 circular tracks (depending upon the model) along which the data are recorded. Usually, data are recorded *serially* along a single track, as shown in Fig. 3-9.

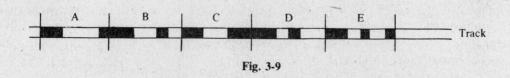

Fig. 3-9

Each disk face is divided into an assigned number of sectors, as pictured in Fig. 3-10. A *storage segment* is a specific sector of a specific track on a specific disk face. A storage segment will store one or several records of a file, depending upon the size of the records. Since each storage segment is uniquely identified by an address (consisting of a disk face number, a track number, and a sector number), a particular record can be directly accessed.

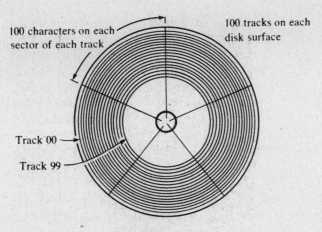

100 characters on each sector of each track

100 tracks on each disk surface

Track 00

Track 99

Fig. 3-10

In some magnetic disk units each track has its own recording head. In this type of unit the recording heads are fixed, reducing the access time even further. Also, in some models, the stack of disks can be removed from the shaft and replaced by a different stack. A removable stack of disks is called a *disk pack*.

A fourth-generation innovation, called the *floppy disk*, is similar to a 45 rpm record stored in an envelope. One disk at a time is placed in an input/output device where it is read or written upon. The storage capacity and access speed of a floppy disk are much less than those of a disk pack. However, the floppy disk is less expensive, easier to maneuver, and is quite suitable for the minicomputers.

The storage capacity of a disk unit varies from model to model, but a fixed disk stack can store up to several hundred million characters. A replaceable disk pack can store up to 50 million characters, which is about the storage capacity of a reel of high-density magnetic tape. A floppy disk can store about 600 000 characters.

As compared to magnetic tape, magnetic disks have the following *advantages*:

(1) The access time of disk storage is a fraction of the access time of tape. Thus disk storage is particularly efficient when a comparatively small number of records of a file must be frequently updated.

(2) Disk storage is much more durable than tape storage. Data on a disk are less likely to be lost because of mishandling or a poor storage environment.

and the following *disadvantages*:

(1) Disk storage is more expensive than magnetic tape. For example, a disk pack costs 20 times as much as a reel of tape with the same storage capacity.

(2) A disk pack is heavier and more difficult to replace than a reel of tape. When a variety of files are to be processed in a relatively short period of time or have to be transported from one data processing center to another, the time gained in faster access may be lost in file replacement time.

3.10   MAGNETIC DRUM

A magnetic drum is similar in many respects to a fixed stack of magnetic disks. It is a rotatable cylinder whose surface is coated with a magnetically sensitive compound. The surface is divided into a number of tracks, each track having one or more fixed reading and recording heads (Fig. 3-11). As in the case of a magnetic disk, data are recorded serially along the tracks, from

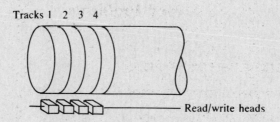

Fig. 3-11

which any particular item may be directly accessed.   With a fixed recording head, no time is lost in
moving the head, and so access time is negligible.   Magnetic drums are commonly used when very
fast access and transfer speeds are required.   They have one disadvantage, however, in that they
cannot be removed from a unit and replaced, as can a disk pack.

3.11   MAGNETIC STRIP

A magnetic strip is a plastic strip about 2 by 12 inches on which data are magnetically
recorded.   Ten of these strips make up a *subcell*, and twenty subcells are stored on a data *cell drive*
(Fig. 3-12).   To read or record data on a strip, the cell drive rotates to the subcell containing the
strip.   Then the strip drops out of the cell drive, moves under a read/write head where the selected
record is read or recorded, and then is replaced in the drive.

Although magnetic strip storage is slower then magnetic disk storage, it is much cheaper and
still can accommodate a reasonably large amount of data.

Fig. 3-12   (*Courtesy of IBM*)

Solved Problems

CHARACTERS, DATA ITEMS, RECORDS, FILES

3.1   What are the three types of characters used in data processing?

   (1) The twenty-six letters of the alphabet;   (2) the ten digits 0 through 9;   (3) certain special characters, such as +, −, /, *.   The number and type of special characters vary from one computer system to another.

3.2   Discuss the relationship among characters, records, data items, a data base, and files.

   The character is the smallest particle of data processed.   Characters are combined to form data items, such as a person's name, a date, an invoice number, etc.   Related data items combine to form a record.   For example, a hospital record may contain the patient's ID number, his name, his address, date of his admission, etc.   Related records are combined to form files.   Thus, an inventory file would contain an inventory record for each item in stock.   A structured collection of files makes up a data base.

3.3   Briefly describe, and give an example of,   (a) a master record,   (b) a detail record,   (c) a summary record.

   (a)   A master record contains relatively permanent data.   For example, a master inventory record for an item in stock would include the item number, a brief description of the item, the name and address of the supplier (or a code number representing the supplier), the minimum number of items to be kept on hand, and the current number of items in stock.

   (b)   A detail record contains data corresponding to a single transaction.   For example, a detail record of a sales transaction might include the date, the item number of the item sold, the number of such items sold, and the price per item.

   (c)   A summary record summarizes a number of detail records.   For example, a monthly summary record of a particular salesperson might include his ID number, his name, and the total amount of his monthly sales.

3.4   The following three records pertain to a sales agent:

(a)	Name Alice Smith	Address 28 First Avenue, Little Town, N.J. 08648		Yearly Salary $18 000.00
(b)	Name Alice Smith	Monthly Sales $8078.50	Monthly Expenses $156.25	Number of Trips 12
(c)	Name Alice Smith	Destination Invest Corp., Westport, Conn.		Expenses $34.75

What type of record is each?   How many data items are there in each record?

   (a)   Since the information is relatively permanent, this would be a master record.   There are three data items.

   (b)   Since the record summarizes sales and expenses for the month, it would be a summary record. There are four data items.

   (c)   Since the record refers to expenses on a particular trip, it would be a detail expense record.   There are three data items.

3.5 Briefly describe and discuss the difference between: (*a*) a sequential-storage medium, and (*b*) a random-access storage medium.

(*a*) In a sequential-storage medium the records of a file are stored in some order, and one obtains information in a particular record by examining each record in the sequence until one reaches the required record.

(*b*) In a random-access storage medium each record in a file can be reached independently of the others. A file which must be quickly and often referred to, such as the reservation file for a particular airplane flight, would normally be stored in a random-access medium.

3.6 If a file of 250 records is stored in a sequential-storage medium, say in a deck of 250 cards, how many times must one examine the file in order to update four given records?

Assuming that the file has been sorted with respect to some data item, record A will be followed in the file by record B, then by record C, and finally by record D. Then one need only examine the file once. Specifically, one searches the file sequentially until he comes to record A, then continues until he comes to record B, and so on. On the other hand, if the file were not sorted in any way, one might have to run through the file four times, once for each record to be updated.

3.7 Briefly define *header* and *trailer* records.

A header record is a special record at the beginning of a sequential file that contains information about the file itself. A trailer record is such a record at the end of the file.

THE 80-COLUMN CARD

3.8 Using Table 3-1, decode the data recorded on the punched card shown in Fig. 3-13.

Table 3-3 lists the rows punched and the corresponding characters represented.

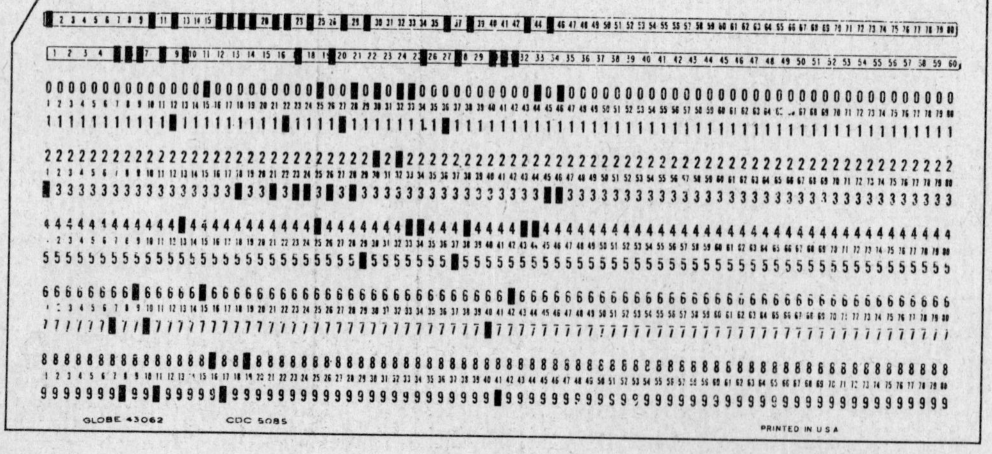

Fig. 3-13

Table 3-3

Rows Punched	12, 3	none	none	none	none	none	11, 7	11, 9	11, 6	12, 7	11, 9	12, 1
Character	C	space	space	space	space	space	P	R	O	G	R	A
	11, 4	none	0, 6	12, 8	12, 9	12, 3	12, 8	none	12, 3	12, 1	11, 3	12, 3
	M	space	W	H	I	C	H	space	C	A	L	C
	0, 4	11, 3	12, 1	0, 3	12, 5	0, 2	none	0, 2	0, 4	11, 4	none	12, 1
	U	L	A	T	E	S	space	S	U	M	space	A
	11, 5	12, 4	none	11, 7	11, 9	11, 6	12, 4	0, 4	12, 3	0, 3		
	N	D	space	P	R	O	D	U	C	T		

3.9 Commas are not punched when numbers are recorded in a numerical field. Also, an integer is always punched right-justified in its field, i.e. so that the last digit appears in the last column of the field. (This guarantees that the units digit in each record appears in the same column, the tens digit in the same column, and so on.) Frequently, one also requires that the left-hand columns be filled with zeros instead of blanks, to guard against any digit's being omitted. Suppose 1,235 is to be punched in a field of width 6, say columns 5–10. Which cards in Fig. 3-14 are punched correctly?

(a) Punched incorrectly, since the number is not right-justified.

(b) Punched incorrectly, since it contains a comma.

(c) Punched correctly, unless it is also required that the field be filled out with zeros on the left.

(d) Punched correctly.

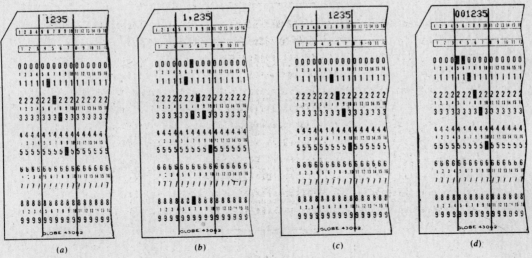

Fig. 3-14

3.10   Dollar amounts are recorded the same way as integers, i.e. without commas, right-justified in their fields, and with the fields filled out with zeros on the left. In addition, dollar amounts are recorded without dollar signs and without decimal points. (*a*) Given a field of width 8, how would one record the following dollar amounts?

$$\$3,444.75 \qquad \$33.88 \qquad \$77,888.22$$

(*b*) What is the largest dollar amount that can be recorded in the above field of width 8? (*c*) Suppose that fields of width 6 contain the following data:

$$123456 \qquad 004488 \qquad 000666 \qquad 777000$$

If the fields represent dollar amounts, how much money is recorded in each field?

(*a*)   One punches only the digits (no dollar signs, commas, or decimal points) right-justified in the field, with zeros on the left to fill out the field. This yields:

$$00344475 \qquad 00003388 \qquad 07788822$$

(*b*)   The largest number that could be recorded in a field of width 8 would consist of 8 nines, i.e. 99999999. This represents the dollar amount $999,999.99.

(*c*)   One inserts a decimal point before the last two digits. Thus:

$$\$1,234.56 \qquad \$44.88 \qquad \$6.66 \qquad \$7,770.00$$

3.11   Blank spaces are permitted in fields with alphabetic data. Unlike numerical data, alphabetic data are punched left-justified in their field, so that the first character appears in the first column of the field. This guarantees that the first character in each record appears in the same column, the second character in the same column, and so on. Suppose that the last names of the employees of a company are to be punched in a field of width 15, say the first 15 columns of the card. Which names in Fig. 3-15 are incorrectly punched?

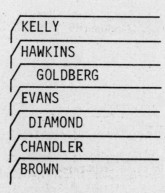

Fig. 3-15

The names Diamond and Goldberg are incorrectly punched. There is one space before Diamond and two spaces before Goldberg, so they are not punched left-justified in their fields.

3.12   Dates are denoted by 6 digits, with the first two digits denoting the month, the next two the day, and the last two the year (assumed to belong to the 20th Century). (*a*) What dates are represented by the following?

$$120775 \qquad 062362 \qquad 010331$$

(*b*)   How would one represent the following dates?

Feb. 28, 1977   July 4, 1980   Sept. 2, 1925

(*a*)   The 12 denotes the 12th month, December; the 07 denotes the 7th day of the month; and the 75 denotes the year, 1975; which give Dec. 7, 1975.   Similarly, 062362 denotes June 23, 1962, and 010331 denotes Jan. 3, 1931.

(*b*)   February is the second month and is represented by 02, so the date is represented by 022877.   Similarly, July 4, 1980, is represented by 070480, and Sept. 2, 1925, by 090225.

3.13   Certain data items are to be recorded on an 80-column card as follows:

Data Item	date	invoice number	salesman number	item number	description	quantity	amount
Columns	1–6	7–11	12–14	15–18	19–38	39–42	43–49

Find the field widths of the data items.

A field width is the number of columns reserved for a particular data item.   Hence the field widths are, respectively, 6, 5, 3, 4, 20, 4, and 7.

3.14   Suppose that on Nov. 3, 1979, salesman number 12 sold one refrigerator, item 321, for $531.75.   How is the record punched, if the invoice number is 1,235 and the format is that of Problem 3.13?

The date is punched as 110379 in columns 1–6.   The invoice number, salesman number, item number, and quantity are punched as

01235   012   0321   0001

in their corresponding fields.   The amount is punched as 0053175 in the amount field, and RE-FRIGERATOR is punched beginning in column 19.   Thus the punched card appears as in Fig. 3-16.

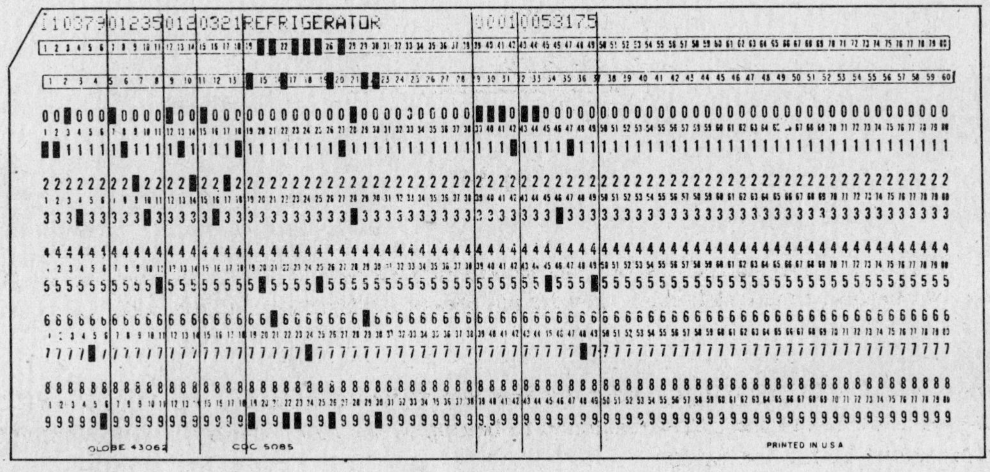

Fig. 3-16

3.15   Describe a unit record data processing system.

A unit record data processing system is a punched-card processing system which uses a single card with the same format for each record.

3.16   A department store is to use a unit record system for its customers. Design a Customer Sales Record for an 80-column card, to contain the following information: customer number, customer name, invoice date, invoice number, and invoice amount.

One must know the maximum values before one can format a card. Suppose that the maximum number of customers is 99,999 (field of width 5), the longest name has 20 characters (field of width 20), the maximum invoice number is 99,999 (field of width 5), and the maximum invoice amount is $99,999.99 (field of width 7). Then Fig. 3-17 gives the card format, where 6 columns are reserved for the date.

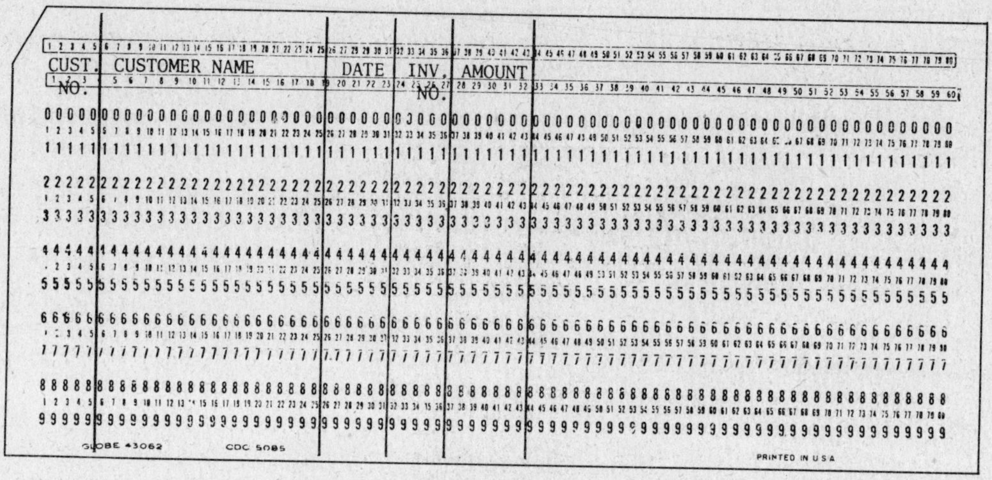

Fig. 3-17

THE 96-COLUMN CARD AND PUNCHED PAPER TAPE

3.17   Give two advantages of the 96-column punched card over the 80-column punched card.

(1) The 96-column card is smaller than the 80-column card and is therefore easier to handle. (2) The 96-column card accommodates about 20% more information than the 80-column card, since it can record 16 (20% of 80) more characters than the 80-column card.

3.18   Why is punched paper tape less widely used as an input/output or storage medium than the 80-column card?

(1) Since paper tape is a continuous strip of paper, it is difficult to correct or insert a character in a record of a file. (2) Cards last longer and are easier to store than tape.

3.19   How many different characters can be recorded on paper tape that has 6 punching positions for each character, excluding the check channel?

A paper tape with only two punching positions (channels) to represent a character could record a maximum of $2^2 = 4$ different characters, as shown in Fig. 3-18. Note that column D, where no hole is punched, is included as representing a character.

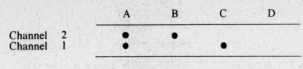

Fig. 3-18

If the tape had 3 punching positions, then the number of different characters possible would be

$$2^3 = 2 \cdot 2 \cdot 2 = 8$$

and for 6 punching positions, $2^6 = 2 \cdot 2 \cdot 2 \cdot 2 \cdot 2 \cdot 2 = 64$ different characters.

In general, if a two-state medium (e.g. punched or not punched) has N possible recording positions, then 2^N different characters can be recorded.

3.20 Using the coding shown in Fig. 3-4, find the data recorded on the segment of paper tape shown in Fig. 3-19.

Fig. 3-19

See Table 3-4.

Table 3-4

Channels Punched	2	C	0, 2, 1	X, 0, C, 8, 1	X, C, 4	X, 0, C, 4, 1	0, C, 2
Character	2	space	T	I	M	E	S
	C	2	C	X, 0, C, 4, 1	X, C, 8	0, C, 4	X, 0, 1
	space	2	space	E	Q	U	A
	X, 2, 1	0, C, 2	C	4			
	L	S	space	4			

MAGNETIC TAPE

3.21 The coding of characters on a 7-track magnetic tape is similar to the coding on the 96-column card, except that the 7-track tape has an additional recording position for each character. What is this additional channel called and what is its purpose?

It is called the **parity-check channel**. It is used to give all characters the same parity (oddness or evenness), thereby providing a check against loss of a magnetic spot.

3.22 The 9-track magnetic tape has two more recording positions for each character than the 7-track tape. (*a*) What are the advantages in having these two additional channels? (*b*) How many more different characters can be recorded on a 9-track tape than on a 7-track tape?

(*a*) The additional channels allow the tape to accommodate a greater variety of characters, such as lowercase letters and additional special characters.

(*b*) With N tracks, one of which is reserved for the parity check, 2^{N-1} characters can be accommodated (see Problem 3.19). Thus the 9-track tape allows

$$2^8 - 2^6 = 256 - 64 = 192$$

more characters.

3.23 Figure 3-20 is a picture of data recorded on a section of 9-track magnetic tape having an odd-parity check channel. Without referring to a coding table, determine which one of the characters is incorrectly recorded.

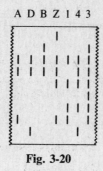

A D B Z 1 4 3

Fig. 3-20

Since the tape contains an odd-parity check channel, each character must have an odd number of spots magnetized. The numeral 1 has an even number (4) of spots; therefore it is the one in error.

3.24 Briefly define (*a*) a *block* of magnetic tape, (*b*) an *interrecord gap*, (*c*) *multirecord blocks.*

(*a*) A block of magnetic tape is a section of the tape that is treated as a unit when data are transmitted to or from the computer.

(*b*) An interrecord gap is a gap between successive blocks of magnetic tape.

(*c*) Multirecord blocks are blocks of a tape, each of which contains more than one record of a file.

3.25 Discuss the reason for formatting a magnetic tape so that several records are in each block, when a file consists of short records.

The blocking of several records speeds the input and output of data, since a block is transmitted to and from the computer at one time.

3.26 State two advantages of magnetic tape storage over punched-card storage.

(1) Data stored on magnetic tape are more compact and easier to handle. (2) Magnetic tape costs less and can be reused.

3.27 Suppose that the density of a certain magnetic tape is 800 characters per inch and that data can be recorded at a tape speed of 75 inches per second. What is the *transmission rate* of the tape (the number of characters recorded in one second)?

The number of characters which can be recorded in one second is equal to the number of characters recorded on one inch of tape times the number of inches the tape travels in one second. That is, transmission rate T equals density D times tape speed S. Thus the transmission rate is

$$T = D \cdot S = 800 \cdot 75 = 60\,000 \text{ characters per second}$$

MAGNETIC DISK, DRUM, AND STRIP STORAGE

3.28 What is the difference in the ways data are recorded on a magnetic disk and on a magnetic tape?

On a magnetic disk data are recorded serially along a single track rather than along several tracks (channels), as on magnetic tape.

3.29 State two advantages of magnetic disk storage over magnetic tape storage.

(1) The access time of magnetic disk is much less than that of tape. (2) Disk storage is longer lasting than tape storage.

3.30 State two advantages of magnetic tape storage over magnetic disk storage.

(1) It is less expensive than disk storage for an equivalent amount of storage capacity. (2) A reel of magnetic tape is lighter, hence easier to handle and transport, than a magnetic disk pack of equal storage capacity.

3.31 Briefly define (*a*) access time, (*b*) read/write head, (*c*) floppy disk.

(*a*) The access time is the time needed to retrieve a particular record of a stored file.

(*b*) A read/write head is a device that picks up data from or records data on a magnetic storage medium.

(*c*) A floppy disk is a small removable magnetic disk used with small computers.

3.32 Compare the access time and the capacity of magnetic drum storage with those of magnetic strip storage.

The access time of magnetic drum storage is less than that of magnetic strip storage (which is an advantage), but its capacity is smaller than that of magnetic strip storage (a disadvantage).

3.33 A company plans to purchase a computer, primarily to process the weekly payroll. The company has the option of using either magnetic tape or magnetic disk packs as a storage medium. Which might be better in this case, and why?

Magnetic tape. Payroll processing usually requires processing every record of a payroll file at the end of the week. Hence there is no major advantage in having a direct-access storage medium such as magnetic disk packs. In this case, the lower cost and easier handling of magnetic tape are decisive.

Review Questions

CHARACTERS, DATA ITEMS, RECORDS, FIELDS

3.34 What is the smallest unit of data which is processed?

3.35 Which are the alphanumeric characters? How many are there?

3.36 Which of the following are true? (*a*) The characters are combined to form data items; (*b*) data items are combined to form records; (*c*) records are combined to form files; (*d*) all of the above.

3.37 A record which contains data that are relatively permanent is called (*a*) a master record, (*b*) a detail record, (*c*) a summary record, (*d*) none of the above.

3.38 The following data items appear in three different types of records that a department store has for its charge card customers: (*a*) charge number, name, address, maximum charge; (*b*) charge number, name, date, amount of sale; (*c*) charge number, name, monthly payment, monthly charge. Which type of record (master, summary, detail) is each?

3.39 Which type of storage medium, sequential or random-access, does each of the following statements describe? (*a*) The records appear in a given order. (*b*) Each record can be directly accessed. (*c*) Before obtaining data in a given record, one must examine the records up to the given record. (*d*) The file is quickly and often accessed.

3.40 Suppose that one has a sequential-storage medium containing a file with 300 records and that the file has been sorted with respect to some data item. How many times must one run through the file in order to update (*a*) one record, (*b*) five records, (*c*) fifty records?

3.41 In a unit record processing system: (*a*) a file consists of one record; (*b*) a record occupies exactly one punched card; (*c*) each record has one data item; (*d*) none of the above.

THE 80-COLUMN CARD

3.42 (*a*) How many punching rows does the 80-column card have? (*b*) Which are the zone-punch rows? (*c*) Which are the digit-punch rows? (*d*) What is the name given to the top edge of the card? (*e*) What is the name given to the bottom edge of the card?

3.43 How many holes are used to represent (*a*) the digits, (*b*) the alphabetic characters, and where are these holes punched?

3.44 Consider the single series transaction recorded on the punched card shown in Fig. 3-21. (*a*) What

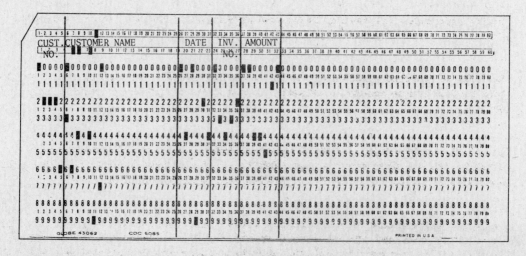

Fig. 3-21

kind of record (master, detail, summary) is stored on the card? (*b*) What is the field width of each item? (*c*) What characters are recorded in each field? (*d*) What are the date and the amount of the sale?

3.45 How would one record (*a*) May 4, 1959; (*b*) Jan. 23, 1974; (*c*) Oct. 3, 1982?

3.46 Which dates are denoted by (*a*) 062873, (*b*) 112233, (*c*) 030570, (*d*) 141275?

3.47 In a numerical field of width 6, how would one record the following numbers: (*a*) 567, (*b*) 1,234, (*c*) 22,555, (*d*) 4,666,777?

3.48 In a field of width 8 reserved for dollar amounts, how would one record (*a*) $333.44, (*b*) $6,666.77, (*c*) $444.00, (*d*) $2,444,888.00?

3.49 What is the largest dollar amount that can be recorded in a field of width (*a*) 6, (*b*) 8, (*c*) 10?

3.50 Dollar signs, commas, and decimal points are not usually punched when recording dollar amounts because: (*a*) it saves punching time, (*b*) it saves column space, (*c*) it is less confusing, (*d*) none of the above.

3.51 In a field of width 12, how would one record the words (*a*) *sailboat*, (*b*) *used table*, (*c*) *new chairs*, (*d*) *used television*?

THE 96-COLUMN CARD, PUNCHED PAPER TAPE, MAGNETIC TAPE STORAGE

3.52 The 96-column punched card: (*a*) is larger than the 80-column card; (*b*) contains about 20% more information than the 80-column card; (*c*) contains 8 recording positions for each character, like the 8-channel paper tape; (*d*) all of the above.

3.53 Punched paper tape: (*a*) was used as the input medium for the EDVAC, (*b*) lacks the storage ease of the punched card, (*c*) is difficult to correct, (*d*) all of the above.

3.54 The 8-channel punched paper tape: (*a*) has 6 punching positions for each character, (*b*) uses a check channel and an end-of-line channel, (*c*) can record 64 different characters, (*d*) all of the above.

3.55 The 7-track magnetic tape: (*a*) has 6 recording positions and one parity-check position for each character, (*b*) is a direct-access storage medium, (*c*) uses entirely different coding than either the 96-column punched card or the 8-channel punched paper tape, (*d*) all of the above.

3.56 The 9-track magnetic tape: (*a*) has one more check channel than does the 7-track magnetic tape, so that both an even and an odd method of checking can be used; (*b*) has an end-of-record channel; (*c*) has two more channels than does the 7-track magnetic tape, so that a greater variety of characters can be recorded; (*d*) none of the above.

3.57 Magnetic tape: (*a*) stores data in a more compact form than do punched cards; (*b*) costs less than punched cards, for the same amount of storage capacity; (*c*) is generally easier to handle than punched cards; (*d*) all of the above.

3.58 The density of a certain magnetic tape is 1000 characters per inch and the tape speed is 50 inches per second. Then the number of characters that can be recorded in one minute is (*a*) 12 000, (*b*) 3 000 000, (*c*) 63 000, (*d*) none of the above.

3.59 Figure 3-22 shows a section of 7-track magnetic tape with a parity-check channel. Which one of the characters is incorrectly recorded?

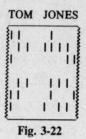

Fig. 3-22

MAGNETIC DISK, DRUM, AND STRIP STORAGE

3.60 True or false: Access time is essentially the time needed to position a read/write head with respect to the storage medium.

3.61 Data stored on a magnetic disk: (*a*) can be reached more quickly than data stored on magnetic tape, (*b*) are less likely to be destroyed than data stored on magnetic tape, (*c*) can be directly accessed, (*d*) all of the above.

3.62 A magnetic disk pack is (*a*) less expensive than a reel of magnetic tape of the same storage capacity, (*b*) lighter than a reel of magnetic tape of the same storage capacity, (*c*) usually of much larger storage capacity than a reel of magnetic tape, (*d*) none of the above.

3.63 A floppy disk is (*a*) a first-generation computer invention, (*b*) smaller and lighter than a disk in a fixed disk stack or a disk pack, (*c*) most often used with very large computers, (*d*) none of the above.

3.64 Magnetic drum storage: (*a*) has a shorter access time than magnetic strip storage, (*b*) has greater capacity than magnetic strip storage, (*c*) is a sequential-storage medium, (*d*) all of the above.

3.65 Which of the following mass storage media are sequential-storage media and which are direct-access storage media? (*a*) punched cards, (*b*) magnetic drum, (*c*) punched paper tape, (*d*) magnetic disk, (*e*) magnetic tape, (*f*) magnetic strip.

Chapter 4

Punched-Card Recording
and Processing

4.1 INTRODUCTION

The punched card is still widely used as a medium for recording data. Once recorded on punched cards, the data (*a*) can be fed into a modern electronic computer which stores and processes the data and outputs the results, or (*b*) can be stored and processed, and the results outputted, by means of various electromechanical devices such as sorters, collators, and tabulators. Such devices are collectively known as Electric Accounting Machines (EAM). They are sometimes also called *unit record machines* (see Section 3.5).

Punched-card data processing has certain *advantages*:

(1) Cards are less expensive than other storage media.

(2) EAM are cheaper and simpler than electronic computers.

On the other hand, such data processing has major *disadvantages*:

(1) Processing of data with punched cards is relatively slow.

(2) The EAM require manual intervention at different stages of the data processing.

(3) Punched cards require large amounts of storage space.

In fact, with the development of the fourth-generation microprocessor (Section 2.4), and more efficient and less expensive computers, the punched-card EAM are being used less and less. However, one still studies these EAM, mainly because certain concepts, such as fields and records, and certain operations, such as sorting and merging, are most easily understood in the context of punched-card data processing.

4.2 CARD-PUNCHING MACHINE

Punching data onto a card, called *keypunching*, is accomplished by means of a *card-punching machine* (or *keypunch*) such as is pictured in Fig. 4-1. We list the various parts of this machine and their functions.

Keyboard. The keyboard looks and operates like a typewriter keyboard. When a key is pushed, the corresponding character is punched in the card. The keyboard also contains functional control switches, program selector, auto feed, etc.

Card hopper. The card hopper, located in the upper right-hand corner of the machine, holds the blank cards (about 500 of them). Cards should be put in the hopper with the 9-edge down and facing the operator.

Punching station. Cards are fed from the card hopper into the punching station, where data are punched onto them.

Reading station. When a card has been punched, it moves into the reading station. Here the data on the card can be read, and can be duplicated onto the following card in the punching station by depressing the duplication key, DUP, on the keyboard.

Card stacker. Cards from the reading station are collected in the card stacker. Like the card hopper, the card stacker can accommodate approximately 500 cards.

Column indicator. This tells the operator which column is next to be punched.

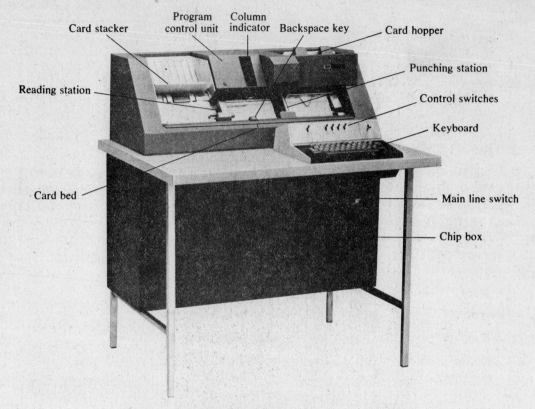

Fig. 4-1.   Card-Punching Machine (*Courtesy of IBM*)

Backspace key.   Depression of this key causes the cards in the punching and reading stations to be backspaced one column.

Program control unit.   In this unit a *program card*, wrapped around a *program drum*, is used to instruct the machine to perform the operations of skipping, duplicating, and shifting.

4.3   VERIFIER

Once data have been punched onto a card, it is essential that the card be checked for accuracy. This task can be done by means of a *verifier*, a machine which looks very much like a card-punching machine. (In fact, some machines, such as the IBM 129, can perform both card punching and verifying.) To verify a punched card, the operator feeds the card into the verifier and, referring to the original source document, strikes the same keys as should have been struck when the card was originally punched. If the holes in the column of a punched card do not correspond to the character entered via the keyboard, the machine locks and a signal is given to the operator. The operator then checks the accuracy of the punched card, and punches a new card if indeed there is an error.

Once a card has been checked for accuracy—that is, when no error has been detected by the verifier or when a new card has been punched correcting an error—this verification is indicated on the card by means of some special punch. For example, the verifier may punch a notch on the right side of the card, as in Fig. 4-2(*a*), or it may punch holes in an added column 81, as in Fig. 4-2(*b*).

4.4   CONTROL PANEL

The various punched-card processing machines (reproducer, sorter, tabulator, etc.) can process cards in more than one way. A specific task is programmed by means of a wired control panel that

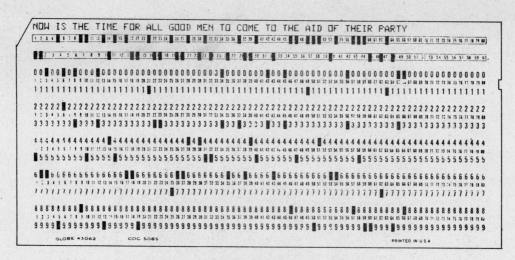

(*a*)　Verified Card with Notch on the Right

(*b*)　Verified Card with Holes Punched in Added Column 81

Fig. 4-2

is inserted into the machine.　Instructions on wiring the control panel usually come with each machine.

4.5　REPRODUCER AND INTERPRETER

Reproducer

Since punched cards are subject to wear, one may want to reproduce a deck of punched cards.　This task can be accomplished by means of the *reproducer* [Fig. 4-3(*a*)].　In fact, the reproducer can be programmed, by means of a control panel, to punch all or part of the data from original cards onto other columns of the same cards or onto new cards.　Besides card-to-card duplication, the reproducer can punch the data from a single *master card* onto a whole deck of *detail cards*.　This process is called *gang punching*.

Interpreter

As it punches character data onto a card, the keypunch normally prints the characters along the top of the card.   On the other hand, the reproducer never prints the characters that it punches in a duplicating deck.   As indicated in Fig. 4-3(*b*), the *interpreter* is a machine that accepts a punched card and prints on the card the characters that were punched into the card.

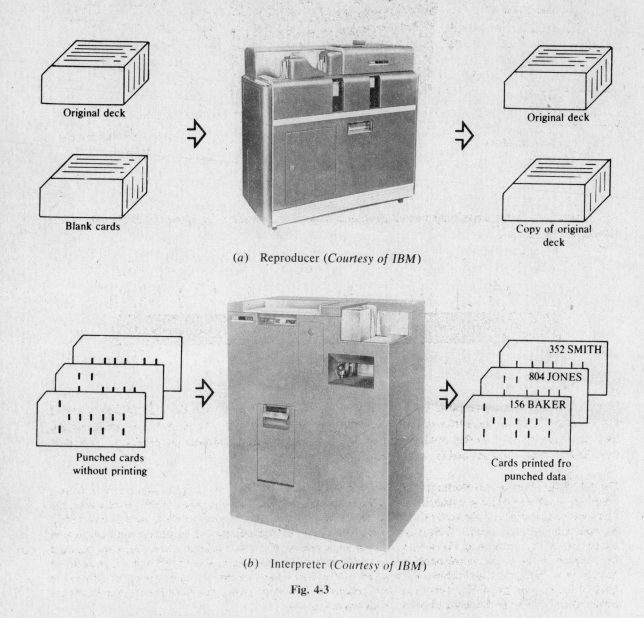

Original deck

Blank cards

Original deck

Copy of original
deck

(*a*)   Reproducer (*Courtesy of IBM*)

Punched cards
without printing

352 SMITH

804 JONES

156 BAKER

Cards printed fro
punched data

(*b*)   Interpreter (*Courtesy of IBM*)

Fig. 4-3

4.6   SORTER AND COLLATOR

Sorter

Recall from Section 1.5 that sorting a file of records means arranging the records in some particular order (numerical or alphabetical).   The *sorter* is the EAM which accomplishes this task, as indicated in Fig. 4-4.

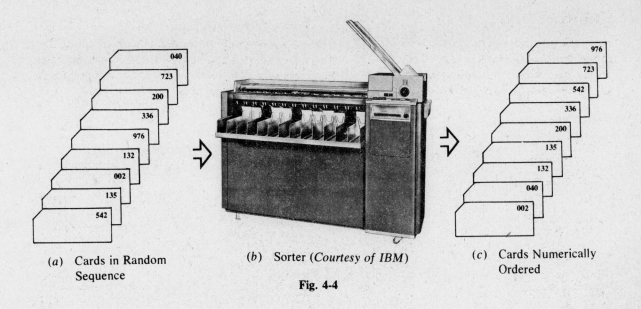

(a) Cards in Random   (b) Sorter (*Courtesy of IBM*)   (c) Cards Numerically
     Sequence   Ordered

Fig. 4-4

Actually, a sorter sorts only one column at a time.   The 13 receiving pockets of the sorter are labeled as in Fig. 4-5.

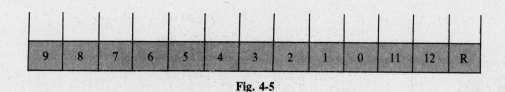

| 9 | 8 | 7 | 6 | 5 | 4 | 3 | 2 | 1 | 0 | 11 | 12 | R |

Fig. 4-5

The first 12 pockets correspond to the 12 rows of an 80-column card, and the last pocket is called the *reject pocket*.   If the sorter detects a hole in, say, the 5-row of the column that is being sorted, then the card is sent to the pocket labeled 5; but if the column contains no punches, or if it is punched incorrectly, the card is sent to the reject pocket R.

EXAMPLE 4.1 (Numerical Sorting) Suppose that we want to sort the deck of cards shown in Fig. 4-4(a), where the numbers appear in columns 41–43.   Since a sorting machine can sort only one column at a time, the cards must be run through the sorter three times, once for each column.   Usually one first sorts the units digit, then the tens digit, and so on.   (This is called *reverse digit sort*.)   Accordingly, one places the deck of cards in the hopper of the sorter as in Fig. 4-6(a) and then sorts column 43.   After column 43 has been sorted, each card appears in the pocket corresponding to its units digit.   The cards are now collected and put back in the hopper, as in Fig. 4-6(b), and column 42 is sorted.   After this second sorting, the cards are collected and put back in the hopper, as in Fig. 4-6(c) and then column 41 is sorted.   After this third sorting, the cards are collected and will be in the required order, as shown in Fig. 4-4(c).

Since each alphabetic character is represented in a column of a card by two punched holes (see Table 3-1), a deck of cards must normally be run two times through a sorter in order to alphabetize a single column.   This is illustrated in Problem 4.17.

Besides numerical and alphabetical sorting, the sorter can perform other general types of sorting, as follows:

Selection sorting.   Here certain cards are sent to the corresponding pockets, and all other cards are sent to the reject pocket.   For example, from a file of class cards, we may want to select all

Cards in hopper before sort

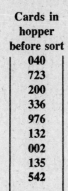

Cards in pockets after sort

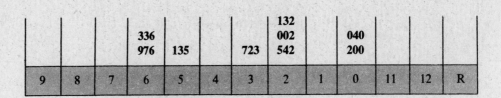

Cards in hopper before sort
040
723
200
336
976
132
002
135
542

9	8	7	6	5	4	3	2	1	0	11	12	R
			336				132		040			
			976	135		723	002		200			
							542					

(a) Column 43 (Units Digit) Sorted

Cards in hopper before sort
336
976
135
723
132
002
542
040
200

9	8	7	6	5	4	3	2	1	0	11	12	R
		976			542	336			002			
					040	135	723		200			
						132						

(b) Column 42 (Tens Digit) Sorted

Fig. 4-6

Cards in hopper before sort
976
542
040
336
135
132
723
002
200

9	8	7	6	5	4	3	2	1	0	11	12	R
976		723		542		336	200	135	040			
								132	002			

(c) Column 41 (Hundreds Digit) Sorted

students whose last name begins with the letter B. We emphasize that in such a selection sort the order of the unselected cards will not be changed.

Major, intermediate, and minor sorting. Frequently card sorting involves more than one field. Thus, sales transaction cards may be sorted numerically according to department number (major sort), then alphabetically according to salesman's name (intermediate sort), and finally numerically according to customer's charge number (minor sort).

Block sorting. Large files of cards might take hours to sort. Rather than sort an entire file before bringing the cards to the next step in the data processing, one sometimes subdivides the file into "blocks" and sorts the blocks one at a time. This is called *block sorting*, and is illustrated in Problem 4.18.

Collator

Recall from Section 1.5 that merging two sorted files of records means combining the two files into one sorted file of records. Figure 1-4 indicates how two decks of cards can be merged. The *collator* (Fig. 4-7) is the EAM that accomplishes this task.

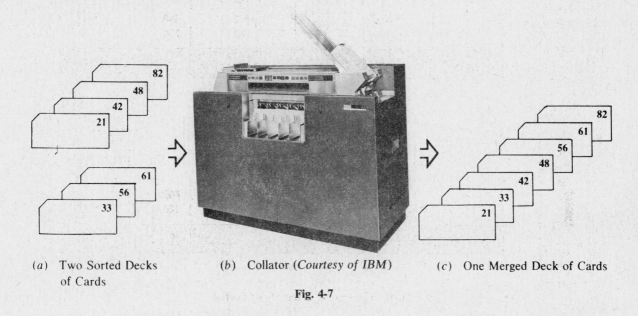

(*a*)   Two Sorted Decks   (*b*)   Collator (*Courtesy of IBM*)   (*c*)   One Merged Deck of Cards
         of Cards

Fig. 4-7

Collators have two input hoppers and several (usually four or five) output pockets. The main property of a collator is that it can read two cards at a time and tell if they are punched identically, and, if not, tell which precedes the other in some ordering. Thus, it merges two numerically sorted decks of cards by reading the two first cards in the decks and sending the lower-numbered to the receiving pocket. This is the same as the algorithm illustrated in Fig. 1-4.

Besides merging, a collator can perform:

Sequence checking. The collator can check if the cards in a sorted deck are in correct order by reading each two successive cards in the deck and seeing if the two cards are in the correct order. Note that all cards except the first and last are read twice when the whole deck is examined.

Selecting. The collator can select from a deck all cards with a specific property, without disturbing the rest of the deck. For example, from an alphabetical file of records containing names and addresses, one can program the collator to send all those cards with a specific ZIP code into one receiving pocket and the remaining cards into another pocket.

Matching. Given two sorted decks of cards, the collator can select any pairs of identical cards, one from each deck. These "matched cards" can either be sent to different pockets, as in Fig. 4-8(*a*), or merged into one pocket ("matched-merged"), as in Fig. 4-8(*b*).

4.7   ACCOUNTING AND CALCULATING MACHINES

Accounting Machine

The *accounting machine* (or *tabulator*), pictured in Fig. 4-9, is an EAM made up of three units:

The *reading* (input) *unit* "reads" all or part of the data on the input cards, and sends this data to the calculating and/or printing unit.

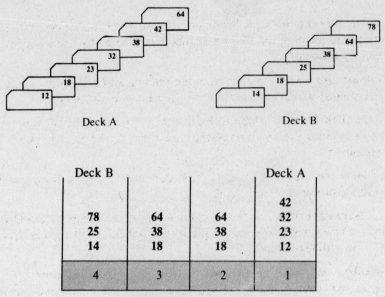

Deck B			Deck A
			42
78	64	64	32
25	38	38	23
14	18	18	12
4	3	2	1

(*a*)   Pockets After Matching

Deck B			Deck A
		64	
		64	
		38	42
78		38	32
25		18	23
14		18	12
4	3	2	1

(*b*)   Pockets After Matching-Merging

Fig. 4-8

(*a*)   Data Punched on   (*b*)   Accounting Machine (*Courtesy of IBM*)   (*c*)   Printed Reports
        Cards

Fig. 4-9

The *calculating unit* performs the operations of addition and subtraction on the input data, and sends the results to the printing unit. The results may also go to a reproducer, to be punched on cards (*summary punching*).

The *printing* (output) *unit* prints the data from the reading and calculating units in final reports, using print forms (pages) which are continuously fed into the machine.

The format of the final reports is controlled by means of a punched paper tape, called the *carriage tape*, which is fed into the machine at the same time as the print forms. There are three general types of printing:

Detail printing. Here part or all of the data from each card are printed on a line, i.e. each card will correspond to exactly one line of print.

Group printing. Here data from a group of cards are used to calculate data that will appear on one line of print. For example, one might print the total sales for a given department, where each sale appears on a different card.

Multiple-line printing. Here the data from one card are printed on more than one line. For example, the name and address of a customer might appear on a card, and one would want this information printed in the usual form of three lines.

Calculating Machine

The *calculator*, pictured in Fig. 4-10, can also perform numerical calculations, but it can record its results only on punched cards, not on printed reports as can the tabulator. However, the calculator is superior to the tabulator in two respects:

(1) The tabulator can only add and subtract, whereas the calculator can also multiply and divide.

(2) The tabulator can record its results on summary cards, whereas the calculator can also record its results on the input cards themselves.

(a) Input Data on   (b) Calculator (*Courtesy of IBM*)   (c) Results on
     Punched Cards   Punched Cards

Fig. 4-10

4.8 AN EXAMPLE OF PUNCHED-CARD DATA PROCESSING

A punched-card data processing system may use some or all of the EAM. We show how this is done in the following example.

Suppose that a factory keeps a master inventory file in which each record consists of an item number and the number of (unsold) items bearing that number in stock. Each day, salesmen send in handwritten sales orders that list, among other things, item numbers and the numbers of such items sold. Figure 4-11 shows how the factory can update its master inventory file. The procedure consists of the following steps:

(1) The item number and number of such items sold on each sales order are punched onto a card, forming a deck of *detail sales records*.

(2) The detail sales records are sorted with respect to the item number.

(3) Since the same item may appear on several detail sales records, a tabulator is used to output a *summary sales record* (a punched card) for each item. Each summary record contains the item number and the total number of such items sold. A printed summary is also produced by the tabulator.

(4) The deck of summary sales records and the *master inventory file* are matched-merged, using a collator. The output consists of an *incomplete master inventory file* and a sorted deck of *matched-merged records* (in which each item is represented by a summary sales record and a master inventory record).

(5) A tabulator is used to produce an *updated inventory record* for each item by subtracting the number of such items sold from the number of such items in stock. The tabulator can also print a report giving items in short supply or out of stock.

(6) The updated inventory records are merged with the incomplete master inventory file to give an *updated master inventory file*.

Solved Problems

PUNCHED-CARD PROCESSING

4.1 Name two ways that data recorded on punched cards may be processed.

The data on the punched cards can be fed into an electronic computer which will process the data and output the results, or the data can be processed by various electromechanical devices.

4.2 What is the translation and meaning of EAM?

EAM is short for electric accounting machines. It is a collective name for all electromechanical devices used in punched-card data processing.

4.3 What is meant by a *unit record system*?

EAM require that each record be contained on exactly one punched card. The use of a single card for each record constitutes a unit record system.

4.4 Punched cards are an example of a random-access storage medium. (True or false.)

False. Punched cards are a classical example of a sequential-storage medium. In order to obtain the information on any given card, it is necessary to examine each card in the deck until one comes to

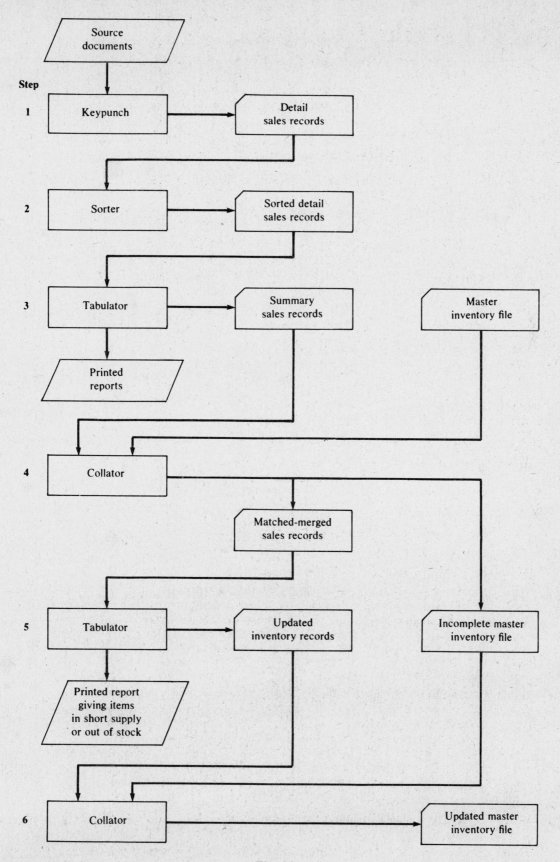

Fig. 4-11

the required card.   As indicated in Problem 3.6, files recorded on punched cards should be sorted for efficient processing.

CARD-PUNCHING MACHINE

4.5   Give the purpose of the   (a) card hopper,   (b) card stacker.

(a)   The card hopper contains the cards before they are processed by the machine.

(b)   The card stacker contains the cards after they have been processed.

4.6   Give the purpose of   (a) the column indicator,   (b) the backspace key,   (c) the main line switch,   (d) the auto feed switch.

(a)   Indicates the next column to be punched.

(b)   As with a typewriter, depressing the backspace key causes the cards in the punching and reading stations to be moved backward one column.

(c)   The machine does not operate unless the main line switch has been turned on.

(d)   When the auto feed switch is on, a new card is automatically fed from the card hopper whenever the card being punched is released.

4.7   Refer to Fig. 4-1.   Where is the wired control panel located?

The keypunch is programmed not by a wired panel, but by a punched card wrapped around a control drum.

VERIFIER, REPRODUCER, INTERPRETER

4.8   Briefly describe the main purpose of the   (a) verifier,   (b) reproducer,   (c) interpreter.

(a)   Checks the accuracy of a punched card.

(b)   Duplicates all or portions of a card.

(c)   Prints the characters punched on a card.

4.9   How does a verifier   (a) recognize whether an error occurred during the punching of a card?   (b) indicate that a card has been punched without any errors?   (c) indicate that an error was made when the card was punched?

(a)   The operator of the verifier depresses the same keys as should have been struck when the card was originally punched.   The verifier detects if the depressed key does not correspond to the punched character.

(b)   The verifier punches a notch in the right edge of the card.

(c)   A signal is given to the operator and a notch is punched at the top of the column in which the error occurred.

4.10   (a) How does the reproducer "know" which columns are to be duplicated?   (b) What is meant by *gang punching* by the reproducer?   (c) Give a case where gang punching might be employed.

(a)   There is a wired control panel that is inserted into the machine, which determines which columns are to be duplicated.

(b)   The reproducer punches data recorded on one card onto a whole deck of cards.

(c)   Suppose that an employee had to insert a card with his name and ID number with each sales order.   Rather than punch a number of cards one at a time, a master card would be punched and then a whole deck of copies would be generated using a reproducer.

4.11   There are two popular ways of checking whether all the cards of a deck have the same punch (same row and same column).   In *sight checking*, the deck of cards is held up to the light, as shown in Fig. 4-12(*a*).   If all the cards have the required punch, then one will be able to see the light at the other side.   In *needle checking*, a blunt needle (like a knitting needle) is glided through the deck at the required spot, as shown in Fig. 4-12(*b*).   If the needle goes through the entire deck, then all the cards have the required punch.   Where in a data processing operation could one of the above methods be used to advantage?

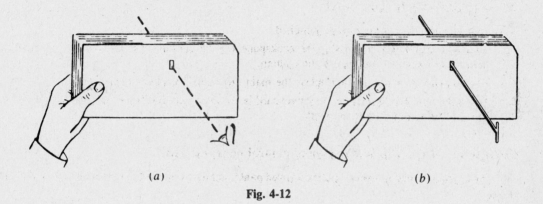

(*a*)   (*b*)

Fig. 4-12

        Either in checking the output of gang punching by a reproducer or in checking the output of a pocket of a sorter.

SORTER

4.12   What is meant by the *key* to a sorting?

        Cards may be sorted in more than one way.   For example, customer account cards may be sorted alphabetically by name or numerically by account number.   The particular field being sorted is called the *key* to the sorting.

4.13   Distinguish among   (*a*) sequence sorting,   (*b*) group sorting,   and   (*c*) selection sorting.

(*a*)   Here all the cards are ordered one after the other, i.e. form a sequence.   We assume that any two cards are punched differently, so that the sequencing is unambiguous.

(*b*)   Here the cards are divided into groups.   Two cards in the same group have the same punch in some fixed field.

(*c*)   Here the cards with a certain punch are sorted out of the deck.

4.14   The time required to sort a given number of columns of a given number of cards can be computed from the formula

$$\text{sorting time} = \frac{(\text{number of columns}) \times (\text{number of cards})}{\text{speed of the sorter}} \times (\text{handling factor})$$

Unless otherwise stated, it is assumed that the handling time is approximately 25% of the actual machine sorting time, in which case the handling factor is $125\% = 1.25$. (*a*) Find the time to sort 6 columns of 9300 cards with a sorter which can sort 1000 cards per minute. (Round off the time to the nearest minute.) (*b*) Find the time to do the same job if the handling time can be reduced to 20% of the machine sorting time.

(*a*)
$$\text{sorting time} = \frac{6(9300)}{1000} \times 1.25 = 70 \text{ minutes}$$

(*b*)
$$\text{sorting time} = \frac{6(9300)}{1000} \times 1.20 = 67 \text{ minutes}$$

4.15 Suppose that one is sorting a deck according to a field of width 5. How many times must he run the cards through the sorter if the field consists of (*a*) digits, (*b*) letters?

(*a*) Five times, once for each digit.

(*b*) Ten times, twice for each letter, because each letter is determined by two punches, one a zone punch and the other a digit punch.

4.16 (*a*) What is meant by *reverse digit sort*? (*b*) Show what can go wrong if one does not use reverse digit sort.

(*a*) In reverse digit sort the units digit is sorted first, then the tens digit, then the hundreds digit, and so on; that is, one sorts the last column of the number field first, the next-to-last column second, and so on.

(*b*) Imagine four cards punched with the numbers 14, 28, 18, and 24. With the tens digit sorted first, the cards will fall into the pockets as shown in Fig. 4-13(*a*). Now, after sorting the units digits, the cards will fall into the pockets as shown in Fig. 4-13(*b*). Observe that the cards are mixed up again. Thus one must use reverse digit sort in this case.

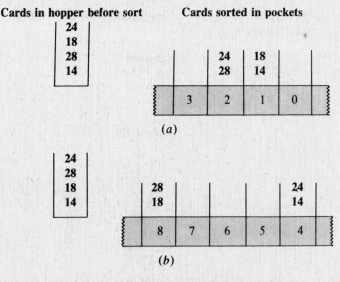

Fig. 4-13

4.17 Show how one sorts a deck of 26 cards, each of which has one letter of the alphabet punched in a given column.

Recall first (Table 3-1) that each alphabetic character is represented by two punched holes in the column, one being a digit punch and the other a zone punch. Accordingly, one first sorts according to the digit punch in the column, so that the cards fall into the pockets of the sorter as shown in Fig. 4-14(a). Collecting the cards in the order of the digit punch, one then runs them through the sorter a second time, this time sorting them according to the zone punch. The cards will fall into the pockets as shown in Fig. 4-14(b). The cards are now alphabetized in the given column.

IRZ	HQY	GPX	FOW	ENV	DMU	CLT	BKS	AJ				
9	8	7	6	5	4	3	2	1	0	11	12	R

(a)

									Z Y X W V U T S	R Q P O N M L K J	I H G F E D C B A	
9	8	7	6	5	4	3	2	1	0	11	12	R

(b)

Fig. 4-14

4.18 Suppose that the names and ID numbers of 4000 students are to be printed in order of the ID numbers rather than alphabetically. Suppose, also, that the ID number is a 5-digit number punched in columns 21–25. Show how one can use block sorting to shorten the time required to print all the names.

   One can first sort the file according to column 21. This divides the file into 10 blocks as in Fig. 4-15. Now the cards in the 0-pocket are sorted according to columns 25 to 22 (reverse digit sort). Then this 0-block can be printed while the 1-block, i.e. the cards from the 1-pocket above, is being sorted; and so on.

90 to 99	80 to 89	70 to 79	60 to 69	50 to 59	40 to 49	30 to 39	20 to 29	10 to 19	00 to 09			
9	8	7	6	5	4	3	2	1	0	11	12	R

(numbers in thousands)

Fig. 4-15

4.19 How does a sorter recognize which hole, if any, is punched in the selected column?

   The punched card passes through the sorter with the 9-edge first, and the selected column passes through a roller and brush. The card acts as an insulator between the roller and brush. However, when a hole in the column is reached, contact is then made between the roller and brush, and an electric circuit is completed. From the length of time it takes for the brush to go from the 9-edge until contact, the sorter can ascertain which hole in the column is punched. The sorter then sends the card to its appropriate pocket. Figure 4-16 shows how this works for a card with a hole punched in the 2-position of the column.

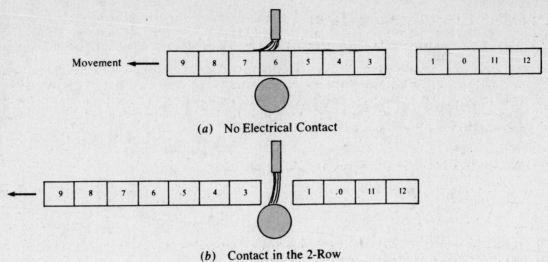

(a) No Electrical Contact

(b)   Contact in the 2-Row

Fig. 4-16

COLLATOR

4.20 How does a collator merge two numerically sorted decks?

One deck is put in the primary feed and the other in the secondary feed. The collator reads the leading card of each deck, sends the lower one to the receiving bin, and replaces the lower card by the next one in its deck. The process is repeated until one deck is empty. The remaining cards of the other deck are then put in the back of the merged deck. (See Fig. 1-4.)

4.21 Name three operations besides merging performed by a collator and briefly describe them.

(1) *Sequence checking*: Checking whether the cards in a sorted deck are in the correct order. (2) *Selecting*: choosing from a deck of cards all those with a specific data item, without disturbing the rest of the deck. (3) *Matching*: selecting from two sorted decks of cards all those cards appearing in both decks.

4.22 Suppose that two decks contain the following data:

Deck A: 15 17 19 21 23 25 27

Deck B: 14 16 17 19 20 27 28 29

How would the cards appear in the pockets (receiving bins) after the decks are (a) matched, (b) matched-merged?

The collator selects from the decks those cards with identical information and [Fig. 4-17(a)] sends the matched cards to two different pockets, or [Fig. 4-17(b)] merges the matched cards into one pocket.

4	3	2	1
			29
25			28
23	27	27	20
21	19	19	16
15	17	17	14

4	3	2	1
		27	
		27	29
25		19	28
23		19	20
21		17	16
15		17	14

(a)   (b)

Fig. 4-17

TABULATOR, CALCULATING MACHINE

4.23 Show how the entire data processing cycle (Fig. 1-1) is illustrated in the tabulator.

Input takes place in the reading unit, which takes data from punched cards and sends the data to the calculating and/or printing units. *Processing* takes place in the calculating unit, where the input data are subjected to addition and/or subtraction; the results go to the printing unit and/or a reproducer. *Output* is performed by the printing unit, which prints on continuously connected pages the input and/or the calculated data.

4.24 What printing functions are programmed on the carriage tape?

The carriage tape governs such items of format as indention, skipping of lines, and carriage returns.

4.25 If the calculating machine not only adds and subtracts, but multiplies and divides, why is it not always used in preference to the tabulator?

The tabulator is chosen when printed reports are needed; the calculator outputs punched cards only.

Review Questions

PUNCHED-CARD PROCESSING

4.26 Name two or three (*a*) advantages and (*b*) disadvantages of punched-card data processing.

4.27 State true or false: (*a*) Punched cards are mainly used with EAM. (*b*) Unit record systems are necessarily punched-card systems. (*c*) EAM are less sophisticated than electronic computers. (*d*) Punched cards are an example of a sequential-storage medium.

KEY PUNCH

4.28 Blank cards should be placed in the card hopper: (*a*) 12-edge down, facing the operator; (*b*) 12-edge down, facing away from the operator; (*c*) 9-edge down, facing the operator; (*d*) 9-edge down, facing away from the operator.

4.29 If an operator wants to duplicate the data from a punched card onto the next card, (*a*) where should the punched card be? (*b*) what is the appropriate manual operation?

4.30 Card-punching machines can be programmed to perform (*a*) column skipping, (*b*) duplicating, (*c*) column shifting, (*d*) all of the above.

4.31 Card-punching machines are programmed by means of (*a*) a punched paper tape, (*b*) a wired control panel, (*c*) a punched program card, (*d*) none of the above.

EAM

4.32 Which EAM duplicates all or portions of a card? (*a*) duplicator, (*b*) interpreter, (*c*) copier, (*d*) none of the above.

4.33 Which EAM prints characters on a punched card? (*a*) printer, (*b*) reproducer, (*c*) verifier, (*d*) none of the above.

4.34 Which EAM checks the accuracy of punched cards?

4.35 Name two nonmachine methods of checking whether all the cards in a deck have the same punch.

4.36 If data on a certain card are to be punched onto a whole deck of cards, (*a*) which EAM can accomplish this task? (*b*) what is the process called? (*c*) what is the original card called? (*d*) what are the duplicate cards called?

SORTER

4.37 A sorter: (*a*) compares data on two different cards, (*b*) reads only one column at a time, (*c*) can be programmed by means of a punched card and drum, (*d*) all of the above.

4.38 The process of partitioning cards into categories is called (*a*) selection sorting, (*b*) group sorting, (*c*) category sorting, (*d*) none of the above.

4.39 The process of separating from a deck those cards with a specific punch is called (*a*) selection sorting, (*b*) group sorting, (*c*) choice sorting, (*d*) none of the above.

4.40 A particular field is used to sort a deck. What name is given to this field?

4.41 (*a*) Find the time to sort 8 columns of 6500 cards with a sorter which can sort 1000 cards per minute. (*b*) What time would be required if the handling time can be reduced to 20% of the machine sorting time?

4.42 Suppose that a deck is sorted according to a field of width 6. How many times must the cards be run through the sorter if the field consists of (*a*) digits, (*b*) alphabetic letters?

4.43 A deck of 8 cards is punched with the following numbers: 52, 61, 42, 43, 53, 62, 41, 51. If one sorts the units digit first and the tens digit next, how do the cards appear in the pockets after each sort?

4.44 Repeat Question 4.43, but sorting the tens digit first. What happens?

4.45 Problem 4.17 shows how one alphabetically sorts a column by first sorting the digit punch and then the zone punch. Describe another way to sort a column alphabetically.

COLLATOR

4.46 What is the maximum number of columns that can be read simultaneously by a collator?

4.47 How many card hoppers does a collator normally have, and what are they called?

4.48 Besides merging, name three basic operations performed by a collator.

4.49   Suppose that two decks contain the following data:

Deck A: 20 22 24 26 28 30 32 34 36 38 40

Deck B: 21 24 25 27 28 29 30 31 33 34 35 39

How would the cards appear in the pockets after the decks are   (a) matched,   (b) matched-merged?

4.50   State true or false: (a) The collator rearranges cards into a particular order.   (b) The collator mainly reads two cards at a time and can tell if they are punched identically or if one precedes the other.   (c) The collator can merge or match two decks only if the two decks themselves are ordered.   (d) The collator can be programmed by means of a wired panel.   (e) The collator indicates that a deck of cards is out of sequence by stopping and flashing an error light.

TABULATOR, CALCULATOR

4.51   What is another name for the tabulator?

4.52   What arithmetical operations can be performed by the   (a) tabulator,   (b) calculator?

4.53   Name the three units of the tabulator.

4.54   The format of the printed reports of the tabulator is controlled by   (a) a program card,   (b) a wired control panel,   (c) a punched paper tape,   (d) none of the above.

4.55   Which EAM can punch calculated data back on the input card?   (a) accounting machine, (b) tabulator,   (c) calculator,   (d) What EAM is used?

4.56   The tabulator can be connected to another EAM so that the tabulator's output may be punched on cards.   (a) What is this process called?   (b) What EAM is used?

4.57   Match the type of printing on the left with its description on the right.

(1) Detail printing.   (a) Each card yields one line of print.

(2) Multiple-line printing.   (b) Two or more cards yield one line of print.

(3) Group printing.   (c) Each card yields two or more lines of print.

Chapter 5

Electronic Data Processing

5.1 INTRODUCTION

The electronic data processing (EDP) industry, already employing millions of people, is one of the country's largest and fastest-growing. Businesses, government agencies, schools, banks, and hospitals are all users of EDP; in fact, these institutions could hardly function today without it.

Figure 5-1 is a picture of a typical medium-sized EDP system. Small-sized electronic computers are becoming increasingly important. Indeed, as their capabilities grow and their price decreases, they are rapidly making punched-card processing obsolete, even for the small user. In this chapter we treat the components and various devices that make up an EDP system. The next chapter will investigate communicating with electronic computers and will give a number of business data processing applications.

5.2 COMPUTER CLASSIFICATIONS

Digital and Analog Computers

Computers operate in two basically different ways. A *digital* computer represents data in terms of discrete numbers and processes data using the standard arithmetic operations. An *analog* computer, on the other hand, measures continuous types of data and uses a physical quantity, such as electric current, to represent and process the data.

EXAMPLE 5.1 The hand calculator, the adding machine, and the punched-card data processing equipment discussed in Chapter 4 are all digital devices. On the other hand, the centrifugal switch, which shuts off a motor when the rotation speed of the shaft (as measured by the angle made with the shaft by a weight) becomes too great, may be considered a primitive analog computer. A somewhat more sophisticated example would be the cruise control device found in some automobiles. It measures the difference between the electric current generated by the rotation of the wheels and a prescribed constant current. Depending upon this difference, the device adjusts the accelerator so as to maintain the automobile at the prescribed constant speed.

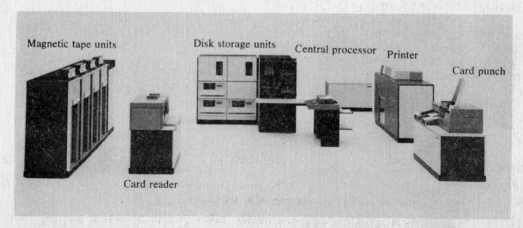

Fig. 5-1. Electronic Data Processing System (IBM 370-135) (*Courtesy of IBM*)

68

We note that the digital computer is much more accurate than the analog computer. The accuracy of an analog computer is limited by the accuracy of measurement of the physical quantity that represents the data.

Some computers combine the digital and analog features into one machine, and they are called *hybrid* computers.

Special-Purpose and General-Purpose Computers

Special-purpose computers are designed to solve a specific problem; the computer program for solving the problem is built right into the computer. For example, the cruise control computer (Example 5.1) is a special-purpose computer. *General-purpose* computers are designed to solve a large variety of problems. That is, they can be given different programs to solve different types of problems.

Most digital computers are general-purpose computers, and it is mainly such computers that are used in business and commercial data processing. On the other hand, most analog computers are special-purpose computers (e.g. flight simulators for training airplane pilots, devices to monitor petroleum distillation).

As this book will be chiefly concerned with general-purpose, electronic, digital computers, the term *computer* shall mean such a computer and its associated devices, unless otherwise specified.

Large and Small Computers

Computers are also classified according to their size. In increasing order, one has: *microcomputers*, *minicomputers*, *medium-sized computers*, and *large-sized computers*. Computer size is determined by a number of factors, e.g. the amount of data that can be stored in the memory and the speed of internal operation. See Section 5.8.

5.3 ADVANTAGES OF ELECTRONIC DATA PROCESSING

Speed and Accuracy

Since a computer is an electronic device, it operates at a speed comparable to the speed of electron flow. A medium-sized computer, for example, can perform 500 000 additions in a second; that is, one every two-millionths of a second. The speed of operation of a computer is thus measured in microseconds or even in nanoseconds (a nanosecond is one *billionth* of a second). At such speeds, a computer can solve in less than a minute problems that would take at least ten hours on a punched-card data processing system.

Finally, a computer can be considered as 100% accurate. Checking circuits are built directly into the computer, so that computer errors that are undetected are extremely rare. (This statement does not apply to *programming* errors.)

Automatic Operation (Stored Program)

Probably the most important advantage of a modern electronic computer over the old punched-card machines is that it can carry out a sequence of many different data processing operations without human intervention. The various operations are executed automatically by way of a stored computer program. See Section 2.4.

Decision-Making Capability

A computer can perform certain decision instructions automatically. Here a decision consists of two steps:

(i) Determining whether a certain statement is true or false.

(ii) Based on that result, choosing one or the other course of action out of alternatives included in the computer program.

Decision-making is often called *branching*, since step (ii) above amounts to branching out to different places in the computer program.

Besides branching, a computer can also be instructed to repeat a list of instructions again and again; this is known as *looping*. Branching and looping will be treated in detail in Chapter 8.

EXAMPLE 5.2 A company wants to compile a list of salespersons whose current total sales exceeds $50 000. It maintains a SALES-FILE of which each record contains the data items RECORD-NAME and TOTAL-SALES, the name and current total sales of a salesperson. The following is the PROCEDURE DIVISION of a program (written in COBOL) that can accomplish the given task:

```
PROCEDURE DIVISION.
PROCEDURE-1.
    READ SALES-FILE RECORD; AT END GO TO END OF JOB.
PROCEDURE-2.
    IF TOTAL-SALES IS GREATER THAN 50000.00,
    DISPLAY RECORD-NAME ON PRINTER.
    GO TO PROCEDURE-1.
END OF JOB.
```

It is called the PROCEDURE DIVISION of the program because it contains the actual instructions for processing the data.

The above program segment contains two PROCEDURE subsegments, which do the following:

(*a*) PROCEDURE-1 instructs the computer to input the first or next record, and to transfer to the END OF JOB statement after all the records have been processed.

(*b*) PROCEDURE-2 instructs the computer to test whether or not TOTAL-SALES exceeds $50 000, and, if it does, to output RECORD-NAME. In either case, the GO TO statement transfers control back to PROCEDURE-1 to input the next record.

Note that there are two decisions in the program. In Procedure-1 the computer has to test whether the last record has been processed, and in PROCEDURE-2 it has to test if TOTAL-SALES exceeds $50 000. Observe also that there is a loop: control is continually transferred from Procedure-2 back to PROCEDURE-1 to repeat the program segment until the last record has been read and processed.

We have written the program segment in the programming language called COBOL. Although the exact details of the language lie beyond the scope of this outline, programming languages are discussed in general in Section 6.8.

Compact Storage

Recall (Section 3.8) that two 10-inch reels of magnetic tape can store as much data as a million punched cards (a stack nearly 600 feet high!). With information in this country doubling every ten years, the ability to store data in a compact and easily retrievable form has become a necessity.

5.4 OVERVIEW OF THE ELECTRONIC COMPUTER

Figure 5-2 indicates the five basic components of the modern electronic computer. The memory unit is also called the *primary storage unit*. Together, the memory, arithmetic, and control units make up the *central processing unit* (*CPU*), or *processor*. Sometimes the input and output units are collectively referred to as the *input/output*, or *I/O*, units.

In addition to the five basic units, a larger computer will normally have one or more mass storage units (Section 2.4), which input and output data that are stored in a compact medium such as magnetic tape or magnetic disks. The relationship between the mass storage units and the five basic components is pictured in Fig. 5-3. The reader should note the similarity between Fig. 5-3 and Fig. 1-2, which schematizes the expanded data processing cycle. Although a mass storage device feeds data into and retrieves data from the CPU, we reserve the term *I/O device* for those

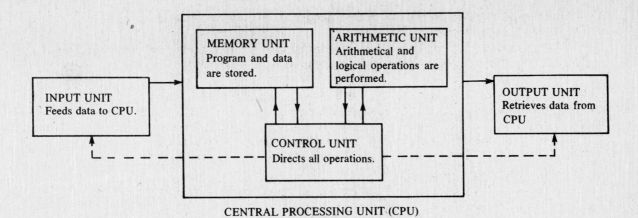

CENTRAL PROCESSING UNIT (CPU)

Fig. 5-2

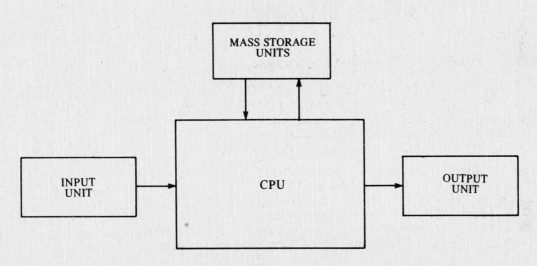

Fig. 5-3

devices by means of which an operator can input/output data to/from the CPU in a form which can be easily read and understood, e.g. typewriter terminal, card punch, card reader. I/O devices are considerably slower than mass storage devices (see Section 5.5). Hence, the latter have become essential for the efficient processing of any large volume of stored data (e.g. master inventory files) and for storing programs which must be quickly accessed.

Peripherals is the term applied to all devices that are connected to the CPU but are not part of the CPU. These include the I/O and mass storage devices discussed above, and other computer devices such as analog-to-digital converters. The collection of all peripheral equipment is called the *computer configuration.*

EXAMPLE 5.3 Figure 5-4 is a picture of a Digital Equipment Corporation PDP-8 computer system. The computer configuration consists of a typewriter terminal for source data input and printed output, two magnetic tape mass storage devices, a magnetic disk storage device, and an analog-to-digital converter. The last device converts input data in the form of a continuous electrical signal into discrete numbers that can then be processed by the CPU.

Magnetic disk device

Analog-to-digital converter

Two magnetic tape devices

Typewriter terminal

CPU

Fig. 5-4   (*Courtesy of Digital Equipment Corporation*)

A computer center may also have various auxiliary devices that are not directly connected to the CPU, such as keypunches, card sorters, and so on.   These are called *off-line* devices.   The term *on-line* devices refers to equipment that is connected to the CPU; hence *on-line devices* and *peripherals* are synonymous.

5.5   INPUT/OUTPUT AND MASS STORAGE UNITS

The input/output and mass storage units feed data into and retrieve data from the CPU.   When inputting, they convert the data, which are recorded in some medium, into a string of electrical impulses which are transmitted to the CPU.   On output, the process is reversed.

Table 5-1.   I/O Devices

Device	Function	Medium	Rate of Data Transfer
Card Reader	input	punched card	300–2000 cards/min
Card Punch	output	punched card	100–500 cards/min
Tape Reader	input	punched paper tape	350–2000 characters/sec
Tape Punch	output	punched paper tape	20–300 characters/sec
Line Printer	output	paper	300–3000 lines/min
Typewriter Terminal	input/output	paper	6–30 characters/min
CRT Terminal	input/output	cathode-ray tube	250–10 000 characters/min
Magnetic-Ink Reader	input	magnetic ink	750–2000 documents/min
Optical Scanner	input	paper	100–3000 documents/min

Table 5-1 gives a list of the most common I/O devices, their functions (input or output or both), and the rates at which they transmit data to or from the CPU. A detailed investigation of these units and their advantages and limitations appears in Chapter 6. When Table 5-1 and the following Table 5-2 are compared, it is seen that the I/O devices are very much slower than the mass storage devices and the (even faster) CPU; this constitutes a serious obstacle to efficient data processing. Various ways of overcoming this obstacle are considered in Section 6.5.

Table 5-2 lists the most common mass storage devices, their types (see Section 3.3), their storage capacities, and the rates at which they transmit data. The media which they handle have been discussed in Chapter 3; the units themselves will be considered in detail in Chapter 6.

Table 5-2. Mass Storage Devices

Device	Medium	Type	Capacity (million characters)	Rate of Data Transfer (thousand characters/sec)
Magnetic Tape Reel	magnetic tape	sequential	1–20	15–800
Magnetic Disk Pack	magnetic disk	direct-access	2–200	100–800
Floppy Disk	magnetic disk	direct-access	0.1–0.5	50–500
Magnetic Drum	magnetic drum	direct-access	1–4	275–1200
Magnetic Strip Handler	magnetic strips	direct-access	100–400	25–45

5.6 CENTRAL PROCESSING UNIT (CPU)

The components of the CPU, as indicated in Fig. 5-2, will be discussed individually.

Control Unit

The control unit supervises all other units of the computer. As indicated by the dashed lines in Fig. 5-2, it selects the appropriate I/O device and causes data to flow between this device and the memory unit. It fetches the proper computer instruction from the memory unit and routes data, referenced by the instruction, from the memory unit to the arithmetic unit and back to the memory unit.

Arithmetic Unit

The arithmetic unit is where the arithmetic and logical operations are performed, as directed by the control unit in accordance with the computer instructions. Chapter 7 and some sections of Chapter 8 will indicate how the computer accomplishes the arithmetic and logical operations.

Memory Unit

The memory unit of the CPU is the place where the computer program and data are stored during processing. It is a random-access storage device consisting of thousands upon thousands of *storage locations*, each of which can be directly reached by the control unit. Each storage location is distinguished by a unique number, its *address*.

During a processing procedure, different data may be stored in any given storage location, but the address of the storage location is always fixed. (The memory unit is often compared to a post office. At various times *different letters* are placed in a postal box, but the *box number* is always the same.)

The data that are to be stored in the memory unit for processing are described by the computer program, and the particular storage locations which are to receive these data are assigned when the program is loaded into memory. In general, each data item (field) is assigned a storage location, so that the item may be directly accessed by means of the address of the storage location and then processed.

The size of a computer is often measured in terms of the number of storage locations in its memory. Because of the way computers are designed, the number of storage locations is always a multiple of the number $K = 1024$. A small computer may have only 4K, or 4096, storage locations; a large computer may have as many as 8192K, or 8 388 608, storage locations. Each storage location itself consists of a given number of positions, where each position is an electronic device having two possible states (see Section 5.7). The two states are represented by the binary digits 0 and 1; we say that each position stores one *bit* (from *bi*nary dig*it*). The number of bits which make up a storage location ranges from 8 to 64, depending on the computer.

The internal representation of data in the memory unit is discussed in detail in Chapter 7. Here we simply mention that a computer normally uses a 6-bit or an 8-bit code for each character. Hence, in the former case, the name ADAMS could be stored in three, adjacent, 12-bit storage locations, as shown in Fig. 5-5.

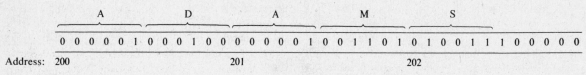

Address: 200   201   202

Fig. 5-5

Observe that the second half of the third storage location contains a blank character (1 0 0 0 0 0).

It should be pointed out that any data in a storage location are automatically erased as new data are entered.

EXAMPLE 5.4 Reconsider the company in Example 5.2, that wanted to compile a list of salespersons whose total sales exceeded $500 000. Example 5.2 discussed the PROCEDURE DIVISION segment of such a program (in COBOL), the segment which contains the actual instructions for processing the data. The complete program will also contain a DATA DIVISION segment such as the one shown in Fig. 5-6(a). This DATA DIVISION segment, which would appear before the PROCEDURE DIVISION segment of Example 5.2, describes the data to be stored in memory. Specifically, it tells the computer to reserve a section of the memory for a record called SALES-RECORD which will contain two data items, RECORD-NAME (the name of the salesperson) and TOTAL-SALES (his current total sales). The "PICTURE" phrases describe the data items:

(i) PICTURE X(20) states that RECORD-NAME is a nonnumeric data item consisting of 20 characters (some of which may be blank characters).

(ii) PICTURE 9(6)V9(2) COMPUTATIONAL states that TOTAL-SALES is a numeric data item consisting of 6 digits before an assumed decimal point and 2 digits after the assumed decimal point (as, for example, the number 123,456.78 would be recorded in a field of width 8, without the comma and the decimal point).

When the computer program is stored in memory, storage locations are assigned to each of the data items, as illustrated in Fig. 5-6(b). More than one storage location might be required to store a particular data item, as would be the case when storing RECORD-NAME (20 characters). The number 332 in Fig. 5-6(b) indicates the address of the first storage location containing RECORD-NAME. Similarly, the number 342 is the address of the first storage location containing TOTAL-SALES (should more than one storage location be required).

```
DATA DIVISION.
FILE SECTION.
FD SALES-FILE;........; DATA RECORD IS SALES-RECORD.
01   SALES-RECORD
     02   RECORD-NAME PICTURE X(20)
     02   TOTAL-SALES PICTURE 9(6)V9(2) COMPUTATIONAL
```

(*a*)

```
                          MEMORY

            ┌─────────────────────────────┐
            │      COMPUTER PROGRAM        │
            └─────────────────────────────┘

              RECORD-NAME      TOTAL-SALES
            ┌───────────────┐  ┌───────────┐
            │ ADAMS  TOM B  │  │ 034000.00 │
            └───────────────┘  └───────────┘
                332               342
```

(*b*)

Fig. 5-6

Fourth-generation small computers combine random-access memory (RAM), as described above, with *read-only* memory (ROM), consisting of storage locations from which data can only be read.   ROM is made of permanently wired, integrated circuits that are designed to perform specific tasks such as processing certain computer instructions or performing certain numerical calculations.

Computer Console

Besides the three units of the CPU discussed above, there is usually a panel on the front of or near the CPU which contains numerous lights and switches.   This *computer console* allows the

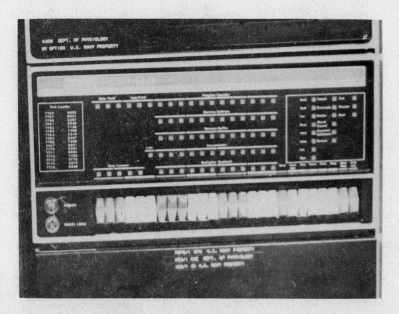

Fig. 5-7   (*Courtesy of Digital Equipment Corporation*)

operator to (i) turn the computer on and off, (ii) start or stop the execution of a program, (iii) display or change the contents of any storage location, (iv) display or change the data in the arithmetic or control unit. Figure 5-7 shows a typical computer console.

5.7   MEMORY DEVICES

The structure of the memory unit is perhaps the most important characteristic of a computer system. Some desirable features in the design of a memory unit are (i) fast, direct accessibility of the data; (2) compactness; (3) low cost; (4) durability and security (i.e. a *nonvolatile* memory). Leaving aside early devices (see Chapter 2) and devices still under development (see Problem 5.25), there are three types of memory that require discussion.

Magnetic Core Memory

Most computers in use today have this type of memory device. It consists of tiny (less than 0.05 inch in diameter) doughnut-shaped objects, called *cores*, made of ferromagnetic material. A basic principle of physics states that if a core is threaded by a wire carrying an electric current, the core will be magnetized in a certain direction, called its *polarity*, which depends upon the direction of the current through the wire. This is pictured in Fig. 5-8. Observe that the core can be put into one of two states, i.e. one of two polarities. Furthermore, once the core is magnetized, it will keep its polarity even when the current is removed. It will change its polarity only when a current is sent through the wire in the opposite direction.

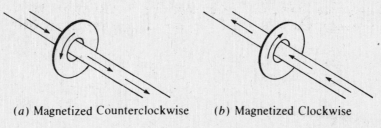

(*a*) Magnetized Counterclockwise   (*b*) Magnetized Clockwise

Fig. 5-8

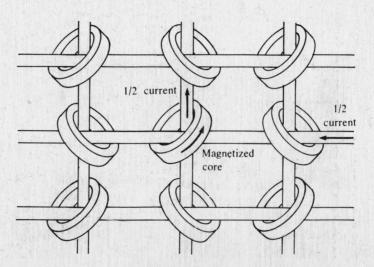

Fig. 5-9

Now, one wants to be able to magnetize one core at a time; but it would be extremely inefficient to have one wire for each core. Therefore, cores are threaded by a screen of wires such that each core is threaded by two of the wires which are perpendicular to each other, as shown in Fig. 5-9. Then, if currents of half the required strength are sent through the two wires threading a certain core, only that core is magnetized.

Reading the polarity of a given bit requires two additional wires, a *sense* wire and an *inhibit* wire, passing through the core (Fig. 5-10). First, the computer will polarize the core in some given direction, say 0; then the computer will polarize the core in the opposite direction, 1. If initially the core was 0, then no change in the polarity of the core takes place in the first step; in particular, no current flows through the sense wire, which informs the computer that that core is 0. In the second step, in this case, the computer will simultaneously put a current through the inhibit wire while it attempts to write a 1. This will prevent a change in polarity of the core, so that it remains 0 after it is read. (The current in the inhibit wire is opposite in direction to that in one of the current wires, and thus cancels the effect of the latter current.) On the other hand, if the core was initially 1, the first step will change the polarity of the core to 0. This will send a current through the sense wire, informing the computer that the core initially contained a 1. The second step restores the core to 1.

The magnetic cores are stacked in parallel planes for the actual storage of data. If the computer uses, say, 12-bit storage locations, the memory will have a stack of 13 planes (one plane for parity check), with a storage location represented by 13 similarly placed cores in the 13 planes, as indicated in Fig. 5-11.

Thin-Film Memory

Thin-film memory consists of spots of a nickel-iron alloy deposited on a very thin plate of glass or plastic. The spots are connected by very thin copper wires etched into the plate. See Fig. 5-12. Each spot operates like a core, and the plate of spots is like a plane of cores. Thin-film

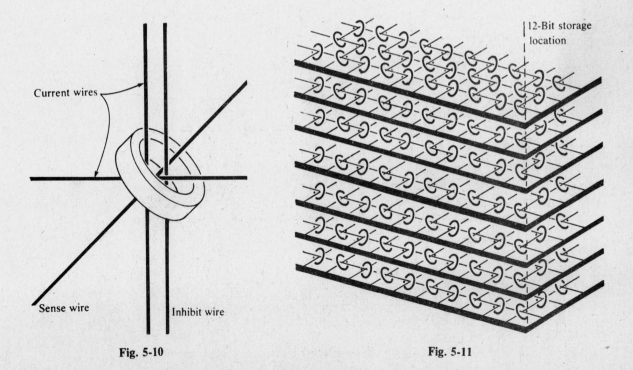

Fig. 5-10

Fig. 5-11

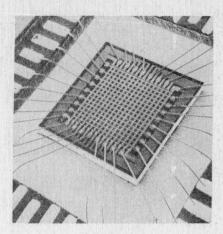

Fig. 5-12

memory is much more compact than core memory; each plane of spots is smaller than a single core. It is also faster and is just as stable. Although production costs were at first rather high, new production methods have brought thin-film units within a practical price range.

Semiconductor Memory

Semiconductor memories consist of integrated electronic circuits etched onto silicon chips. A single chip (see Fig. 2-4) contains over a thousand circuit elements that form the basis for 128 memory circuits and support circuits. Since 1971, when the semiconductor memory was first introduced, its cost has dropped significantly, and this type of memory is replacing magnetic core memory in most of the newer computers. An important advantage of semiconductor memories is their small size and their speed; a disadvantage is that they may be volatile and lose the data stored in them when the computer power goes off.

5.8   COMPUTER SIZES

As applied to a computer, *size* means data processing capability; it is codetermined by (1) the amount of data that can be stored in memory, (2) the speed of internal operation of the computer, (3) the number and type of peripheral devices, and (4) the amount and type of software (programs) available for use with the computer.

Microcomputers

The Radio Shack TRS-80, shown in Fig. 5-13, is an example of a microcomputer, essentially a fourth-generation device. Microcomputers have from 4K to 32K storage locations (Section 5.6) and range in price from $500 to $5000, depending upon memory size and peripheral equipment. They are quite capable of handling small, single-business applications such as sales analysis and payroll.

Minicomputers

A typical minicomputer, the PDP-8 made by Digital Equipment Corporation, is shown in Fig. 5-4. Although the speed of operation of the minicomputer is the same as that of the microcomputer, minicomputers usually have larger memory (from 4K to 128K storage locations), more numerous and faster I/O devices, and a greater variety of software. As in the case of the microcomputer, modern memory and mass storage devices have made these computers affordable and quite capable of servicing a single medium-sized business. Other examples of minicomputers

Fig. 5-13 *(Courtesy of Radio Shack—A Division of Tandy Corporation)*

are the IBM SYS/3, the Honeywell 200 and 1200 computers, and the Hewlett-Packard series 2000 computers. Minicomputers range in price from $5000 to $100 000, depending upon memory size and peripheral equipment.

Medium-Sized Computers

The IBM System 370, model 135, pictured in Fig. 5-1, exemplifies the medium-sized computer. As compared to a minicomputer, a medium-sized computer usually has a larger capacity for storing data (32K to 512K storage locations) and operates at a higher speed. Medium-sized computers can serve the needs of a large bank, insurance company, or university. A computer of this size also may be used on a time-sharing basis, whereby several small companies purchase computer time from the owner of the computer. Some other medium-sized computers are the Burroughs 3500 system and NCR Century 200 system. Medium-sized computers range in price from $200 000 to $1 000 000.

Large-Sized Computers

Large-sized computers have storage capacities of from 512K to 8192K, and some such computers have internal operating speeds measured in terms of nanoseconds, as compared to smaller computers where speed is measured in terms of microseconds. Prices of large-sized computers vary from $500 000 up, depending upon the number and type of peripheral devices.

Computer manufacturers often refer to "logical growth systems" that can be expanded from a medium-sized configuration to a large size as the need presents itself and at a minimum cost. The possibility of increasing the data processing capability of a computer by adding devices, such as additional memory or peripheral devices, is called *expandability*. The possibility of increasing the capability of the computer by replacing one or more devices of the system by newer and faster models is called *upward mobility*. Both of these means of growth are provided for by most of the manufacturers of medium and large computers.

EXAMPLE 5.5   The IBM System 370 is a logical growth system.   Table 5-3 compares the CPU's of the IBM System 370, from model 115, which is a medium-sized computer, to model 168, which is considered a large-sized computer.

Table 5-3

SYS/370 Model	Storage Capacity	Speed (million instructions per second)
115-0	64K–192K	0.087
125-0	96K–256K	0.087
135	96K–512K	0.185
145-2	256K–2048K	0.340
158-1	512K–6144K	0.860
168-0	1024K–8192K	2.100

Solved Problems

TYPES OF COMPUTERS

5.1   Briefly describe the difference between a digital and an analog computer, and give an example of each.

A digital computer, such as a hand or desk calculator, represents data in terms of discrete numbers, whereas an analog computer represents data in terms of some continuous physical quantity.   A household thermostat is an elementary analog computer.

5.2   Briefly distinguish between a general-purpose and a special-purpose computer, and give an example of each.

A general-purpose computer is designed to solve a variety of problems (or, at least, a family of similar problems), whereas a special-purpose computer is designed to solve a specific problem.   The automobile cruise control device is a special-purpose computer; the typical hand calculator is a general-purpose computer.

5.3   What is a hybrid computer?   Give an example.

A hybrid computer is one with both digital and analog devices.   These can be general-purpose or special-purpose.   The electronic calculating scale, as used in food stores, is an example of a special-purpose hybrid computer.

5.4   Which type of computer might the following companies use to solve their problem? (*a*) The Nevasink Aircraft Corporation want to simulate flight conditions in order to train their pilots.   (*b*) The Munificent Loan Company want to send monthly up-to-date bills to their customers.   (*c*) Osmosis Oil, Ltd., want to monitor their natural gas production. (*d*) Heist Sales Incorporated want to keep a weekly inventory of their goods.

(*a*)   A special-purpose analog computer.

(*b*)   Digital computers are always used for calculations.

(c) An analog computer or possibly, if calculations are to be performed on the monitored information, a hybrid computer.

(d) Digital computers are always used for searching and numerical-type operations.

5.5 In general, how does the accuracy of an analog computer compare with the accuracy of a digital computer?

The digital computer is usually more accurate than the analog computer, since the accuracy of an analog computer is fixed by the measuring devices used in the computer.

5.6 What is the correlation among digital, analog, special-purpose, and general-purpose computers?

Most digital computers are general-purpose, whereas most analog computers are special-purpose.

ADVANTAGES OF EDP

5.7 Name four major advantages of electronic data processing.

(1) Speed and accuracy, (2) automatic operation, (3) ability to make decisions, (4) compact data storage.

5.8 What is a computer program?

An explicit set of instructions given to the computer for solving a problem.

5.9 Briefly describe how a computer can perform a complicated series of data processing operations automatically.

It initially stores the computer program in its memory and then follows the instructions of the program step by step until the processing is complete.

5.10 There are two steps involved in having a computer make a decision. What are these steps, and why is decision-making called *branching*?

The steps are: (1) determining whether a certain statement is true or false; and (2) based upon the result of (1), continuing along one or the other *branch* of the computer program.

5.11 (a) What is *looping*? (b) What determines how many times a loop is executed?

(a) The repetition of a sequence of instructions in a computer program.

(b) The number of repetitions may be fixed, but it is often variable and under the control of a branching decision (see Problem 5.10). For instance, a numerical algorithm may be repeated until the results have a desired accuracy.

5.12 Figure 5-14 is the PROCEDURE DIVISION segment of a computer program written in COBOL. The input is a master inventory file whose records include the item number, the number ordered of that item, and the current number in stock of that item. What does the program instruct the computer to do?

The program instructs the computer to read each inventory record and to determine whether the number of items in stock is less than the number ordered. If so, the computer is instructed to output the item number. Thus the computer compiles a list of items which are to be purchased.

```
PROCEDURE DIVISION.
PROCEDURE-A.
  READ INVENTORY-FILE RECORD; AT END GO TO END OF JOB.
PROCEDURE-B.
  IF CURRENT-NUMBER IS LESS THAN NUMBER-ORDERED,
    DISPLAY ITEM-NUMBER ON PRINTER.
  GO TO PROCEDURE-A.
END OF JOB.
```

Fig. 5-14

OVERVIEW OF THE COMPUTER

5.13 State the five basic units of the computer, name the three which make up the CPU, and give the function of each of the five units.

The five basic units are as follows: (1) input unit, (2) output unit, (3) memory unit, (4) arithmetic unit, (5) control unit. The last three make up the CPU. The functions of the units are: (1) feeds data into the CPU; (2) retrieves data from the CPU; (3) stores the computer program and the data that are to be immediately processed; (4) performs the arithmetical and logical operations; (5) directs the other units of the computer.

5.14 What is the function of a mass storage unit, and how does it differ from the I/O units?

A mass storage unit inputs and outputs data that are stored on such media as magnetic tape or magnetic disk. The I/O units are used mainly to input source data or output summary documents, whereas the mass storage units transfer data that have already been processed and stored, such as master files and computer programs.

5.15 Using Table 5-1, calculate the rate of transfer of data, in characters per second, of the fastest card reader and compare this result with the rate of transfer of data of the slowest magnetic tape unit, as given in Table 5-2.

According to Table 5-1, the fastest card reader transfers data at 2000 cards per minute. Since there are 80 characters on a card, the rate of transfer T is

$$T = 2000 \times 80 = 160\,000 \text{ characters per minute}$$

or

$$T = \frac{160\,000}{60} = 2667 \text{ characters per second}$$

On the other hand, by Table 5-2, the slowest magnetic tape unit can transfer 15 000 characters per second, which still is 5.6 times faster than the card reader.

5.16 Briefly define (*a*) peripheral device, (*b*) off-line device, (*c*) computer configuration.

(*a*) A device that is connected to the CPU.

(*b*) A device that is not connected to the CPU (but is used in conjunction with it).

(*c*) The totality of devices connected to the CPU, i.e. all the peripherals.

THE CENTRAL PROCESSING UNIT

5.17 Which one of the three units of the CPU is described in each of the following statements? (*a*) It is a storage area for the computer program. (*b*) It calls upon the I/O devices when data are to be fed to or from the CPU. (*c*) It is a random-access storage medium. (*d*) It acts as an intermediary between the other two units. (*e*) It performs arithmetic operations. (*f*) It fetches computer instructions from the memory unit and interprets them.

(*a*) memory   (*c*) memory unit   (*e*) arithmetic unit
(*b*) control unit   (*d*) control unit   (*f*) control unit

5.18 Define: (*a*) storage location in memory, (*b*) address of a storage location.

(*a*) The smallest section of the memory which can be directly accessed.

(*b*) A number assigned to a storage location by means of which that particular storage location may be accessed.

5.19 How does one measure the size of a computer memory?

The size of a computer memory is measured in terms of the number of its storage locations. Because of the way that computers are designed, this number will always be a multiple of the number $K = 2^{10} = 1024$. Thus, for example, one will say that a computer has 38K, or 54K, or 64K, storage locations.

5.20 Suppose that a computer has 32K storage locations. (*a*) Approximately how many storage locations are there? (*b*) Exactly how many storage locations are there? (*c*) What is the percent difference between the answers in (*a*) and (*b*)?

(*a*) Since K is approximately 1000, there are approximately 32 000 storage locations.

(*b*) Since K = 1024, there are exactly (32)(1024) = 32 768 storage locations.

(*c*) The percent difference between 32 768 and 32 000 is

$$\frac{768}{32\,768} = \frac{24}{1024} = 0.023 = 2.3\%$$

This 2.3% difference, which is equal to the percent difference between K and 1000, will be the same for any computer size, although the numerical difference will be larger for larger computers.

5.21 If a 12-bit storage location is to be used to store the nonnegative integers $0, 1, 2, \ldots$, what is the largest integer that can be stored in the location?

Recall (Problem 3.19) that a two-state storage medium with N positions can store at most 2^N different characters. Thus a 12-bit storage location can store at most $2^{12} = 4096$ different characters. It follows that, beginning with 0, the largest integer which can be stored in the location is 4095.

5.22 In view of Problem 5.21, how may computers with 12-bit storage be programmed so that numbers larger than 4095 can be processed?

Computers with storage locations having fewer than 32 bits are usually programmed to use more than one location to store a number. Thus, computers with 12-bit locations normally use 3 locations to store a number. With one bit reserved for the sign, this permits integers as large as 2^{35} (strictly, $2^{35} - 1$) to be stored. Furthermore, using the exponential form of a number, such computers can store numbers as large as 10^{38} with 7-significant-figure accuracy. (Chapter 7 gives a full discussion of this representation of numbers in computer memory.)

5.23 What are four operations which a computer operator can perform using the lights and switches on a computer console?

(1) Turn the computer on or off. (2) Start or halt the execution of a program. (3) Display or change the contents of any storage location. (4) Display or change the data in the arithmetic or control unit.

MEMORY DEVICES

5.24 Briefly describe each of the following types of memory devices: (*a*) magnetic core, (*b*) thin-film   (*c*) semiconductor.

(*a*)   Magnetic core memory consists of toroidal magnetizable objects transfixed at the intersections of a wire screen.

(*b*)   Thin-film memory consists of spots of magnetic material deposited on a thin film of glass or plastic.

(*c*)   Semiconductor memory consists of electronic circuits etched into silicon chips.

5.25 A type of memory that is still in the experimental stage is *cryogenic* (low-temperature) *memory*.   What might be the advantage in using extremely cold electronic circuits?

At temperatures near absolute zero certain materials lose essentially all of their electrical resistance, becoming superconductors.   As discovered in 1962 by Brian Josephson, applying an external magnetic field instantly deprives a circuit element of superconductivity, while removing the field instantly restores superconductivity.   One thus has the basis for an extremely fast, two-state (memory) device.

5.26 What basic principle of physics underlies the magnetic core memory?

The principle is that moving electric charges always generate a magnetic field.   In the case of an electric current in a wire, the lines of magnetic force circle the wire in the clockwise or counterclockwise sense, depending on the direction of the current.   If, then, a ferromagnetic (highly magnetizable) object is brought near the wire, it will be magnetized in one of two directions, according to the current direction.

5.27 Consider a magnetized magnetic core.   (*a*) What is meant by its *polarity*?   (*b*) What is the function of the sense and inhibit wires through the core?

(*a*)   The polarity of a core is the direction in which the core is magnetized.

(*b*)   The sense and inhibit wires are used to read the polarity of the core.

5.28 Find the number of magnetic cores in the memory of a computer having 32K storage locations, each consisting of 13 bits, including a check bit.

Each core corresponds to a bit; hence the number of cores in each storage location is 13.   As the computer has

$$32K = (32)(1024) = 32\,768$$

storage locations, the total number of cores in memory is

$$(32\,768)(13) = 425\,984$$

5.29 Relative to magnetic core memory, state   (*a*) two advantages and   (*b*) one disadvantage of semiconductor memory.

(*a*)   Smaller size, higher speed.

(*b*)   Volatility: semiconductor memory may lose the data stored in it when the power to the computer is shut off.

5.30 Distinguish between RAM and ROM.

Data may be transferred into or out of RAM (random-access memory), but may only be transferred out of ROM (read-only memory).   ROM contains permanently stored information, not subject to change by a particular program.   For instance, if the computer contained a built-in checking routine that involved the values of certain constants, these values would be stored in ROM.

COMPUTER SIZES

5.31 Which four factors determine the data processing capability (size) of a computer?

(1) The number of storage locations in the memory unit; (2) the working speed of the CPU; (3) the number and type of peripheral devices; (4) the available software.

5.32 If computer A is larger in size (data processing capability) than computer B, would you expect it to be larger in physical size?

Yes; each factor in Problem 5.31 is positively related to physical size.

5.33 Define the terms (a) *computer expandability*, (b) *upward mobility*

(a) Computer expandability is the ability of a medium-sized computer system to increase in data processing capability by addition of such devices as mass storage devices, I/O devices, and primary storage locations.

(b) Upward mobility is the ability of a medium-sized computer system to increase in data processing capability by the substitution of larger or more efficient computer devices.

Review Questions

TYPES OF COMPUTERS AND ADVANTAGES OF EDP

5.34 Match the type of computer on the left with its description on the right.

(1) Digital computer.   (a) A computer designed to solve a specific problem.

(2) Analog computer.   (b) A computer which represents data by numbers.

(3) General-purpose computer.   (c) A computer which represents data in terms of a continuous physical quantity.

(4) Special-purpose computer.   (d) A computer designed to solve a large variety of problems.

5.35 What is the name given to a computer having both digital and analog devices?

5.36 The *planimeter* measures the area of a plane figure by tracing its periphery.   Which type of "computer" is this?

5.37 An analog computer is (a) often used to simulate a physical phenomenon, (b) usually less accurate than a digital computer, (c) usually a special-purpose computer, (d) all of the above.

5.38 Which type of computer is usual in business data processing?

5.39 Electronic data processing: (a) is fast and accurate, (b) can automatically make decisions of a certain type, (c) provides compact storage, (d) all of the above.

5.40 What do we call a set of instructions given to the computer to solve a particular problem?

5.41   Match each term on the left with the phrase on the right which best describes it.

(1)   Branching.

(2)   Looping.

(3)   GO TO statement.

(a)   An instruction in a computer program which transfers control to another part of the program.

(b)   A term used to describe the decision-making part of a computer program.

(c)   A term used to describe the repetition of a sequence of instructions in a computer program.

OVERVIEW OF THE COMPUTER; THE CPU

5.42   Match each of the five basic units of the computer on the left with the phrase on the right that best describes its function.

(1)   Input unit.

(2)   Output unit.

(3)   Memory unit.

(4)   Arithmetic unit.

(5)   Control unit.

(a)   Retrieves data from the CPU.

(b)   Performs the arithmetic and logical operations.

(c)   Directs the other units.

(d)   Stores the computer program and the data which are to be immediately processed.

(e)   Feeds data into the CPU.

5.43   Which unit, outside the CPU, supplements the memory unit?

5.44   Match each term on the left with the phrase on the right which best describes it.

(1)   Peripheral.

(2)   Computer configuration.

(3)   Off-line device.

(a)   A computer device which is not connected to the CPU.

(b)   A device which is connected to the CPU.

(c)   The totality of devices connected to the CPU.

5.45   (a) Using Table 5-1, calculate the rate of data transfer, in characters per second, of the fastest punched paper tape reader.   (b) How much faster is the fastest disk pack device, as given in Table 5-2?

5.46   Using Table 5-2, determine how much more data can be stored in a magnetic disk pack of largest capacity than on a magnetic tape of largest capacity.

5.47   The memory unit of the computer is   (a) a direct-access storage device,   (b) a storage area for the computer program as it is being executed,   (c) a storage area for data which are about to be processed,   (d) all of the above.

5.48   The control unit of the computer: (a) performs logical operations on the data,   (b) is a device for manually operating the computer,   (c) directs the other units of the computer,   (d) all of the above.

5.49   A storage location in memory: (a) is a section of memory which can be directly tapped;   (b) may have several identifying numbers, or addresses;   (c) may have different data stored in it at different times;   (d) all of the above.

5.50   The two possible states of a position in the memory of a computer are normally represented by   (a) the words *right* and *left*, depending upon the polarity of the core;   (b) the words *on* and *off*;   (c) the digits 0 and 1;   (d) none of the above.

5.51   Match each term on the left with its description on the right.

(1) DATA DIVISION.	(a) A phrase in a COBOL program which states that a certain data item is nonnumeric and consists of 20 characters, including blanks.
(2) PROCEDURE DIVISION.	(b) The segment of a COBOL program which describes the data to be stored in memory.
(3) PICTURE X(20).	(c) The segment of a COBOL program which contains the instructions for solving the problem.

5.52   An operator can run the computer manually by means of the (a) on-line devices, (b) control unit, (c) computer console, (d) peripherals.

5.53   What is the acronym used to denote the one-way storage locations in the memory of a computer?

5.54   A certain small computer has a 4K RAM and a 12K ROM. How many locations in memory are available both for introducing and retrieving data?

MEMORY DEVICES AND COMPUTER SIZES

5.55   Desirable characteristics in the design of a memory unit are (a) speed, (b) compactness, (c) durability, (d) all of the above.

5.56   Match each of the three types of memory units on the left with its description on the right.

(1) Magnetic core.	(a) Spots of magnetic material deposited on a thin film of glass or plastic.
(2) Thin-film.	(b) Integrated electronic circuits etched into silicon chips.
(3) Semiconductor.	(c) Doughnut-shaped magnetizable objects around intersections of a wire lattice.

5.57   Semiconductor memory: (a) is somewhat larger than magnetic core memory, (b) is somewhat slower than magnetic core memory, (c) may lose the data stored in it when power is shut off, (d) none of the above.

5.58   State whether the following are true or false. (a) The available software for a computer does not affect the data processing capability of the computer. (b) Increasing the size of the memory of a computer usually increases the data processing capability of the computer. (c) The smaller computer will usually have more peripheral devices in order to compensate for its size.

5.59   State whether the following are true or false. (a) Microcomputers are fun to play with, but are too small for practical applications. (b) Computers which can service a medium-sized business run to millions of dollars and are therefore always rented. (c) Usually, to increase the data processing capability of a medium-sized computer, entirely new equipment must be purchased.

Chapter 6

Communicating with the Computer

6.1 INTRODUCTION

This chapter continues the study of electronic data processing (EDP), with further discussion of I/O devices, efficient ways to input/output data, and computer software. In addition there is given a brief description of some of the more popular high-level programming languages, such as COBOL, FORTRAN, and BASIC. A number of business data processing applications are considered.

6.2 I/O DEVICES

Devices That Employ Punched Cards or Paper Tape

In electronic data processing, punched cards are used chiefly for inputting source data. They are not ordinarily used for data storage if mass storage facilities are available. The relative disadvantages of punched cards as a storage medium were discussed in Section 3.8.

The unit that inputs data on punched cards is called a *card reader*; the output unit is called a *card punch*. The two are often housed in the same cabinet, as shown in Fig. 6-1.

Fig. 6-1 (*Courtesy of IBM*)

To input data, the deck of punched cards is placed in the *read hopper*. On command from the CPU, a card is moved through two devices, each of which senses the holes in the card (by the brush-and-roller technique of Problem 4.19 or by means of photoelectric cells which register light passing through the holes) and transmits the data electrically to the CPU. Two reading stations are used, in order to detect any errors in reading. See Fig. 6-2(*a*). The card is then deposited in the *output stacker*.

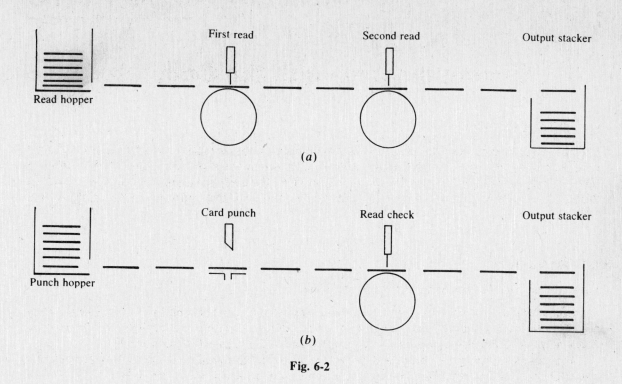

Fig. 6-2

To output data, a stack of blank cards is placed in the *punch hopper*, as pictured in Fig. 6-2(*b*). A card is moved past dies that punch it in accordance with electrical signals from the CPU. The card then passes a read sensor to detect any punching errors. The card is then deposited in the output stacker.

Punched paper tape has never been as popular as punched cards for general-purpose data processing (see Section 3.7). It does, however, serve as output medium in certain special devices such as cash registers and Teletype machines.

Since both punched-card and paper tape I/O devices are comparatively slow, a variety of off-line devices are manufactured which transfer data directly from cards or paper tape onto a mass storage medium. These punched-card-to-magnetic-tape or punched-card-to-magnetic-disk converters are used while the computer is processing some other problem, thus conserving computer time. The magnetic tape or magnetic disk is later deposited in an on-line mass storage device and the stored data processed.

Line Printers

Almost every computer will include a device that outputs data in readable form. A small computer might only have a single cathode-ray tube (like the picture tube in a television set) on which the output appears temporarily. Most computer applications, however, require *hard copy*, i.e. output which is printed on paper, so that the computer configuration will include a typewriter terminal for low-volume output and one or more line printers for high-volume output.

There are essentially two types of line printers: an *impact* printer prints by means of type striking an inked ribbon and paper; a *nonimpact* printer prints by chemical or photographic means. Both differ from the typewriter in that several characters of a line, or even the complete line, of output is printed at one time.

Figure 6-3 is a picture of an impact printer and Fig. 6-4 indicates its mechanism, which consists of 132 bars corresponding to the 132 characters composing a line of print. In front of the paper and ribbon is a rotating chain of five 48-character sections of type. As the characters pass in front of the positions on the line where they are to be printed, the bar behind the paper presses the paper

Fig. 6-3   (*Courtesy of IBM*)

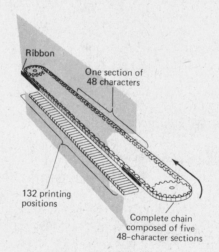

Fig. 6-4

against the type, thereby printing the characters.   This particular device, called a *chain printer*, can print as many as 2500 lines per minute.   Another common type of impact printer, the *wheel printer*, consists of 132 wheels of type, each containing 48 characters.   The wheels are aligned horizontally along the width of the mechanism and are positioned to print simultaneously.

Among the nonimpact printers, one kind operates by an electronic beam passing through a mask containing the various characters and then impinging upon an electron-sensitive film.   The film is later developed and used to transfer the output data onto hard copy.   This type of printer can print as many as 64 000 lines per minute.   Although nonimpact printers are much faster than impact printers, they do not make carbon copies and the quality of the output is not as good.

In business applications of the computer, the output of a line printer comes in almost every conceivable format.   Figure 6-5 shows part of a bank account statement; observe that elements such as headings and ruled lines are printed commercially before processing.

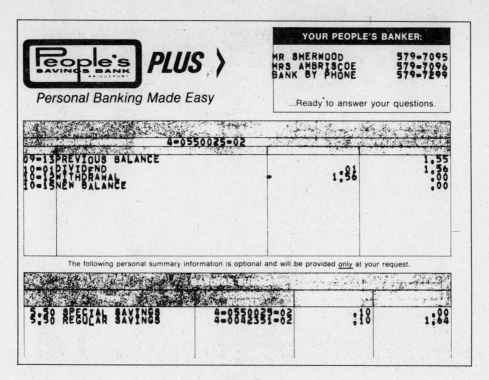

Fig. 6-5

Keyboard Devices

The *typewriter terminal* (Fig. 6-6) and the *cathode-ray terminal*, or *CRT* (Fig. 6-7), are the most popular I/O devices for low-volume input and output. Here the input is typed on a keyboard similar to that of an ordinary typewriter. The devices are reasonably inexpensive and require a minimum amount of training to operate. The typewriter terminal is both an input and an output device, and both input and output data are printed on paper. The output is printed character by character, at a speed of up to 30 characters per second. The CRT is also both an input and an output device, the data appearing on a cathode-ray tube. CRT output, being electronic, is faster than the output of the electromechanical typewriter terminal. However, the CRT gives only a transitory record, whereas the output of a typewriter is hard copy.

Keyboard terminals are particularly useful for computer applications that require entering and retrieving small amounts of data rather quickly and often at some distance from the computer center. Programs and input data can be typed directly into the computer from the terminal, and the output data can be automatically transmitted to the terminal as directed by the computer program. If the terminal is not located at the computer center, it is connected to the computer either through a company-owned communications network or through the telephone system.

EXAMPLE 6.1 A major airline has hundreds, or perhaps thousands, of keyboard terminals scattered throughout the country. They are located at the various airport terminals, airline sales offices, and telephone reservation centers. The computer system provides the customer with immediate and efficient flight bookings, flight information, and special passenger service.

Regardless of how automatic a computer may be, at times an operator will have to communicate with the computer directly. This is usually accomplished by means of a keyboard device, located near the CPU, called the *console terminal*. (This terminal is distinct from the *computer console*, which was discussed in Section 5.6.) The terminal is used, for example, to input

Fig. 6-6   *(Courtesy of Digital Equipment Corporation)*

Fig. 6-7   *(Courtesy of IBM)*

the program for a particular processing task, or, when necessary, to interrupt the computer during processing so that some special output may be obtained.

EXAMPLE 6.2 In order to copy a file from one magnetic tape onto another, the operator of a certain computer first types the special character ⌐C. In response the computer types a *monitor prompter* in the form of a period. See Fig. 6-8. The prompter signals the operator that she must answer with the name of the program she wishes to use. The operator then types "R PIP" which stands for "Run the program called PIP." PIP is the system program (Section 2.5) which is used to transfer files. Since more information is required by the computer, the computer responds with another prompter, an asterisk. This prompter tells the operator that she must answer with the name of the file to be copied, the name of the mass storage device containing the file, the name of the new file, and the name of the new mass storage device. The operator then types

$$TAPE2:DATA \leftarrow TAPE1:DATA$$

which stands for "Copy the file called DATA, which is on the mass storage device TAPE1, onto the mass storage device TAPE2, giving the new file the same name, DATA." After the program has been executed, the computer returns with the monitor prompter for further instructions, if any.

Fig. 6-8

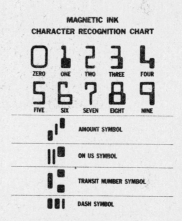

Fig. 6-9

Like punched-card devices, keyboard devices are rather slow, and so off-line converters are frequently employed to transfer data directly from keyboard to magnetic tape or disk.

Magnetic-Ink Readers

In the late 1950s the American Bankers Association recognized the need to automate the processing of bank checks. A system, called Magnetic-Ink Character Recognition (MICR), was developed whereby certain data are precoded on a check in a magnetic ink. These data can later be read into a computer for processing. The fourteen MICR characters are shown in Fig. 6-9.

EXAMPLE 6.3 When a customer opens a checking account, the bank prints in magnetic ink its identification number and the customer's account number at the bottom of each of his checks. After a check is filled out but before it is processed, the amount of the check is also encoded. This is illustrated in Fig. 6-10. For processing, checks are fed into a magnetic-ink reader-sorter. Here the encoded information is read into a computer and at the same time the checks are sorted so that they can be easily returned to the issuing bank. The reader-sorter shown in Fig. 6-11 can process as many as 2000 checks per minute.

SARAH FRAGNER
MARTIN M. LIPSCHUTZ

No. 1093

8/3 19 79 60-117/310 19

PAY TO THE
ORDER OF _Cash_____ $190.00

One Hundred and Ninety and no/100 _____ DOLLARS

CONTINENTAL
BANK
NORRISTOWN, PENNSYLVANIA

FOR _____

⑆031001175⑆ ⑈49⑈7⑈380⑈6⑈   ⑆00000190000⑆

HARLAND N08

Bank identification   Customer account number   Amount of check

precoded

Fig. 6-10

Fig. 6-11   (*Courtesy of IBM*)

MICR has three *advantages*:

(1) The characters are easily read by a person.

(2) There is a high accuracy in reading the characters by the input device.

(3) The input devices are reasonable in cost.

A major *disadvantage* is that the number of characters is limited, whence the system is unsuitable for general-purpose data processing.

Optical Character Readers

These are photoelectric devices which scan a document and recognize characters by comparing their shapes with internally stored patterns. The first practical reader, developed in the early

1950s, was able to read typewritten characters only. Today, however, optical readers are manufactured which can recognize handwritten characters, with a rejection rate of less than one percent of the total number of documents scanned. Also, some of these readers can process as many as 3000 documents per minute.

Since optical readers read the source documents directly, they eliminate the bottleneck of having a person transfer the data from the source document onto a computer input medium. However, at present the optical readers are still rather expensive, ranging from $200,000 up to $1 million for machines which can read a full page. When manufacturing costs are reduced and when better methods are developed for recognizing imperfectly handwritten characters, the optical reader will no doubt take over the work of most of the keypunch and keyboard input devices.

6.3   MASS STORAGE UNITS

The distinction between mass storage devices and I/O devices in general was made in Section 5.4.

Magnetic Tape Units

By far the most popular sequential-storage medium (Section 3.3) is magnetic tape. Figure 6-12 is a picture of a magnetic tape unit, used both for input and output of data. The operator mounts the reel of tape to be read or written upon on the left side of the drive and an empty, *take-up* reel on the right. The tape from the left reel is then threaded past the *read/write head* onto the take-up reel. The operator then engages a switch that gives control of the tape unit to the CPU. It is not necessary to erase a tape before recording new data on it: the recording process automatically obliterates any previously stored data.

Fig. 6-12   (*Courtesy of IBM*)

In addition to the switch noted above, every magnetic tape unit will have a *rewind* control, which is used to rewind the tape from the right reel back onto the left reel when processing is completed, and a *write-lock* switch which, when engaged, prevents the computer from recording onto the tape. It is important that the write-lock switch be engaged when a tape is only to be read from, so that the data on the tape might not be destroyed if the computer were to "crash" and attempt to record data onto the tape.

Most computer centers will have more than one magnetic tape unit, since magnetic tape may be used to store different kinds of information (e.g. several data files and computer programs), all of which may be used at the same time in a data processing application.

Magnetic Disk Units

The most popular random-access storage medium (Section 3.3) is the magnetic disk.   There are three types of magnetic-disk mass storage units: one where the magnetic disks are fixed, one where the disks can be removed in the form of a disk pack, and one which accommodates the small, floppy disk.   Figure 6-13 shows a unit containing a disk pack.

Fig. 6-13   (*Courtesy of Prime Computer, Inc.*)

According to Table 5-2, a disk pack can store up to 200 million characters of data.   Also, each storage segment of a disk can be accessed directly and the rate of data transfer is extremely high.   Thus a disk pack unit considerably enhances the data processing capability of a computer.   Initial cost of a disk pack is the major disadvantage of disk storage as compared to magnetic tape storage.

The operation of the disk pack unit was described in Section 3.9.   As in the case of magnetic tape units, it is not necessary to erase data on a disk: new data are simply recorded over the old.   Also, it is quite common in large computer systems to have several magnetic disk units in use at the same time.

Magnetic Drum and Magnetic Strip Units

Two other secondary storage devices in use are the magnetic drum unit and the magnetic strip unit (see Sections 3.10 and 3.11).   Both are random-access devices used either for input or output.   The magnetic drum has smaller storage capacity than the magnetic strip unit (Table 5-2);

on the other hand, its access time is much less.   In general, both of these storage media are being phased out in favor of magnetic disk storage, which is more versatile.

6.4   EXAMPLE OF A FILE MAINTENANCE PROCEDURE

In Section 4.8 we showed how a master file might be updated using EAM with punched-card input and output.   Here we indicate how a similar task might be accomplished on the computer, with magnetic tape as the medium.

We begin with two tape files, the old master file, to be updated, and the *transaction file*, containing the information to be used in the updating.   Both files are assumed to be sorted with respect to increasing values of the same key (Section 1.5), which might be employee's payroll number in the case of a master personnel file, or part number in the case of a master inventory file.

As shown in Fig. 6-14, the old master file, the transaction file, a tape containing the "file update" computer program, and a blank reel of tape which will contain the new master file are each placed on one of four magnetic tape units.   On command from the console terminal, the program is read into the memory of the computer and execution is begun.

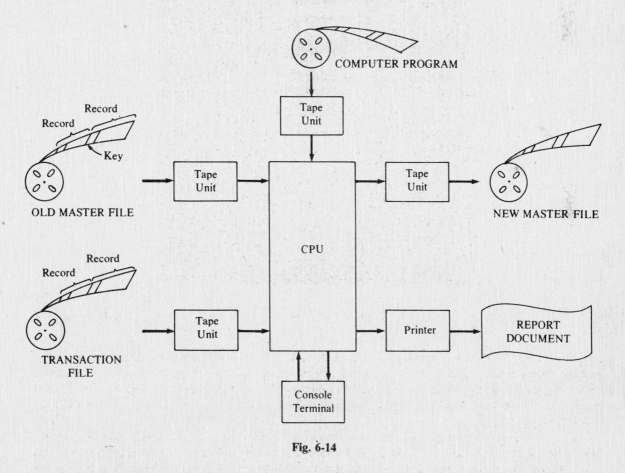

Fig. 6-14

The program directs that a record of the old master file and a record of the transaction file be read into the memory of the computer and then, in the arithmetic unit, that the key values of the two records be compared.

   (i)   If the key value of the master record is *less than* the key value of the transaction record, no change is to be made in the master record, and the master record is copied on the blank tape exactly as it was in the old master file.

(ii) If the key value of the master record is *equal to* the key value of the transaction record, then either the master record is to be deleted, in which case nothing is written on the blank tape, or the master record is to be changed. In the latter case the appropriate changes are made to the master record in the CPU, and the new master record is written on the blank tape. It is the transaction record itself that tells which to do, to drop or to change and copy.

(iii) If the key value of the master record is *greater than* the key value of the transaction record, then the transaction record is a new record which is then copied onto the blank tape.

Figure 6-15 shows how the above procedure would work in a particular case. Here the key value (122) of the first master record is less than the key value (124) of the first transaction record, so the master record is simply copied as it is onto the new master file and the next master record is compared with the same transaction record. Now both records have the same key value (124); also, the transaction record states that the master record is to be changed. The changed record is outputted and the next two records are compared. Again both records have the same key value (126). But now the transaction record states that the master record is to be deleted. This is done, and the next master record and the next transaction record are then compared. This time the key value (129) of the master record is greater than the key value (128) of the transaction record. This transaction record is a new record, which is outputted next. When all the records in the old master file and the transaction file have been read into the CPU, the computer stops. The records appearing on what was the blank tape make up the new master file.

Finally, as shown in Fig. 6-14, at the same time that the new master file is generated, a report

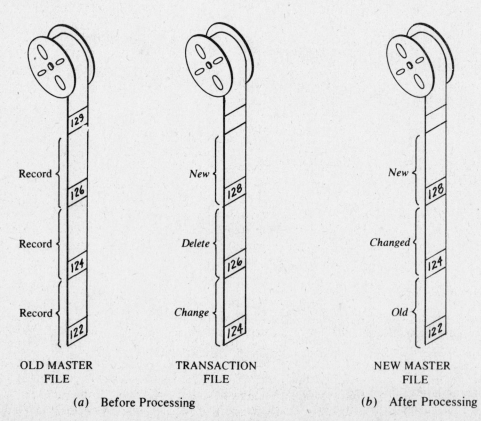

OLD MASTER   TRANSACTION   NEW MASTER
    FILE   FILE   FILE

(*a*) Before Processing   (*b*) After Processing

Fig. 6-15

document would be printed, detailing certain changes in the master file. Thus, if the master file were a personnel file, the report document might be a list of the names of the employees who have been dropped and the names of the new employees.

6.5 INPUT/OUTPUT SYSTEMS AND PROCEDURES

An electronic computer operates at a speed comparable to the speed of electron flow, which at ordinary temperatures is on the order of one hundredth the speed of light. (Research is in progress on *optical memory*, where the two states 0 and 1 would be represented by right circular polarization and left circular polarization of a light beam. Such a computer would operate at essentially the speed of light.) For example, a medium-sized computer can perform approximately 500 000 additions per second. However, the various I/O devices cannot input/output data from the CPU at anywhere near the rate at which the CPU can process the data. This difference in speed has constituted a serious bottleneck to the efficient use of the computer since the beginning of electronic data processing. Various methods have been developed to compensate for this difference; we discuss some of them below.

Buffers

A *buffer* is a temporary storage area between the I/O device and the CPU. The buffer stores the data from the I/O device until they are ready to be used by the CPU, or vice versa. See Fig. 6-16. Once the data are in the buffer they are transferred to or from the CPU at speeds comparable to the speed of the CPU. The buffer may be physically a part of the I/O device or a part of the memory of the CPU.

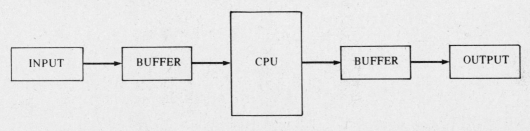

Fig. 6-16

Specifically, a buffer works as follows. Processing a file normally comprises reading a record, processing this record, outputting the result; and then repeating these steps until the end of the file is reached. Without buffers the CPU would remain idle while each record was inputted and outputted, as shown in Fig. 6-17(*a*). With input and output buffers, on the other hand, the records can be continuously fed into the input buffer while previous records are being processed and outputted, and also records can be continuously retrieved from the output buffer while succeeding records are inputted and processed. See Fig. 6-17(*b*).

Multiplexor and Selector Channels

A *channel* is a connection between the CPU and one or more I/O devices.

Even though a buffer permits the continuous flow of data to or from the CPU, the bottleneck persists. Thus, in Fig. 6-17(*b*), the CPU is still idle between the processing of records. To help solve this problem, third-generation computers (Section 2.4) were designed so that they could input data from several I/O devices simultaneously. This is done by means of *multiplexor* channels, which interleave single characters from the various I/O devices into one fast stream of data that is transmitted to the CPU. Multiplexor channels are used with slow devices, such as card readers and keyboard terminals; they can serve as many as 200 of these devices at a time.

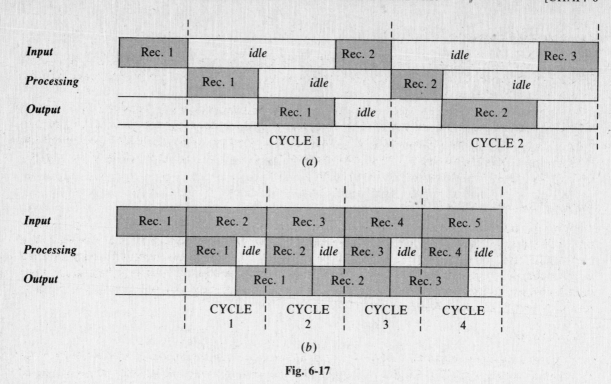

Fig. 6-17

A *selector* channel is like a switch which simply connects one out of several I/O devices to the CPU. Normally, selector channels are used to connect the CPU with a fast device, such as a mass storage unit, or with another CPU.

Multiprogramming and Multiprocessing

The hardware developments described above allowed third-generation computers to process more than one problem at a time, and led to the notions of multiprogramming and multiprocessing.

In *multiprogramming*, several programs are executed concurrently on a single computer under the control of an overall system program (Section 2.5). For example, a system program could use the idle time in Fig. 6-17(*b*) to execute another program. In certain multiprogramming systems each program is allotted a fixed "slice of time," say 0.1 second, after which control is transferred to another program. A given program will generally require a number of these slices, which alternate with the slices devoted to other programs. This kind of multiprogramming is called *time-sharing*.

In *multiprocessing*, the CPU's of several computers are linked, or else (the more modern alternative) the CPU of a single computer is provided with more than one arithmetic unit. These CPU's or arithmetic units operate in parallel, thereby allowing simultaneous execution of several programs or of several parts of the same program.

Batch Processing and Real-Time Processing

There are basically two modes of data entry. In *batch processing*, the data to be processed are accumulated over a period of time and then processed all together. In *real-time processing*, each transaction is processed as soon as it is received.

In early EDP, batch processing was the only practical procedure. Why load a computer program and read through a sequential file just to update one or two records? The drawback, of course, was the time delay incurred in processing a transaction. When multiprogramming and fast, direct-access, mass storage devices became available, real-time processing became viable. It is used especially in computerized reservations systems and the like, where an immediate response is required. (See Example 6.4.)

6.6 TELEPROCESSING

As a business expands, management often sets up branch offices or plants in distant cities.   The method of processing data when the input and output devices are in a different location from the CPU is known as *teleprocessing*.

A teleprocessing system may be relatively simple, consisting of a few I/O devices connected to a CPU in the same building, or it may be a complex nationwide network, composed of one or two large CPU's at the home office, which is connected to a number of branch offices throughout the country, with each branch office connected to several I/O devices located in outlying areas.   In any case, three basic processes occur in the system.

Remote Input and Output of Data

This is most commonly accomplished by means of the terminals discussed in Section 6.2.   (The appropriateness of the name "terminals" is now apparent, for the I/O devices are at the end of the line, with the CPU as home base.)   Besides the keyboard terminals, new, special-purpose terminals appear on the market almost daily.   There are *badge readers*, which scan credit card numbers or other badge numbers, as well as the graphic display terminals and audio response terminals mentioned in Section 2.4.

Data Transmission

Data transmission is the process whereby data are sent from the terminals to the CPU (or the reverse) or from one CPU to another.   Data can be transmitted via telephone lines, radio waves, or microwaves.   The science of transmitting data from one location to another is called *telecommunications*; one often refers to teleprocessing as a combination of data processing and telecommunications.

Data transmission involves a transmission *channel*—either a telephone line or the combination of a telephone line and a radio or microwave beam—and a *coupler*—a device that connects the terminal or CPU to the channel.   We discuss each of these separately.

Transmission channels are classified according to *directionality* (Table 6-1) and *grade, i.e.* rate at which data can be transmitted (Table 6-2).   The simplex type is the least expensive to rent, and the

Table 6-1

Channel Type	Directionality
simplex	Data can be transmitted in only one direction.
half duplex	Data can be transmitted in both directions, but only in one direction at a time.
full duplex	Data can be transmitted in both directions simultaneously.

Table 6-2

Channel Grade	Transmission Rate
narrow-band	Up to 300 bits per second.
voice-band	From 300 to 4000 bits per second.
broad-band	Above 4000 bits per second.

full duplex the most expensive; the latter type is used to establish a two-way connection between a more sophisticated terminal and the CPU or between two CPU's.   The narrow-band channel is the one which is normally provided by Western Union.   It is used for a single low-speed I/O device, such as a typewriter terminal or a punched paper tape terminal.   The voice-band channel is the one generally provided by the telephone system.   It is the grade most often used, and can service as many as 45 terminals on a multiplexor channel.   The broad-band channel, which can accommodate a very large flow of data, is sometimes split among several users.

Couplers are also called *modems* or *interface devices*.   A *hard-wired* coupler is permanently connected between the terminal or CPU and the transmission channel, and forms a direct electronic bridge between them.   An *acoustic* coupler converts electronic signals from the terminal into audible signals for transmission over ordinary telephone lines.   It is not a permanent connection, so that a terminal and coupler can be used in conjunction with any available telephone line, as shown in Fig. 6-18.

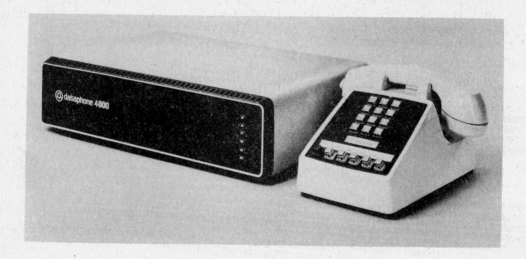

Fig. 6-18   (*Courtesy of A. T. & T.*)

Data Processing

Data processing from a remote terminal can be either batch or real-time processing.   In batch processing, the data are accumulated at the remote location and then transmitted to the CPU using a punched-card or paper tape reader.   The output is usually obtained on a line printer or typewriter terminal.   A batch-processing job inputted at a remote terminal is called a *remote job entry*.

EXAMPLE 6.4   It is only with real-time processing that teleprocessing realizes its full potential.   Consider a bank with several branch offices.   There will be real-time teller terminals at each branch which are connected to a CPU at the main office.   When a customer makes a deposit or withdrawal, the teller keys in the account number and the amount of the transaction.   In a matter of seconds, the computer accesses the customer's account, posts the transaction, updates the account, and outputs a hard copy of the transaction at the terminal for the customer.

6.7   HIERARCHY OF LANGUAGES

Machine Language

On the bottom rung is machine language.   Every computer has its own machine language, which is the only language understood by the computer.   Originally, programs were written in machine language. Today, programs are written in special programming languages, but these programs must still be translated into the machine language of the computer before the program can be executed.

Machine-language instructions are represented by binary numbers, i.e. sequences consisting of 0's and 1's. For example,

001010001110

could represent a 12-bit machine-language instruction. The instruction is divided into two parts, an *operation code* (or *op code*) and an *operand*, e.g.,

Op Code   Operand
001   010001110

The op code specifies the operation (add, multiply, move,...) and the operand is the address (Section 5.6) of the data item that is to be operated on. Besides remembering the dozens of code numbers for the operations, the programmer also has to keep track of the addresses of all the data items. Thus programming in machine language is highly complicated and subject to error. Also, the program is machine dependent, i.e. good only for the particular machine, since different computers use different machine languages.

Assembly Language

Here, the sequences of 0's and 1's that serve as operation codes in machine language are replaced by *mnemonics* (memory-aiding, alphabetic codes), such as TAD for addition. Operands are symbolized ad hoc, in letters chosen by the programmer.

Each assembly-language instruction may have three parts, not all of which need occur in a given instruction. The first part is the *label* or *tag*. These are the programmer-defined symbols that give the address of the instruction. Then follow the op code and the operand, as with the machine-language instruction.

EXAMPLE 6.5 Figure 6-19 is a very simple program written in the assembly language PAL III. The program instructs the computer to add the numbers 1 and 2, initially stored in NUMA and NUMB respectively, and to deposit the sum in storage location NUMC. Specifically:

(*a*) CLA sets the *accumulator*, a storage location in the arithmetic unit which holds running sums, equal to zero.

(*b*) TAD NUMA adds the contents in storage location NUMA, i.e. 1, to the contents of the accumulator, yielding 1 in the accumulator.

(*c*) TAD NUMB adds the contents in NUMB, i.e. 2, to the accumulator, yielding 3 in the accumulator.

Label	Op Code	Operand
	CLA	
	TAD	NUMA
	TAD	NUMB
	DCA	NUMC
	HLT	
NUMA,	0001	
NUMB,	0002	
NUMC,	0000	

Fig. 6-19

(*d*) DCA NUMC deposits the contents of the accumulator, now 3, in the storage location NUMC.

(*e*) HLT, the last instruction, stops the computer.

High-Level Language

Today one normally writes computer programs in "almost-English" computer languages such as FORTRAN, COBOL, BASIC, PL/1, etc. These are called *high-level languages* to distinguish them from the *low-level languages*, machine and assembly languages. They are also called *compiler languages*, since they each require a special program, called a *compiler*, which translates programs written in that language into machine language. The original program written in the high-level language is called the *source program*, and its translation in machine language is called the *object program*. The next section will discuss high-level languages in much more detail.

6.8 HIGH-LEVEL LANGUAGES

High-level languages share three important *advantages*:

Simplification. Since the terminology in high-level languages is "almost English," the languages can be easily learned and understood. In fact, most people can write simple programs after a few days' study.

Standardization. The high-level languages have been standardized (up to slight modifications). Thus, programs written in, say, FORTRAN can be understood by people throughout the world. In particular, these languages are machine independent, insofar as a high-level-language program can be accepted by any computer which has a compiler for that language.

Diagnostic error detection. Each high-level language has its own syntax, or set of rules that govern the writing of statements in the language. Hence, before a program is translated and executed, the compiler checks each statement in the program for syntactical errors. All such errors are outputted, and translation is not begun by the compiler until all the errors have been corrected.

FORTRAN

FORTRAN (FORmula TRANslation), developed in 1957, was one of the first high-level languages. As its name suggests, its syntax is similar to that of mathematical formulas, and it is commonly used in statistical and scientific applications. FORTRAN's primary advantages are its excellent mathematical capability and its compactness. Furthermore, its compiler needs a relatively small amount of memory and thus can be used in the smaller computer.

COBOL

COBOL (COmmon Business Oriented Language) was developed in the late 1950s as a universal language for business applications. Three important *advantages* of COBOL are:

(1) It closely resembles English, so that programs written in COBOL can be followed by nonprogrammers.

(2) It can easily handle I/O operations. Thus it is particularly useful for processing large data files.

(3) It can easily manipulate alphameric data. For example, it is easy to convert 0123456 to $1234.56 in COBOL, while it is difficult to do so in FORTRAN.

A *disadvantage* of COBOL is that its compiler requires a large amount of memory and so the use of COBOL is limited to medium and large computers.

BASIC

BASIC (Beginner's All-purpose Symbolic Instruction Code) was created in the late 1960s at Dartmouth College, mainly to make it easier for students to use the computer for simple problems. It is similar to FORTRAN, with slightly more English-like qualities and with more ease in handling input and output data. Although initially the language was rather limited, features are continually being added, and the language is increasingly being used for general-purpose applications, including business applications.

An important advantage of BASIC is that it is an *interactive language*, one where the program is compiled instruction by instruction as it is read into the computer and where the compiler has various editing features that allow the program to be modified as it is inputted. Thus the programmer can directly *interact* with the computer via a keyboard terminal, quickly writing, correcting, and obtaining partial results of his program (which themselves may lead to modifications of the program). To put it another way, *real-time programming* is possible with BASIC.

Finally, we note that BASIC is the language normally used with microcomputers. Here the compiler is permanently wired into the ROM (Section 5.6) of the computer, so that BASIC is, in effect, the machine language. (This has led to the comment that microcomputers "know" BASIC.)

RPG

RPG (Report Program Generator) is a limited-purpose language that was designed primarily to produce management reports. It is used in installations where a very limited amount of computation generates a large volume of printed output. RPG is also suited to small computers which do not have sufficient memory to implement COBOL or PL/1.

PL/1

PL/1 (Programming Language 1) was developed by IBM in the middle 1960s as a general-purpose programming language. It was designed to incorporate the best features of FORTRAN and COBOL, along with features not found in either. The language allows real-time programming in addition to conventional (noninteractive) business and scientific programming. Although PL/1 is powerful and not too difficult to learn, it has not been as successful as had been hoped. Instead, many of the new features of the language are being incorporated into FORTRAN and COBOL.

6.9 OPERATING SYSTEM PROGRAMS

Operating system programs (Section 2.5) fall into two broad categories, which we discuss separately.

Control Programs

These are the programs which supervise the operations of the computer. Medium- and large-sized computers will normally have three such programs:

The *monitor program* provides the communication between the operator and the computer by effecting the commands from the console terminal. These commands include fetching, loading, and starting the various other system programs. Thus, the monitor program controls the overall scheduling of the computer.

The *input/output control program* operates the various I/O devices as called for by the application program (Section 2.5). It prepares the I/O devices for use, it opens and closes the channels between the I/O devices and the CPU, and it continuously monitors the I/O devices for a possible breakdown.

The *job control program* is used to schedule jobs for processing, so that there may be a steady flow of work for the computer. The program also directs the processing of jobs in multi-programming and time-sharing modes.

Processing Programs

These are the operating system programs that help the application program to do the actual data processing. There are basically two types of such programs:

Language translators are the compilers and assemblers (Section 2.5) which are respectively used to translate programs in high-level and assembly languages into machine language. A larger computer may support several high-level and assembly languages by having a compiler or assembler for each language.

Service programs are "canned" programs that execute tasks frequently required in data processing. They save the programmer time and effort by making it unnecessary for him to detail these tasks in his program. Among service programs, the *editor* is used to create or modify files. By means of the editor, a data file or a computer program can easily be written and edited on a keyboard terminal, and then stored in a mass storage medium. Furthermore, files and programs already stored in a mass storage medium can easily be modified or updated. *Sort/merge programs*, which perform the indicated operations, are almost indispensable in business data processing. Similarly, *utility programs* perform tasks such as transferring files from one mass storage medium to another or formatting a magnetic tape into blocks so that files can be efficiently processed.

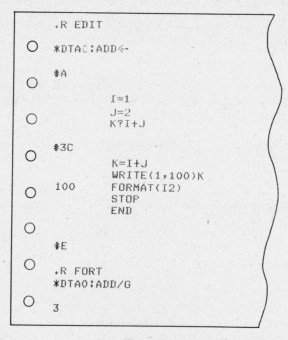

Fig. 6-20

EXAMPLE 6.6 Figure 6-20 is a typewriter terminal printout, having to do with a simple computer program written in FORTRAN. We discuss each line of the printout individually, to indicate how the operator communicated with the computer as the program was written and compiled.

Line 1   .R EDIT

When the computer is turned on, the monitor program prints a period, the monitor prompter (compare Example 6.2). In response, the operator types R EDIT, informing the computer that he wants to run the editor program, EDIT.

Line 2   *DTAO : ADD <

Since more information is needed, the monitor replies with an asterisk, the command prompter. In response, the operator types DTAO : ADD<, announcing that the computer program he wishes to write is to be recorded in mass storage device DTAO and that the name of his program is ADD.

Line 3   #A

The editor program, which has been started after Line 1, now types the "number" symbol, #, called the *editor prompter*. The operator responds with the letter A, which informs the computer that the statements following are to be recorded. The operator now begins to write the computer program.

Line 4   I = 1

This is the first statement of the computer program. When the program is executed, it will instruct the computer to store the integer 1 in the storage location designated by the letter I. Note that the program is now just being recorded on a storage medium. Later, when it has been completely written, it will be compiled and then executed.

Line 5   J = 2

This statement will instruct the computer to store the integer 2 in storage location J.

Line 6   K?I + J

An error was made in typing this statement. The operator recalls the editor prompter, #, by typing a special character not seen on the printout.

Line 7   #3C

Here the operator follows the editor prompter with 3C. This informs the computer that the next line to be typed is to be a correction to the third statement of the program (line 6).

Line 8   K = I + J

This is now the third statement of the computer program. It will instruct the computer to add the integers stored in I and J and then to store the sum (which is 3) in storage location K.

Line 9   WRITE(1,100)K

This statement will instruct the computer to print out the integer in storage location K on the typewriter terminal.

Line 10   100 FORMAT(I2)

This statement is associated with the WRITE statement above. It will tell the computer that the output is an integer to be written in a field of width 2.

Line 11   STOP

Here the computer will be instructed to stop.

Line 12   END

This END statement is the last statement of the computer program. It will inform the compiler, which will translate the program into machine language that it has reached the end of the program. This statement itself is not translated into machine language; it is information only for the compiler. Having written the program, the operator recalls the editor prompter, #.

Line 13   #E

The operator follows the prompter with the letter E, which informs the editor program that his program is complete.

Line 14   .R FORT

After the command E, the monitor automatically returns with the monitor prompter. Since the operator now wants his program to be executed, he responds with R FORT, which instructs the computer to run the FORTRAN compiler.

Line 15   *DTAO: ADD/G

Following the monitor's command prompter, printed in response to line 14, this line instructs the computer that the program to be compiled is located in the storage device DTAO and has the name ADD. The operator also types /G, which informs the computer that the program is to be executed after it has been compiled.

Line 16   3

This is the output of the computer program, the integer in storage location K.

Solved Problems

I/O DEVICES

6.1 Why are there a second read station in a card reader and a read station in a card punch?

These read stations are used to check for errors.

6.2 What are the two sensing methods used to read punched cards?

A wire brush makes electrical contact with a metal drum only where there is a hole in the card; a photoelectric cell registers light passing through a hole in the card.

6.3 What is the purpose of having off-line devices which convert data stored on punched cards or punched paper tape onto magnetic tape or magnetic disks?

Stored magnetically, the data can later be transmitted to the CPU at a much faster rate than they could be from punched cards or punched paper tape. This saves costly computer time.

6.4 Briefly describe the two types of line printers.

Impact printers use type, the face of which strikes against an inked ribbon and paper; *nonimpact printers* print by means of a chemical or photographic process.

6.5 Name the two most common keyboard I/O devices. What are the advantages and disadvantages of one compared to the other?

The typewriter terminal and the cathode-ray terminal. The output on a CRT is faster than on a typewriter terminal, but the typewriter terminal can provide the user with a hard copy.

6.6 What is a *console terminal*?

A console terminal is a keyboard device near the CPU that enables an operator to control the computer. It is used, for example, to input a program or interrupt the execution of a program for some special purpose.

6.7 How can a computer center compensate for the fact that a keyboard device is slow for inputting a large amount of data?

Off-line, key-to-magnetic-tape or key-to-magnetic-disk devices can first be used to transfer the data onto a mass storage medium.

6.8 What is the major disadvantage of MICR as a general-purpose input medium?

The number of characters that can be recorded with present techniques is very limited. Moreover, the characters cannot be read repeatedly without losing their magnetism.

6.9 At present, what is a major disadvantage of optical character readers?

Their high cost.

MASS STORAGE DEVICES

6.10 List the five most common mass storage devices.

(1) Magnetic tape drive, (2) magnetic disk pack, (3) floppy disk unit, (4) magnetic drum unit, (5) magnetic strip unit.

6.11 Mass storage devices have a write-lock switch, but no read-lock switch. Explain.

Recording data on a mass storage medium will destroy any previous data and store the new data in their place. Hence a write-lock switch is necessary to prevent accidental destruction of stored data. But reading out data from a mass storage medium does not destroy those data, and so there is no need for a read-lock switch.

6.12 Answer each of the following by referring to Table 5-2. Which mass storage device (*a*) normally stores the most data? (*b*) normally stores the least amount of data? (*c*) normally has the highest rate of data transfer? (*d*) normally has the lowest rate of data transfer?

(*a*) Magnetic strip unit.

(*b*) Floppy disk unit.

(*c*) Magnetic drum unit.

(*d*) Magnetic strip unit.

6.13 Why would a computer system normally have several mass storage devices?

Often, in the course of a single data processing problem, several files are used simultaneously. As it is usually much more efficient to have an I/O device for each file, several mass storage devices are provided.

6.14 The file maintenance procedure in Section 6.4 presupposes that the transaction file, as well as the old master file, is sorted. Figure 6-21 shows the old master file and transaction file of Fig. 6-15(*a*), but with the first two records of the transaction file out of order. Describe where the first error in processing would occur.

Since the key value (122) of the first master record is less than the key value (126) of the first transaction record, the first master record would be copied onto the new master file, as it should be. When the next master record is compared with the transaction record, its key value (124) is also less than 126, and so it too would be copied onto the new master file, which would be an error in processing the data.

6.15 An old master file and a transaction file have records as shown in Fig. 6-22. Describe the first five records of the new master file if the records are processed as in Section 6.4.

(430) is a new record; (431) is to be deleted; (436) is copied onto the new file; (437) is changed; (442) is copied onto the new file; (443) is deleted; (445) is copied onto the new file. The first five records of the new master file are shown in Fig. 6-23.

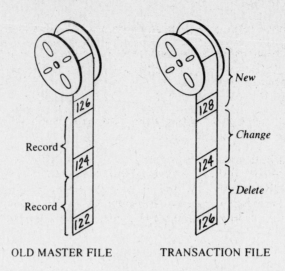

OLD MASTER FILE   TRANSACTION FILE

Fig. 6-21

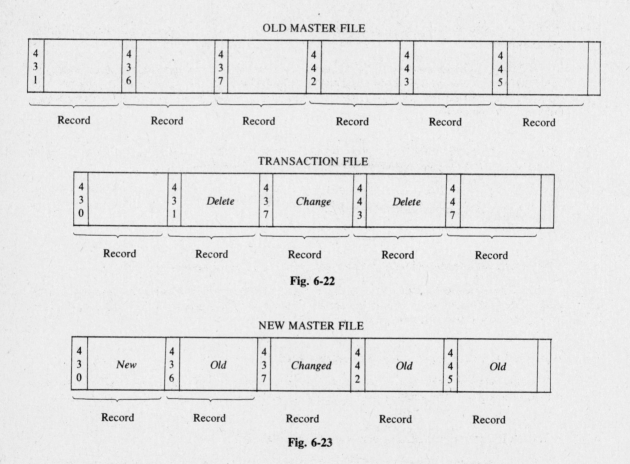

OLD MASTER FILE

4 3 1		4 3 6		4 3 7		4 4 2		4 4 3		4 4 5		

Record · Record · Record · Record · Record · Record

TRANSACTION FILE

4 3 0		4 3 1	*Delete*	4 3 7	*Change*	4 4 3	*Delete*	4 4 7		

Record · Record · Record · Record · Record

Fig. 6-22

NEW MASTER FILE

4 3 0	*New*	4 3 6	*Old*	4 3 7	*Changed*	4 4 2	*Old*	4 4 5	*Old*	

Record · Record · Record · Record · Record

Fig. 6-23

INPUT/OUTPUT SYSTEMS AND PROCEDURES

6.16 Why have I/O devices presented a bottleneck to efficient use of the computer?

I/O units transfer data to and from the CPU at a much slower speed than that at which the CPU processes the data.

6.17   What two means have been developed to compensate for the low speed of I/O devices?

(1) Buffers, or fast-access units that temporarily store data from an input device (or the CPU) until needed by the CPU (or output device);   (2) multiplexor channels, or channels that input data from several I/O devices simultaneously.

6.18   Refer to Fig. 6-17.   Show that the use of an input and an output buffer cuts the time needed to process a file by approximately 50%.

Take as the unit of time the average time required by the CPU to process one record.   Then, a conservative estimate for the average time needed to input or to output a record would be 100 units.   From Fig. 6-17(a) it is seen that the length of the processing cycle in the absence of buffers is an input time plus a processing time plus an output time, or 201 units; while, from Fig. 6-17(b), the length of the cycle with buffers is an input time, or 100 units.   Thus, the use of buffers shortens the cycle by a factor of

$$\frac{100}{200} \approx \frac{1}{2}$$

and (disregarding end corrections) the length of the entire job will be reduced by the same factor.

6.19   Briefly describe how a multiplexor channel inputs data from several I/O devices simultaneously.

The channel admits one character from device A, then one character from device B, . . . , then one character from device X; then it repeats the cycle.   In this way, the devices are all served at the same time, yet are distinguished (as is necessary for correct processing of the data by the CPU) by their fixed order in the cycle.

6.20   State the type of channel that would normally be used between a CPU and   (a) three disk pack units,   (b) twenty typewriter terminals,   (c) four magnetic tape units.

(a)   A selector channel (high-speed I/O devices).

(b)   A multiplexor channel (low-speed I/O devices).

(c)   A selector channel (high-speed I/O devices).

6.21   What is the difference between multiprogramming and multiprocessing?

In multiprogramming, one CPU, under a master program, executes several programs concurrently.   In multiprocessing, several processing units are used simultaneously to process several programs or parts of a single program.

6.22   Describe the multiprogramming procedure called time-sharing.

In time-sharing, each user is allocated a set of fixed-length time quanta in which his program occupies the CPU.   An overall *supervisory program* interleaves the quanta of the various users.

6.23   What are the two ways of grouping data for processing?

Batch processing and *real-time processing*.   In batch processing, the data are accumulated over a period of time before being processed en masse; in real-time processing, data items are individually processed as they arrive.

6.24   What hardware developments made real-time processing practical?

Multiplexor channels and high-speed, direct-access, mass storage devices.

TELEPROCESSING

6.25   What is teleprocessing?

Literally, "far-processing": the processing of data when input and output devices are far from the CPU.

6.26   Give the three components of teleprocessing.

Data entry, which is the inputting or retrieving of data by means of a remote terminal; *data transmission*, or sending the data from the terminal to the CPU, from the CPU to the terminal, or from one CPU to another; *data processing* in the CPU.

6.27   Describe each of the following types of terminals: (*a*) badge readers,   (*b*) graphic display devices,   (*c*) audio response devices.

(*a*)   A badge reader is an optical-electronic device that scans numbers on credit cards or other badges and transmits these data to the computer in order to validate the credentials or credit of the bearer.

(*b*)   A graphic display device translates suitable graphs or line drawings drawn by the operator into electrical input to the computer.

(*c*)   An audio response device translates certain simple messages spoken by the operator into electrical input to the computer.   At present, the range of spoken messages comprehensible to the computer is very limited.

6.28   Data transmission channels are ranked in two ways.   Describe these ways.

First, a channel is (i) simplex, (ii) half duplex, or (iii) full duplex, according as it can transmit (i) in one direction only, (ii) in one direction or the other but not in both at once, (iii) in both directions at once.   Second, a channel is ranked in increasing order of transmission rate (measured in bits per second) as narrow-band, voice-band, or broad-band.

6.29   The expected traffic between two CPU's amounts to 9600 bits per second.   What sort of channel (grade and directionality) should be used to link them?

From Table 6-2 it is seen that a broad-band channel will be required.   Further, the channel should be full duplex, as CPU's are involved.

6.30   Briefly describe the difference between a hard-wired and an acoustic coupler.

The hard-wired coupler is a permanent electronic connection between the terminal or CPU and the transmission channel.   The acoustic coupler converts the electronic signal from the terminal into a sound signal, which is then transmitted over an ordinary telephone line. (Electronic-to-sonic conversion of the CPU output is not employed in the hard-wired coupler.)

HIERARCHY OF COMPUTER LANGUAGES

6.31   Briefly define *computer program*.

A computer program is a step-by-step list of unambiguous instructions given to the computer to solve a problem.

6.32   Briefly describe the three levels of computer language.

Machine language is the language understood by the computer.   It varies from one model of computer to another, but may always be represented by binary numbers.   *Assembly language* uses symbolic codes in place of the binary numbers of machine languages.   Assembly languages also vary from one type of computer to another. A *high-level language* is more or less English-like and algebra-like. These languages are relatively machine independent.

6.33   Give the three parts of an assembly-language instruction.

The *label*, the first part, is a programmer-defined symbol (or symbols) representing the address of the instruction. The *op code*, the second part, is a symbolic code (often mnemonic in nature) that specifies the commanded operation. The *operand* is the symbolic address of the data item to be operated on.

6.34   Interpret the assembly-language instruction

INST TAD NUM

where TAD is the symbolic code for adding the number at the given address into the accumulator.

The label, INST, is the address of this instruction. If necessary, this instruction itself can be referenced in some other instruction by using INST as an operand. The information which is actually stored at this address is TAD NUM, where TAD is the op code and NUM the operand. The instruction orders the computer to add the contents of storage location NUM into the accumulator.

6.35   What is a *compiler*?

A compiler is a system program which translates a program (called the *source program*) written in a high-level language into a machine-language program (the *object program*). Each high-level language requires its own compiler.

6.36   In what sense is a language like FORTRAN or BASIC "higher" than assembly or machine language?

A program in a low-level language is hardly more than a list of addresses; at most it might be compared to the pointing of a finger—"this go there." By contrast, a high-level language has, like a spoken language, *words* and a *syntax*, or rules for the correct combination of those words. In short, it has a *grammar*, whereas the low-level language has none.

This does not imply that a high-level language is more *effective* than a low-level language. Indeed, the opposite is true: everything that the computer is capable of doing can be commanded in machine language, but not in high-level language.

HIGH-LEVEL LANGUAGES

6.37   Why is FORTRAN a good language to use for mathematical problems and scientific applications?

Its syntax is similar to the rules for writing standard mathematical formulas.

6.38   State three reasons why COBOL is suited to business applications.

(1) Business people, being for the most part nontechnical, will require a computer language that is quite close to ordinary English, as is COBOL. (2) Business files are often voluminous, and COBOL is specially designed to handle I/O operations. (3) COBOL can easily manipulate the form of alphameric data, as required for business reports.

6.39   "A language like BASIC allows one to program the computer *in the conversational mode*." What is meant by this statement?

The interaction, via keyboard terminal, between the programmer, writing in BASIC, and the computer may be likened to a conversation, since the future actions of either party may be influenced by the information supplied by the other.

Conversational-mode programming is often associated with time-sharing. Certainly, there is a strong economic link between the two: a solitary user could scarcely afford the computer time needed to "converse."

6.40 Point out three differences between BASIC and FORTRAN.

BASIC is   (1) slightly more English-like than FORTRAN;   (2) easier to use than FORTRAN for commanding the input and output of data;   (3) an interactive language, whereas FORTRAN is not. (It should be mentioned that FORTRAN has been modified so as to make it interactive.)

OPERATING SYSTEM PROGRAMS

6.41 What are the principal functions performed by control programs?

They enable the operator to direct the computer from the console terminal (*monitor programs*); they operate the I/O devices as required by the application program (*input/output control programs*); they schedule jobs for processing (*job control programs*).

6.42 What are the principal functions performed by processing programs?

They translate the application program into machine language (*language translators*); they carry out computations or operations that are common to a large number of data processing problems (*service programs*).

6.43 What two system programs are involved when the operator orders the loading of a new program?

The operator's command from the console terminal is accepted by the monitor program, which calls in a utility program known as a *program loader*.   It is the program loader that actually introduces the new program into the memory unit.

Review Questions

I/O AND MASS STORAGE DEVICES

6.44 Match the part of a card reader and punch listed on the left with the phrase on the right that best describes its function.

(1) Punch hopper.   (*a*) The receptacle for cards which have been read or punched.

(2) Stacker.   (*b*) The receptacle for the stack of cards which are to be read.

(3) Read hopper.   (*c*) The receptacle for the stack of blank cards on which data are to be punched.

6.45 Match the term on the left with its description on the right.

(1) Impact printer.   (*a*) It prints by the impact of wheels of type against an inked ribbon and paper.

(2) Nonimpact printer.   (*b*) It prints by chemical or photographic means.

(3) Chain printer.   (*c*) It prints by means of type striking against an inked ribbon and paper.

(4) Wheel printer.   (*d*) It prints by the impact of a chain of type against an inked ribbon and paper.

6.46   An impact printer: (a) is slower than a nonimpact printer, (b) makes higher-quality copy than a nonimpact printer, (c) can make carbon copies, (d) all of the above.

6.47   Keyboard devices: (a) are used for low-volume input and output, (b) are used to supervise the operation of the computer, (c) are often used at a distance from the computer center, (d) all of the above.

6.48   The main purpose of off-line devices is (a) to reduce the number of operator errors in recording data, (b) to save computer time, (c) to save floor space in the computer center, (d) none of the above.

6.49   Match each term on the left with its description on the right.

   (1) Console terminal.   (a) A 14-character system recorded with a special ink.
   (2) Magnetic-Ink Character Recognition.   (b) A keyboard device near the CPU used to supervise
                                                      the operation of the computer.
   (3) Optical character reader.   (c) An input device which recognizes printed characters.

6.50   Magnetic-ink characters are (a) used on bank checks, (b) easily read by a person, (c) too few in number to constitute a general recording medium, (d) all of the above.

6.51   The devices on the left are found on a magnetic-tape mass storage unit. Match each device with its description on the right.

   (1) Take-up reel.   (a) It actually reads data onto the tape or from the tape.
   (2) Read/write head.   (b) It is used to prevent the computer from recording onto the tape.
   (3) Rewind control.   (c) It holds the part of the tape that has been read or written upon.
   (4) Write-lock switch.   (d) It is a switch used in returning the tape to its initial reel, after
                                    processing.

INPUT/OUTPUT SYSTEMS AND PROCEDURES

6.52   A buffer is (a) a device for performing logical operations, (b) a medium of temporary storage between an I/O device and the CPU, (c) a channel for high-speed I/O devices, (d) none of the above.

6.53   The speed at-which data are transmitted between a buffer and the CPU is (a) low, (b) comparable to, (c) much greater than, the speed at which data are transmitted within the CPU.

6.54   Match each term on the left with the phrase on the right that best describes it.
   (1) Channel.   (a) A connection between the CPU and one or more I/O devices.
   (2) Selector channel.   (b) A simultaneous connection between the CPU and several I/O
                                   devices.
   (3) Multiplexor channel. (c) A connection between the CPU and any of a group of I/O devices.

6.55   Multiprogramming was made feasible by the advent of (a) multiplexor channels, (b) fast mass-storage devices, (c) buffers, (d) all of the above.

6.56   Match each term on the left with the phrase on the right that best describes it.
   (1) Time-sharing.   (a) The processing of several programs simultaneously by use of more
                                   than one processing unit.

    (2) Multiprocessing.   (b) Processing several programs concurrently by allowing each program time quanta.

    (3) Batch processing.   (c) Processing data items the moment they are received.

    (4) Real-time processing.   (d) Processing data in groups collected over periods of time.

TELEPROCESSING

6.57 In teleprocessing: (a) data are processed as soon as they are received, (b) data are accumulated for a period of time and then processed, (c) the input and output devices are remote from the CPU, (d) none of the above.

6.58 Match the type of terminal on the left with its description on the right.

    (1) Badge reader.   (a) A terminal where messages spoken by the operator are transmitted for processing.

    (2) Graphic display terminal.   (b) A terminal which scans cards or badges for verification.

    (3) Audio response terminal.   (c) A terminal where pictures are transmitted for processing.

6.59 Telecommunications is (a) the science of processing data by means of several CPU's located at various places, (b) the science of transmitting data from one place to another, (c) the design of audio response and optical display terminals, (d) none of the above.

6.60 Match the type of transmission channel on the left with the phrase on the right that best describes it.

    (1) Simplex.   (a) Data can be transmitted in both directions simultaneously.

    (2) Half duplex.   (b) Data can be transmitted in only one direction.

    (3) Full duplex.   (c) Data can be transmitted in both directions, but only in one direction at a time.

6.61 Match the grade of channel on the left with the transmission capability on the right.

    (1) Narrow-band.   (a) The channel can serve as many as 45 terminals on a multiplex basis.

    (2) Voice-band.   (b) The highest grade; the channel can act as many high-speed channels at once.

    (3) Broad-band.   (c) The channel can service not much more than one low-speed I/O device.

LANGUAGES

6.62 Machine language: (a) is the language that programs were first written in, (b) is the only language understood by the computer, (c) differs from one type of computer to another, (d) all of the above.

6.63 Assembly language: (a) uses alphabetic codes in place of the binary numbers of machine language, (b) is the easiest language in which to write a computer program, (c) need not be translated into machine language when used with a computer, (d) none of the above.

6.64 Match the part of the assembly-language instruction on the left with its description on the right.

    (1) Label.   (a) It identifies the storage location of the instruction.

    (2) Operation code.   (b) It gives the storage location of the quantity to be affected by the instruction.

    (3) Operand.   (c) It identifies the operation to be performed under the instruction.

6.65   A compiler is (a) a program which translates an assembly-language program into machine language, (b) any program written in machine language, (c) a program which translates a high-level language into machine language, (d) none of the above.

6.66   A source program is (a) a program written in machine language, (b) a program to be translated into machine language, (c) the translation into machine language of a program written in a high-level language, (d) none of the above.

6.67   Some important advantages of a high-level language are that (a) it is easier to learn and understand than is machine or assembly language, (b) it can specify procedures that cannot be specified in machine or assembly language, (c) errors in syntax are outputted when a program written in the language is compiled, (d) all of the above.

6.68   Match the high-level language on the left with its description on the right.

(1) FORTRAN.   (a) It is designed primarily for business applications.

(2) COBOL.   (b) It is a recent general-purpose language allowing real-time and systems programming.

(3) BASIC.   (c) It is designed primarily for scientific applications.

(4) RPG.   (d) It is a real-time, general-purpose language, now widely used, though originally designed for college students.

(5) PL/1.   (e) It is a limited-purpose language designed to produce management reports.

OPERATING SYSTEM PROGRAMS

6.69   Control programs are (a) programs used in the execution of a particular processing job, (b) programs which are written in machine language, (c) programs used to supervise the operation of the computer, (d) none of the above.

6.70   Processing programs are (a) programs used in the execution of a particular processing job, (b) programs used to schedule time-sharing on the computer, (c) programs which control the I/O devices, (d) none of the above.

6.71   Match the system program on the left with its description on the right.

(1) Editor program.   (a) It is used to fetch and start all other programs.

(2) Monitor program.   (b) It is used to create or modify files.

(3) Sort/merge program.   (c) It is used to control the flow of processing jobs to the computer.

(4) Job control program.   (d) It is used to put data files in order.

6.72   Match the processing task described on the left with the system program on the right which would be used to perform the task.

(1) To fetch a compiler to translate a source program.   (a) The monitor program.

(2) To sort a data file with respect to a given key.   (b) The editor program.

(3) To write a computer program.   (c) The job control program.

(4) To set up the computer for time-sharing procedures.   (d) A sort/merge program.

(5) To modify an existing source program.

(6) To fetch and start an object program.

Chapter 7

Computer Codes and Arithmetic

7.1 INTRODUCTION

As indicated in Section 5.6, the CPU of a computer is composed of various two-state elements (currents that do or do not flow, cores that are magnetized clockwise or counterclockwise, etc.). The two possible states are denoted by 0 and 1, the digits of the binary number system (called bits for short). Within the computer, then, data are represented as sequences of bits—we say they are expressed in a *binary code*—and the processing of the data follows the laws of binary-system arithmetic. Therefore, we shall investigate the binary number system, beginning with a review of pertinent topics in the more familiar *decimal system*.

7.2 DECIMAL SYSTEM

The decimal system uses the following ten digits: 0, 1, 2, 3, 4, 5, 6, 7, 8, 9.   A *decimal integer* is a string of decimal digits. A *decimal fraction* is a string of decimal digits together with an embedded decimal point.

Any decimal integer can be expressed as the sum of each of its digits times a power of ten.   For example, 74352 can be expressed as:

$$74352 = 7 \times 10^4 + 4 \times 10^3 + 3 \times 10^2 + 5 \times 10^1 + 2 \times 10^0$$
$$= 7 \times 10000 + 4 \times 1000 + 3 \times 100 + 5 \times 10 + 2 \times 1$$

This is called the *expanded notation* of the integer.   The powers of ten,

$$10^0 = 1 \qquad 10^1 = 10 \qquad 10^2 = 100 \qquad 10^3 = 1000 \qquad \ldots$$

correspond respectively to the digits in the integer reading from right to left, and are called the *place values*. The digit 7 in the decimal integer 74352 is said to have *face* value 7, *place* value $10^4 = 10000$;   the digit represents the product $7 \times 10^4 = 70000$.   And so on.

Any decimal fraction may also be expressed in expanded notation, but here the place values of the digits to the right of the decimal point are the negative powers of ten:

$$10^{-1} = \frac{1}{10} \qquad 10^{-2} = \frac{1}{100} \qquad 10^{-3} = \frac{1}{1000} \qquad \ldots$$

For example, 625.417 is expressed in expanded notation as follows:

$$625.417 = 6 \times 10^2 + 2 \times 10 + 5 \times 10^0 + 4 \times 10^{-1} + 1 \times 10^{-2} + 7 \times 10^{-3}$$
$$= 600 + 20 + 5 + \frac{4}{10} + \frac{1}{100} + \frac{7}{1000}$$

The decimal fraction 625.417 is said to have three *decimal places*, or digits to the right of the decimal point.   Observe also that

$$625.417 = 625 + \frac{417}{1000}$$

which is an integer plus a proper fraction whose denominator is a power of ten.

A decimal number (integer or fraction) is written in *exponential form* when it is expressed as some other decimal number times a power of 10.   For example, 37.2 may be written in exponential form in any of the following ways:

$$3.72 \times 10^1 \qquad 0.372 \times 10^2 \qquad 0.00372 \times 10^4 \qquad 372. \times 10^{-1} \qquad 372000 \times 10^{-4}$$

118

We emphasize that all the above represent exactly the same number. In fact, one may even write 37.2 as 37.2×10^0, with a zero exponent of ten. The only difference between one exponential form and another is the position of the decimal point and the exponent of 10. As one moves the decimal point to the left, the exponent increases; as one moves the decimal point to the right, the exponent decreases.

Every nonzero decimal number can be written uniquely in *standard exponential form*, i.e. with the decimal point directly before the first nonzero digit. The numerical part and the exponent of 10 in the standard exponential form are respectively called the *mantissa* and the *exponent* of the number. For example:

Decimal Number	Standard Exponential Form	Mantissa	Exponent
37.2	0.372×10^2	0.372	2
0.05555	0.5555×10^{-1}	0.5555	-1
-777.7	-0.7777×10^3	-0.7777	3
0.6666	0.6666×10^0	0.6666	0

We note that the mantissa will always be

$$not\ less\ than\ 0.1\ but\ less\ than\ 1.0$$

if the number is positive, and

$$greater\ than\ -1.0\ but\ not\ greater\ than\ -0.1$$

if the number is negative.

In computer parlance, a *floating-point number* is a number that is stored and processed in standard exponential form, i.e. where one part of the storage location is reserved for the mantissa and another part for the exponent. If this is not the case, the number is called a *fixed-point number*.

7.3 SIGNIFICANT DIGITS, ROUNDING OFF, TRUNCATING

The modern computer, no matter how large, is limited as to the number of digits that it can handle in any given operation. Hence the topics to be covered in this section are important in the study of data processing.

Significant Digits

The *precision* of a numerical data item is defined to be the number of *significant digits* that are used to measure or store the item. The following rules tell which digits are significant:

(1) Nonzero digits: *always significant.*

(2) Zeros between nonzero digits: *always significant.*

(3) Leading zeros: *never significant.*

(4) Trailing zeros. There are two cases:

　(i) At least one of the zeros appears after the decimal point: *all the zeros are significant.*

　(ii) All the zeros appear before the decimal point: *ambiguous; either none of the zeros is significant or there is a block of significant zeros immediately following the last nonzero digit.*

The first and last significant digits in a number are called the *most significant* digit and the *least significant* digit, respectively. Thus, what is ambiguous in case (ii) of rule (4) is that one does not know which, if any, of the trailing zeros is the least significant digit.

EXAMPLE 7.1   The leading and trailing zeros in the following numbers have been labeled by *No*, *Yes*, or *Maybe* to show which are significant.   (All other digits are significant, by rules (1) and (2).)

Decimal number	0.002340000	23.4000	23400.000	234000.
	No	*Yes*	*Yes*	*Maybe*
Precision	7	6	8	?

Underneath each number is given the number of its significant digits.   The precision of the last number is ambiguous; the possibilities are as follows:

234000.	234000.	234000.	234000.
Yes	*No*	*No*	*No*
6	5	4	3

Scientists frequently write nonzero numbers in *scientific notation*, i.e. in exponential form with the decimal point appearing directly *after* the first nonzero digit.   This notation should not be confused with the standard exponential form in which the decimal point appears before the first nonzero digit.   We also note that in both of these forms there is no ambiguity about the number of significant digits.

Rounding Off to k Decimal Places

Frequently we want to reduce the number of digits in a number by eliminating one or more significant digits on the right.   This is usually done by *rounding off* (or, simply, *rounding*).   First we discuss rounding off a number to k decimal places, and then to k significant figures.

Suppose that a decimal number A has more than k decimal places, and let δ be the digit in the $(k+1)$st place.   Observe that δ is necessarily significant, by the rules given above.   We round off A to k decimal places by first examining δ.   There are two possibilities:

(1) δ is less than 5.   Then δ and all succeeding digits are dropped and the remaining digits are kept unchanged.   (This is called *rounding down*.)   For example, the following numbers are rounded off to two decimal places.:

Decimal number	38.563	158.25489	0.00123
Rounded off	38.56	158.25	0.00

(2) δ is 5 or more.   Then δ and all succeeding digits are dropped, but 1 is added to the digit in the kth decimal place.   (This is called *rounding up*.)   For example, the following numbers are rounded off to two decimal places:

Decimal number	66.666	12.34567	22.9966
Rounded off	66.67	12.35	23.00

The above rule (2) is sometimes modified when δ is 5 and all succeeding digits are zeros (these zeros are also significant).   Then the digit in the kth decimal place is increased by 1 if it is odd, but is left unchanged if it is even.   (This is called the *odd-add rule*.)   For example, the following numbers are rounded off to two decimal places:

Decimal number	44.4450	33.3350	44.44503
Rounded off	44.44	33.34	44.45

The last number is rounded up because there is a nonzero digit following 5.

Rounding Off to k Significant Digits

If a decimal number A has more than k significant digits, with δ being the $(k+1)$st significant digit, we round off A to k significant digits by using the same rules as above, except that it is the kth *significant digit* that we increase by 1 when δ is 5 or more.   For example, the following numbers have been rounded off to 4 significant digits:

Decimal number	3.33333	66.6666	77.998	222.2500	333.3500
Rounded off	3.333	66.67	78.00	222.2	333.4

It is important to keep the two terminal zeros in the third number so that a reader would know that the number has four significant digits.   We used the odd-add rule for the fourth and fifth numbers.

Truncating

Suppose that one simply deletes the digits after a certain digit rather than rounding off the number.   This is called *truncating* or *chopping*.   For example, the following numbers have been truncated to an integer by simply deleting the fractional part of the number:

Decimal number	77.77	−12345.6	8.7654
Truncated	77	−12345	8

Truncating can be used advantageously in certain situations (e.g. as in Problem 7.8).

7.4   NUMBERS TO ARBITRARY BASES

Any positive integer $b > 1$ can be used as the base for a positional numeration system which is similar to the decimal system, of which the base is $b = 10$.   Since computers are composed of various two-state devices, we will be interested primarily in the *binary system*, for which $b = 2$, and secondarily in the *octal* ($b = 8$) and the *hexadecimal* ($b = 16$) *systems*.   However, it is instructive first to investigate numbers to bases in general.

The digits in the number system to the base b are the numbers $0, 1, 2, 3, \ldots, b - 1$.   Any positive integer m can be expressed uniquely in the form

$$m = a_r b^r + a_{r-1} b^{r-1} + \cdots + a_1 b + a_0 \qquad (7.1)$$

where $a_0, a_1, a_2, \ldots, a_r$ are digits and $a_r \neq 0$.   Once b distinct symbols have been chosen for the b digits (if $b > 10$, additional symbols besides $0, 1, \ldots, 9$ will be required), the *expanded notation*, (7.1), for m can be condensed to the representation

$$(a_r a_{r-1} \ldots a_2 a_1 a_0)_b \qquad (7.2)$$

in which each of the a's is the appropriate digit symbol and in which b is expressed as a decimal number.   The digit a_k in (7.2), which represents the number $a_k b^k$ in (7.1), is said to have *face value* a_k and *place value* b^k.   When there is no ambiguity about the base of the number system, the parentheses and/or b may be omitted from the representation (7.2).

Table 7-1 displays the digits for the number systems most used in the computer.

Table 7-1

Number System	Base	Digits
Binary	2	0, 1
Octal	8	0, 1, 2, 3, 4, 5, 6, 7
Hexadecimal	16	0, 1, 2, 3, 4, 5, 6, 7, 8, 9, A, B, C, D, E, F

EXAMPLE 7.2   Convert the following numbers into the decimal system: (a) $(21403)_5$,   (b) $(3E7B)_{16}$.
Write each number in expanded notation and then evaluate the sum in the decimal system.

(a)   Here the base is $b = 5$, so we use powers of 5 in writing the number in expanded notation.   Since the number has five digits, the first digit, 2, will have place value 5^4.

$$(21403)_5 = 2 \times 5^4 + 1 \times 5^3 + 4 \times 5^2 + 0 \times 5 + 3$$
$$= 2 \times 625 + 1 \times 125 + 4 \times 25 + 0 \times 5 + 3$$
$$= 1250 + 125 + 100 + 0 + 3 = 1478$$

(b) Here the base is $b = 16$, the hexadecimal system. As indicated in Table 7-1, the digits E and B denote the (decimal) numbers 14 and 11, respectively. Accordingly,

$$(3E7B)_{16} = 3 \times 16^3 + 14 \times 16^2 + 7 \times 16 + 11$$
$$= 3 \times 4096 + 14 \times 256 + 7 \times 16 + 11$$
$$= 12288 + 3584 + 112 + 11 = 126595$$

EXAMPLE 7.3 Write the decimal integer 1436 in the octal system.

As was shown in Example 7.2, conversion from a nondecimal to the decimal system involves multiplication. It is not surprising, then, that the reverse conversion involves division. First, divide 1436 by the base 8 to obtain a remainder r_0:

$$
\begin{array}{r}
179 \\
8)\overline{1436} \\
\underline{8} \\
63 \\
\underline{56} \\
76 \\
\underline{72} \\
4
\end{array}
\qquad \text{(that is, } r_0 = 4\text{)}
$$

Next, divide the quotient 179 by the base 8 to obtain a remainder r_1:

$$
\begin{array}{r}
22 \\
8)\overline{179} \\
\underline{16} \\
19 \\
\underline{16} \\
3
\end{array}
\qquad \text{(that is, } r_1 = 3\text{)}
$$

Now, divide the above quotient 22 by the base 8 to obtain a remainder r_2:

$$
\begin{array}{r}
2 \\
8)\overline{22} \\
\underline{16} \\
6
\end{array}
\qquad \text{(that is, } r_2 = 6\text{)}
$$

This last quotient, 2, is less than (the base) 8, so 2 becomes our last remainder:

$$r_3 = 2$$

(More precisely, dividing the quotient 2 by the base 8 gives a quotient 0 and remainder 2.)
The octal representation of 1436 is the sequence of remainders *in reverse order*:

$$1436 = (2634)_8$$

We check our answer by writing $(2634)_8$ in the decimal system, following Example 7.2:

$$(2634)_8 = 2 \times 8^3 + 6 \times 8^2 + 3 \times 8 + 4$$
$$= 2 \times 512 + 6 \times 64 + 3 \times 8 + 4$$
$$= 1024 + 384 + 24 + 4 = 1436$$

By using short division, one can compactly obtain the above result in the following manner:

	Remainders
8)1436	4
8)179	3
8)22	6
2	

That is, one continually places the quotient underneath the dividend, and the remainder on the right.   The desired sequence of remainders is then from the bottom up, as indicated by the arrow.

7.5   BINARY NUMBER SYSTEM

The digits in the binary system ($b = 2$) are 0 and 1; the place values of these digits, or bits, in the binary representation of a number are powers of 2.   A few positive powers, together with their decimal and binary representations are listed in Table 7-2, and the binary representations of the first 20 integers are listed in Table 7-3.   Sometimes, for easier reading and checking, one separates a long binary number into 4-bit groups, beginning with the units digit; e.g.

$$11\ 1011\ 0110\ 1110\ 0101$$

Table 7-2

Power	Decimal	Binary
2^0	1	1
2^1	2	10
2^2	4	100
2^3	8	1000
2^4	16	10000
2^5	32	100000
2^6	64	1000000
2^7	128	10000000
2^8	256	100000000
2^9	512	1000000000
2^{10}	1024	10000000000

Table 7-3

Decimal	Binary
0	0
1	1
2	10
3	11
4	100
5	101
6	110
7	111
8	1000
9	1001
10	1010
11	1011
12	1100
13	1101
14	1110
15	1111
16	10000
17	10001
18	10010
19	10011
20	10100

One can convert integers from the decimal system to the binary system and vice versa as in Examples 7.3 and 7.2 (see also Problems 7.11, 7.12, and 7.14).   Conversion into the decimal system is particularly simple because there is only one nonzero face value, 1, in the binary system.   Moreover, just as the decimal system uses a decimal point for representing decimal fractions, so does the binary system use a *binary point* for representing binary fractions.   The place values of digits to the right of the binary point are negative powers of 2.   A few such powers, and their decimal and binary representations, appear in Table 7-4.

Table 7-4

Negative Power	Decimal	Binary
2^{-1}	$1/2 = 0.5$	0.1
2^{-2}	$1/4 = 0.25$	0.01
2^{-3}	$1/8 = 0.125$	0.001
2^{-4}	$1/16 = 0.0625$	0.0001
2^{-5}	$1/32 = 0.03125$	0.00001
2^{-6}	$1/64 = 0.015625$	0.000001
2^{-7}	$1/128 = 0.0078125$	0.0000001
2^{-8}	$1/256 = 0.00390625$	0.00000001

Any negative power of 2 has a terminating decimal representation, since

$$2^{-k} = \frac{1}{2^k} = \frac{5^k}{5^k \times 2^k} = \frac{5^k}{10^k}$$

Consequently, when a terminating binary fraction is converted to the decimal system, using the expanded form of the binary fraction, the result is always a terminating decimal fraction. However, the converse is not true: a terminating decimal fraction may have as its binary representation an infinite, repeating fraction. See Problem 7.16.

Binary numbers can also be written in exponential form; that is, as a binary number times a power of 2. Also, any nonzero binary number can be written in only one way in standard exponential form, i.e. with the binary point directly before the first nonzero digit (which must be 1). Such a form yields a unique mantissa and exponent, as illustrated below.

Binary Number	Standard Exponential Form	Mantissa	Exponent
1111.1	0.11111×2^4	0.11111	4
0.011001	0.11001×2^{-1}	0.11001	-1
-10101	-0.10101×2^5	-0.10101	5

7.6 BINARY ARITHMETIC

This section will take up the addition and subtraction of binary integers. Binary multiplication is simply repeated addition, and is treated in Problem 7.22; binary division is simply repeated subtraction, and is treated in Problem 7.24. Here we will also discuss binary subtraction in terms of the notion of complements. In each case, we show the parallel in the decimal system.

Binary Addition

Recall that we add two decimal numbers by adding pairs of decimal digits and carrying 1 whenever the sum is greater than 9. For example, the sum of 12937 and 4526 is obtained as follows:

$$\begin{array}{r} 1\ 1 \\ 12937 \\ \underline{4526} \\ 17463 \end{array}$$

Binary numbers are added similarly.   First we need to know the sums of pairs of binary digits:

$$0 + 0 = 0$$
$$0 + 1 = 1$$
$$1 + 0 = 1$$
$$1 + 1 = 0, \text{ with a carry of } 1$$

and we note that the last two sums imply that

$$1 + 1 + 1 = 1, \text{ with a carry of } 1$$

Using only the above sums, we are able to do binary addition, as shown below.

We compute the binary sum of 11011011 and 1001110 as follows:

```
   1  1111
  11011011
   1001110
 100101001
```

We add more than two binary numbers by accumulating them to a running total one at a time.   For example,

```
    11101
    10110
     1100
    11011
 +   1001
```

is obtained as follows:

```
   11
   11101    First number
   10110    Second number
  110011    Sum
    1100    Third number
  11111
  111111    Sum
   11011    Fourth number
  11
 1011010    Sum
    1001    Fifth number
 1100011    Final sum
```

We do not use the same technique as with decimal numbers, since that would involve an exorbitant amount of carrying.

Binary Subtraction

Recall that in decimal subtraction we subtract a decimal digit from a smaller decimal digit by borrowing 1 from the next column.   For example, the decimal difference $73426 - 9185$ is obtained as follows:

```
    6  3
  7¹34¹26
 −  91 85
  6 42 41
```

Binary subtraction can be accomplished similarly.   First we need to know the following subtraction facts:

$$0 - 0 = 0$$
$$1 - 0 = 1$$
$$1 - 1 = 0$$
$$0 - 1 = 1, \text{ with a borrow of 1 from the next column}$$

We illustrate with examples:

(i)   Here there is no borrowing.

$$
\begin{array}{r}
1111011 \\
-\ 101001 \\
\hline
1010010
\end{array}
$$

(ii) Here we borrow 1 from the third column because of the difference $0 - 1$ in the second column.

$$
\begin{array}{r}
0 \\
111\!\!\not{1}'01 \\
-\ 100\ 10 \\
\hline
1010\ 11
\end{array}
$$

What if we cannot borrow 1 from the next column because the column contains a 0?   First we look at what happens in decimal subtraction.   The decimal difference $800046 - 397261$ is obtained as follows:

$$
\begin{array}{r}
7999 \\
8\!\not{0}\!\not{0}\!\not{0}'46 \\
-3972\ 61 \\
\hline
4027\ 85
\end{array}
$$

Observe that we borrowed 1 from the sixth column for the second column, since the third, fourth, and fifth columns contained zeros.   After the borrowing, the third, fourth, and fifth columns contain

$$10 - 1 = 9$$

Now, the same thing happens in binary subtraction, except that after the borrowing the zero columns contain

$$10 - 1 = 1$$

For example, the binary difference $110001 - 1010$ is obtained as follows:

$$
\begin{array}{r}
011 \\
1\!\not{1}\!\not{0}\!\not{0}'01 \\
-\ \ 10\ 10 \\
\hline
1001\ 11
\end{array}
$$

Complements

In a method very well suited to the computer, subtraction is transformed into addition by use of the *radix-minus-one complement* or the *radix complement*.   We shall first discuss these complements in the decimal system, where they are called the *nines complement* and the *tens complement*, respectively (the corresponding complements in the binary system are called the *ones complement* and the *twos complement*).   We note that when complements are used for subtraction, all numbers are written with the same number of digits; this can be accomplished by adding 0's at the beginning of a number, if necessary.

The nines complement of a decimal number is obtained by subtracting each decimal digit from

9, and the tens complement is the nines complement plus one.   For example,

Decimal number	456	321	730
Nines complement	543	678	269
Tens complement	544	679	270

Observe that the relationship between a number and its complement is symmetric.   Thus, referring to the above example, the tens complement of 544 is 456 and the nines complement of 678 is 321.

Decimal subtraction can be accomplished by the addition of the nines complement plus one [Fig. 7-1(b)], or the addition of the tens complement [Fig. 7-2(c)].

$$
\begin{array}{cccc}
& & 893 & \\
& & +678 & \\
893 & & \overline{1\ 571} & 893 \\
-321 & & 1 & +679 \\
\overline{572} & & \overline{572} & \overline{1\ 572}
\end{array}
$$

(a) Ordinary   (b) Decimal Subtraction   (c) Decimal Subtraction
     Decimal   by Use of   by Use of
     Subtraction   Nines Complement   Tens Complement

Fig. 7-1

Observe that the leftmost 1 is simply deleted in adding the tens complement, but is subjected to "end-around carry" in adding the nines complement.

Analogously, the ones complement of a binary number is obtained by subtracting each binary digit from 1 or, equivalently, converting each 0 to 1 and each 1 to 0, and the twos complement is the ones complement plus one.   For example,

Binary number	110011	101010	011100
Ones complement	001100	010101	100011
Twos complement	001101	010110	100100

The binary subtraction $110001 - 1010$ is illustrated in Fig. 7-2, where it is arranged that all numbers have exactly six digits.

$$
\begin{array}{cccc}
& & 110001 & \\
& & +110101 & \\
110001 & & \overline{1\ 100110} & 110001 \\
-001010 & & 1 & +110110 \\
\overline{100111} & & \overline{100111} & \overline{1\ 100111}
\end{array}
$$

(a) Ordinary   (b) Binary Subtraction   (c) Binary Subtraction
     Binary   by Use of   by Use of
     Subtraction   Ones Complement   Twos Complement

Fig. 7-2

EXAMPLE 7.4 The theoretical reason why complements work can be explained as follows.   Suppose that a six-digit automobile odometer reads zero:

$$\boxed{0}\boxed{0}\boxed{0}\boxed{0}\boxed{0}\boxed{0}$$

If now we add -1 to the reading, i.e. if we turn back the odometer 1 mile, then the reading becomes

$$\boxed{9}\boxed{9}\boxed{9}\boxed{9}\boxed{9}\boxed{9}$$

Thus we have the identification

$$999999 = -1$$

when we assume that all numbers (readings) have exactly six digits. Suppose now that we want to subtract b from a. Let c be the nines complement of b, so that

$$b + c = 999999 = -1$$

or

$$c + 1 = -b$$

Then we have

$$a - b = a + c + 1$$

The term *overflow* refers to the case where a digit is lost because the result of an operation exceeds the capacity of the register or location where the result is to be stored. Thus, in Fig. 7-1(c) (three-digit storage) or in Fig. 7-2(c) (six-digit storage), the circled 1 is lost by overflow. In general, when subtracting by use of the radix complement, there is overflow when the result of the subtraction is positive or zero, and no overflow when it is negative.

EXAMPLE 7.5   Subtracting 456 from 331 gives

$$
\begin{array}{r}
331 \\
-456 \\
\hline
-125
\end{array}
$$

Suppose that we have a three-digit device and that the decimal subtraction is performed by adding the tens complement:

$$
\begin{array}{r}
331 \\
+544 \\
\hline
875
\end{array}
$$

Observe that there is no overflow and that the negative of the tens complement of the sum 875 is the required difference, -125. The analogous situation obtains in the binary system. That is, if adding the twos complement does not result in any overflow, then the negative of the twos complement of the sum is the actual difference.

7.7   OCTAL AND HEXADECIMAL SYSTEMS

As eight and sixteen are powers of two, there exists a very close relationship between the octal (base-8) and the hexadecimal (base-16) systems and the binary system. (Sometimes *hexadecimal* is abbreviated to just *hex*.)

Table 7-5 gives the 3-bit equivalent of each octal digit, and Table 7-6 gives the 4-bit equivalent of each hexadecimal digit. This is the only information needed to convert from any one of the three systems to any other.

EXAMPLE 7.6   Convert (a) the octal number 6305_8 to its binary equivalent, (b) the hexadecimal number $5D93_{16}$ to its binary equivalent, (c) the binary number 11010100001101 to its octal equivalent, (d) the binary number 101101011011001011 to its hexadecimal equivalent.

(a)   Each octal digit is replaced by its 3-bit equivalent, as follows:

6305

110 011 000 101

Thus, 110011000101 is the binary equivalent of the octal number 6305_8.

Table 7-5

Octal Digit	Three-Bit Equivalent
0	000
1	001
2	010
3	011
4	100
5	101
6	110
7	111

Table 7-6

Hexadecimal Digit	Four-Bit Equivalent
0	0000
1	0001
2	0010
3	0011
4	0100
5	0101
6	0110
7	0111
8	1000
9	1001
A (ten)	1010
B (eleven)	1011
C (twelve)	1100
D (thirteen)	1101
E (fourteen)	1110
F (fifteen)	1111

(b) Each hexadecimal digit is replaced by its 4-bit equivalent, as follows:

$$5D93$$

$$0101 \quad 1101 \quad 1001 \quad 0011$$

Thus, 101110110010011 is the binary equivalent of the hexadecimal number $5D93_{16}$.

(c) Partition the binary number into 3-bit sequences, starting from the right, and then replace each 3-bit sequence by its octal equivalent:

$$011 \; 010 \; 100 \; 001 \; 101$$
$$\downarrow \quad \downarrow \quad \downarrow \quad \downarrow \quad \downarrow$$
$$3 \quad 2 \quad 4 \quad 1 \quad 5$$

Thus, 32415_8 is the octal equivalent of 11010100001101. (Observe that a zero was added at the beginning of the number to make the number of digits a multiple of three.)

(d) Partition the binary number into 4-bit sequences, beginning on the right, and then replace each 4-bit sequence by its hexadecimal equivalent:

$$0010 \; 1101 \; 0110 \; 1100 \; 1011$$
$$\downarrow \quad \downarrow \quad \downarrow \quad \downarrow \quad \downarrow$$
$$2 \quad D \quad 6 \quad C \quad B$$

Thus, $2D6CB_{16}$ is the hexadecimal equivalent of 101101011011001011. (Observe that two zeros were added at the beginning of the number to make the number of digits a multiple of four.)

It is clear that conversions between the octal and hexadecimal systems can be accomplished by combining two steps from Example 7.6.

7.8   WORDS AND BYTES

As discussed in Section 5.6, the memory of a computer consists of various storage locations, each of which can accommodate a certain number of bits (binary digits).   The basic properties of a storage location are:

(i)   Normally it inputs/outputs all its bits at once.

(ii)   It has a unique address, which allows direct access to it.

A *word* is a set of bits processed as a unit, the number of bits being the *length* of the word.   Historically, a word consisted of the bits in one storage location and hence had a fixed length.   Today, words can also have variable length and can consist of the bits occupying more than one storage location.   In either case, the *address* of a word is the address of the leading storage location of the word.

Words are usually partitioned into 8-bit subunits called *bytes*.   (Some computers, such as the CDC 6000–7000 series, still use 6-bit bytes.)   The byte is that part of a word which represents exactly one character (Section 3.2).   The IBM 360/370 series is a byte-addressable computer which contains 32-bit words partitioned into four 8-bit bytes, as follows:

Word

Byte 0	Byte 1	Byte 2	Byte 3

In such byte-addressable machines the word is still used as a unit of information (though not the smallest unit), and the address of a word is the address of its leftmost byte, i.e. the byte whose bits have the highest place values.

7.9   CHARACTER CODES

Normally, two kinds of data may be stored in the memory of a computer—*character data* (names, addresses, etc.) and *numerical data.*   This section will discuss various codes used to represent and process character data.   These codes are also used, to some extent, for numerical data.   However, the representation of numbers for calculations is a more elaborate affair, and we prefer to deal with numerical data separately in Section 7.10.

The 48 characters normally recognized by the computer were presented in Section 3.2.   Since $2^5 = 32$ but $2^6 = 64$,   one must use at least a 6-bit code to represent these 48 characters.   Such 6-bit codes do exist, but most third- and fourth-generation computers use 8-bit codes, which can accommodate the 36 alphameric characters and up to 220 special characters.   For example, some computers recognize the inequality symbols $<$ and $>$, the question mark ?, and so on, besides the special characters listed in Section 3.2.

In the two most popular 8-bit character codes, which we describe below, the representation of each character (i.e. each byte) is divided into two 4-bit portions—a *zone* portion, on the left, and a *numeric* portion, on the right.

Because each portion corresponds precisely to a single hexadecimal digit (obtained by reading Table 7-6 from right to left), a character is also uniquely represented by a two-digit hexadecimal number.   Hence the third column in Tables 7-7 and 7-8 below.

In addition to the 8 bits representing a character, virtually every computer stores an extra bit, called a *check bit* or *parity bit*, usually preceding the zone bits.   The function of the check bit is precisely that of the parity-check channel on magnetic tapes (Section 3.8).   For each character, the value of the check bit is chosen such that the (9-bit) byte for the character contains an even number of 1s, if the computer operates with even parity; or contains an odd number of 1s, if the computer operates with odd parity.

EBCDIC

The Extended Binary-Coded Decimal Interchange Code, or EBCDIC (pronounced "ebb-see-dick"), is an 8-bit code primarily used by IBM and IBM-compatible computer systems.   Thus, the IBM 360/370 series, which uses a 32-bit word, can store up to 4 characters in a particular location.   Table 7-7 gives this code for the 26 alphabetical characters and the 10 digits.   Observe:

   (i)   Each digit has 1111 as the zone portion of its byte and its binary representation as the numeric portion.
   (ii) The alphabetical characters are partitioned into three groups, according as their bytes have 1100, 1101, or 1110 as the zone portion.

Table 7-7

Char.	EBCDIC zone	numeric	HEX	Char.	EBCDIC zone	numeric	HEX
A	1100	0001	C1	S	1110	0010	E2
B		0010	C2	T		0011	E3
C		0011	C3	U		0100	E4
D		0100	C4	V		0101	E5
E		0101	C5	W		0110	E6
F		0110	C6	X		0111	E7
G		0111	C7	Y		1000	E8
H		1000	C8	Z	1110	1001	E9
I	1100	1001	C9	0	1111	0000	F0
J	1101	0001	D1	1		0001	F1
K		0010	D2	2		0010	F2
L		0011	D3	3		0011	F3
M		0100	D4	4		0100	F4
N		0101	D5	5		0101	F5
O		0110	D6	6		0110	F6
P		0111	D7	7		0111	F7
Q		1000	D8	8		1000	F8
R	1101	1001	D9	9	1111	1001	F9

ASCII-8

The American Standard Code for Information Interchange, or ASCII (pronounced "ass-key"), was developed to standardize codes of various data processing equipment; it is primarily used by non-IBM computer systems.   It began as a 7-bit code with a 3-bit zone portion, but was later extended to an 8-bit code, denoted ASCII-8.   Table 7-8 gives this 8-bit code for the 26 alphabetical characters and the 10 digits.   Observe:

(i)   Each digit has 0101 as the zone portion of its byte, and its binary representation as the numeric portion.

(ii) The alphabetical characters are partitioned into two groups, according as their bytes have 1010 or 1011 as the zone portion.

Table 7-8

Char.	ASCII-8 zone	ASCII-8 numeric	HEX	Char.	ASCII-8 zone	ASCII-8 numeric	HEX	Char.	ASCII-8 zone	ASCII-8 numeric	HEX
A	1010	0001	A1	P	1011	0000	B0	0	0101	0000	50
B		0010	A2	Q		0001	B1	1		0001	51
C		0011	A3	R		0010	B2	2		0010	52
D		0100	A4	S		0011	B3	3		0011	53
E		0101	A5	T		0100	B4	4		0100	54
F		0110	A6	U		0101	B5	5		0101	55
G		0111	A7	V		0110	B6	6		0110	56
H		1000	A8	W		0111	B7	7		0111	57
I		1001	A9	X		1000	B8	8		1000	58
J		1010	AA	Y		1001	B9	9	0101	1001	59
K		1011	AB	Z	1011	1010	BA				
L		1100	AC								
M		1101	AD								
N		1110	AE								
O	1010	1111	AF								

7.10   NUMERICAL CODES

There are two basic ways of coding a numerical data item, i.e. a decimal number: coding the individual decimal digits, or coding the entire number.   In the latter method, fixed-point integers and floating-point numbers are coded differently.   A word length of 32 bits is assumed in what follows, though we shall not bother to show leading zeros when illustrating the storage of small numbers.

Numerical Character Codes

Here each digit of the number is individually coded by the character code of the computer, e.g. EBCDIC or ASCII-8, except that the zone of the last digit is reserved for the sign of the number.   The coding of the sign is as given in Table 7-9.

Table 7-9

Last Zone	Sign
1111	unsigned (positive value)
1100	positive
1101	negative

Figure 7-3 shows how the numbers 637, +637, and −637 are coded in EBCDIC.

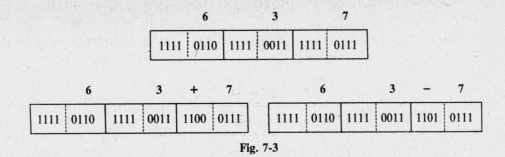

Fig. 7-3

Numerical character codes are not geared towards performing arithmetic operations on the data. Accordingly, most computers convert the character code for numerical data into a more convenient *processing code* before performing arithmetic operations on the data. The results of the arithmetic processing are then converted back to the character code for potential outputting.

One popular processing code is the Binary-Coded Decimal (BCD) system, which uses the 4-bit binary representation of each digit, with the last 4-bit field reserved for the sign. Figure 7-4 shows how 637, +637, and −637 are represented in BCD.

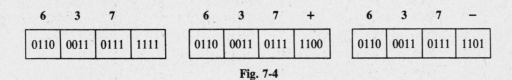

Fig. 7-4

Observe that one can convert numerical data from the 8-bit character code EBCDIC (or ASCII-8) to BCD by simply deleting the zone bits and "packing" together the remaining bits, with the sign transferred to the right. See Fig. 7-5.

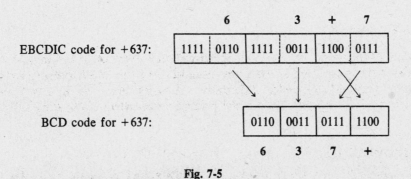

Fig. 7-5

Hence, BCD is frequently called the *packed decimal* system.

Addition in the processing code BCD is by binary addition of the 4-bit representations of the individual decimal digits (see Problem 7.41). The other arithmetic operations, which are all based upon addition, are carried out similarly.

Integer Quantity Codes

It is natural to represent an integer in a storage location by use of its binary representation. This can be done in more than one way.

(1) **Sign-and-magnitude binary representation.** Here the first bit is reserved for the sign, with 0 for positive and 1 for negative, and the remaining bits give the binary representation of the magnitude of the number. For example, 637 and −637 would be stored in 32-bit memory locations as indicated in Fig. 7-6.

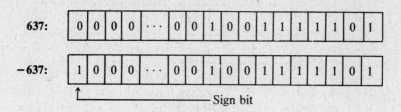

Fig. 7-6

This method of representation is rarely used, since it does not lend itself to arithmetic calculations.

(2) **Twos-complement binary representation.** Here there is no sign bit, and negative integers are stored as their twos complements (Section 7.6). Figure 7-7 shows how 637 and −637 would be stored under this method.

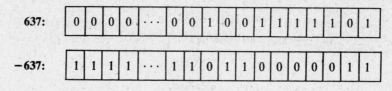

Fig. 7-7

Observe that positive integers are stored identically under the two methods. Furthermore, under both methods, negative integers have a 1 as the first bit. Either way, the largest positive integer that may be stored as a 32-bit word is expressed as a 0 followed by thirty-one 1s. This is the binary representation of

$$2^{31} - 1 \approx 2\,000\,000\,000 \quad \text{(about two billion)}$$

Any attempt to store an integer with more than nine decimal digits would likely result in overflow, with loss of the most significant digit.

Fractional Quantity Codes

Decimal fractions can be represented in memory by their floating-point binary representations; that is, by their binary representations in standard exponential form (Section 7.5). It will be necessary that all mantissas have the same number of bits; this may be accomplished by truncating or rounding off, or by adding zeros. Figure 7-8 shows how the bits are allocated in the storage of a floating-point binary number as a 32-bit word.

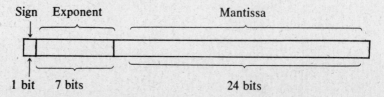

Fig. 7-8

Since an exponent may itself be negative, one has to include the sign of the exponent within the field reserved for the exponent. Rather than reserve a bit for the sign, one uses the *characteristic* of the exponent instead of its true value. When a 7-bit field is reserved for the exponent, the characteristic of an exponent is obtained by adding $2^6 = 64$ to the exponent. Thus:

True Exponent	−64	−63	−62	−61	...	−1	0	1	...	63
Characteristic	0	1	2	3	...	63	64	65	...	127

(In case an 8-bit field is used to store the exponent, one adds $2^7 = 128$ to the true exponent to obtain its characteristic; and so on.) With a 7-bit characteristic, which represents exponents from −64 to 63, the computer can store only numbers whose magnitudes lie between

$$0.1000 \cdots \times 2^{-64} = 2^{-65} \approx 3 \times 10^{-20}$$

and

$$0.1111 \cdots \times 2^{63} \approx 2^{63} \approx 9 \times 10^{18}$$

Finally, we mention that complement forms are seldom used for negative floating-point numbers.

EXAMPLE 7.7 The decimal fraction −45.6875 is represented in standard binary exponential form as

$$-0.1011011011 \times 2^6$$

The true exponent is 6, so the characteristic is $6 + 64 = 70$. The binary representation of 70 being

$$1000110$$

the decimal number −45.6875 is stored internally as follows:

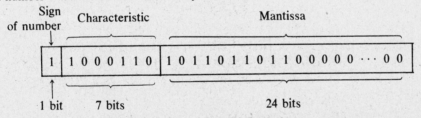

Observe that zeros appear at the end of the mantissa, to fill out the 24-bit field. On the other hand, if a characteristic had fewer than 7 binary digits, then zeros would appear at the beginning of the characteristic, to fill out the 7-bit field for the characteristic.

Solved Problems

DECIMAL SYSTEM

7.1 Evaluate (a) 3^4, (b) 5^2, (c) 10^0, (d) 8^{-1}, (e) 2^{-5}, (f) 16^{-3}.

Recall that, for n a positive integer, $a^n = a \times a \times \cdots \times a$ (n factors); $a^0 = 1$; and $a^{-n} = 1/a^n$.

(a) $3^4 = 3 \times 3 \times 3 \times 3 = 81$ (d) $8^{-1} = \dfrac{1}{8^1} = \dfrac{1}{8}$ (f) $16^{-3} = \dfrac{1}{16^3} = \dfrac{1}{4096}$

(b) $5^2 = 5 \times 5 = 25$

(c) $10^0 = 1$ (e) $2^{-5} = \dfrac{1}{2^5} = \dfrac{1}{32}$

7.2 Write in expanded notation: (a) 3457, (b) 49.135.

The expanded notation of a number is the sum of each digit times its place value.

(a) $3457 = 3 \times 10^3 + 4 \times 10^2 + 5 \times 10 + 7 \times 1$

(b) $49.135 = 4 \times 10 + 9 \times 1 + 1 \times 10^{-1} + 3 \times 10^{-2} + 5 \times 10^{-3}$

7.3 Write each decimal number in standard exponential form to obtain its mantissa and exponent: (a) 123.123, (b) 0.000456456, (c) 5.678×10^{-3}, (d) 0.888, (e) 0.0.

Write the number in exponential form with the decimal point directly in front of the leading nonzero digit. See Table 7-10.

Table 7-10

	Decimal Number	Standard Exponential Form	Mantissa	Exponent
(a)	123.123	0.123123×10^3	0.123123	3
(b)	0.000456456	0.456456×10^{-3}	0.456456	-3
(c)	5.678×10^{-3}	0.5678×10^{-2}	0.5678	-2
(d)	0.888	0.888×10^0	0.888	0
(e)	The number zero has no standard exponential form.			

7.4 Find the number of significant digits in each number: (a) 20.45, (b) 580.00, (c) 0.00555, (d) 0.0055500, (e) 30 000.

(a) Four [by rules (1) and (2), Section 7.3].

(b) Five [rules (1) and (4)(i)].

(c) Three [rules (1) and (3)].

(d) Five [rules (1), (3), and (4)(i)].

(e) Ambiguous [rule (4)(ii); the number could be 0.3×10^5, 0.30×10^5, 0.300×10^5, 0.3000×10^5, or 0.30000×10^5].

7.5 Round off the following numbers to three decimal places: (a) 22.2222, (b) 7.77777, (c) 4.4444, (d) 7.654321, (e) 3.7996.

Delete all digits after the third decimal place, adding 1 to the third decimal place if the digit in the fourth decimal place was 5 or more:

	(a)	(b)	(c)	(d)	(e)
Decimal Number	22.2222	7.77777	4.4444	7.654321	3.7996
Rounded Off	22.222	7.778	4.444	7.654	3.800

Observe that in (e) we add 0.001 to 3.799 to obtain 3.800. We keep the two zeros to show that the number has been rounded off to three decimal places. (If we wrote 3.8, a reader might believe that the number was rounded off to only one decimal place.)

7.6 Round off each number to four significant digits, and then write the number in standard exponential form: (a) 2406.8, (b) 20402., (c) 0.0044446, (d) 0.555555.

Delete all digits after the fourth significant digit, adding 1 to the fourth significant digit if the fifth significant digit was 5 or more:

	(a)	(b)	(c)	(d)
Decimal Number	2406.8	20402.	0.0044446	0.555555
Rounded Off	2407	20400	0.004445	0.5556
Standard Form	0.2407×10^4	0.2040×10^5	0.4445×10^{-2}	0.5556×10^0

7.7 Truncate the following decimal numbers to integers: (a) 234.342, (b) -33.99, (c) 0.056, (d) 5800, (e) -0.77.

Simply drop all digits after the decimal point (no rounding off).

(a) 234   (b) -33 (c) 0   (d) 5800   (e) 0

7.8 Let INT be the function that converts any number to an integer by truncation, e.g.

$$INT(2.6) = 2 \qquad INT(-3.7) = -3$$

Show how one can use INT to determine whether an integer N is even or odd.

If N is even, then $N/2$ is an integer and hence $INT(N/2)$ has the same value as $N/2$. Accordingly,

$$2 \times INT(N/2) = N \tag{1}$$

On the other hand, if N is odd, then $N/2$ is not an integer, and $INT(N/2)$ will not have the same value as $N/2$. Consequently, (1) will not hold. In short, N is even if and only if (1) holds.

NUMBERS TO ARBITRARY BASES

7.9 Convert each of the following into its decimal equivalent: (a) 3104_5, (b) 2456_8, (c) $2D7B_{16}$, (d) 3957_8.

Write each number in expanded notation and then compute.

(a)
$$3104_5 = 3 \times 5^3 + 1 \times 5^2 + 0 \times 5 + 4$$
$$= 3 \times 125 + 1 \times 25 + 0 \times 5 + 4$$
$$= 375 + 25 + 0 + 4 = 404$$

(b) $2456_8 = 2 \times 8^3 + 4 \times 8^2 + 5 \times 8 + 6 = 2 \times 512 + 4 \times 64 + 5 \times 8 + 6$
$= 1024 + 256 + 40 + 6 = 1326$

(c) Recall from Table 7-1 that A, B, C, D, E, and F are the symbols in the hexadecimal system representing the decimal numbers 10, 11, 12, 13, 14, and 15, respectively. Hence:

$2D7B = 2 \times 16^3 + 13 \times 16^2 + 7 \times 16 + 11 = 2 \times 4096 + 13 \times 256 + 7 \times 16 + 11$
$= 8192 + 3328 + 112 + 11 = 11\,643$

(d) The number is meaningless, since 9 cannot be a digit in the octal (base-8) system.

7.10 Represent the decimal integer 3457 as an integer to the base (a) 5, (b) 8, (c) 16.

In each case, divide the given number, 3457, and each successive quotient by the base. The sequence of remainders in reverse order is the required numeral.

(a)

$$
\begin{array}{c|c|c|c|c}
691 & 138 & 27 & 5 & 1 \\
5)\overline{3457} & 5)\overline{691} & 5)\overline{138} & 5)\overline{27} & 5)\overline{5} \\
\underline{30} & \underline{5} & \underline{10} & \underline{25} & \underline{5} \\
45 & 19 & 38 & r_3 = 2 & r_4 = 0 \\
\underline{45} & \underline{15} & \underline{35} & & \\
7 & 41 & r_2 = 3 & & \\
\underline{5} & \underline{40} & & & \\
r_0 = 2 & r_1 = 1 & & &
\end{array}
$$

$r_5 = 1$

Accordingly, $3457 = 102312_5$.

Using short division, one can compactly obtain the above answer as follows:

$$
\begin{array}{rc}
 & \textbf{Remainders} \\
5)\underline{3457} & 2 \\
5)\underline{691} & 1 \\
5)\underline{138} & 3 \\
5)\underline{27} & 2 \\
5)\underline{5} & 0 \\
1 &
\end{array}
$$

The desired number is the sequence of remainders from the bottom up, as indicated by the arrow; i.e. $3457 = 102312_5$.

(b)

$$
\begin{array}{rc}
 & \textbf{Remainders} \\
8)\underline{3457} & 1 \\
8)\underline{432} & 0 \\
8)\underline{54} & 6 \\
6 &
\end{array}
$$

As indicated by the arrow, $3457 = 6601_8$.

(c)

$$
\begin{array}{c|c}
216 & 13 \\
16)\overline{3457} & 16)\overline{216} \\
\underline{32} & \underline{16} \\
25 & 56 \\
\underline{16} & \underline{48} \\
97 & r_1 = 8 \\
\underline{96} & \\
r_0 = 1 &
\end{array}
$$

$r_2 = 13 = D$

Thus, $3457 = D81_{16}$, where D is the digit representing 13.

BINARY SYSTEM

7.11   Convert the binary integer 110110101 to the decimal system.

Method 1

Write the number in expanded notation and compute:

$$110110101_2 = 1 \times 2^8 + 1 \times 2^7 + 0 \times 2^6 + 1 \times 2^5 + 1 \times 2^4 + 0 \times 2^3 + 1 \times 2^2 + 0 \times 2 + 1$$
$$= 1 \times 256 + 1 \times 128 + 0 \times 64 + 1 \times 32 + 1 \times 16 + 0 \times 8 + 1 \times 4 + 0 \times 2 + 1$$
$$= 256 + 128 + 0 + 32 + 16 + 0 + 4 + 0 + 1 = 437$$

Since a face value in the binary system can only be 1 or 0, we can obtain the above by simply adding the place values where a 1 appears.   That is,

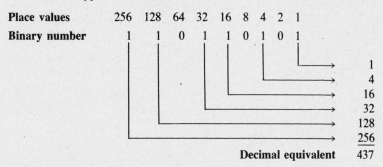

Place values	256	128	64	32	16	8	4	2	1
Binary number	1	1	0	1	1	0	1	0	1

	1
	4
	16
	32
	128
	256
Decimal equivalent	437

Method 2

Another procedure for converting a binary integer to its decimal equivalent, called *double summing*, is as follows:

(i)   Double the leftmost digit and add the next digit.

(ii)   Double each sum and add the next digit.

(iii)   When the rightmost digit is added, the final sum is the required decimal equivalent.

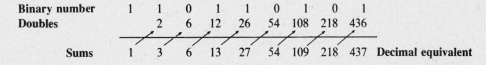

Binary number	1	1	0	1	1	0	1	0	1	
Doubles		2	6	12	26	54	108	218	436	
Sums	1	3	6	13	27	54	109	218	437	**Decimal equivalent**

The reason this method works is that the first 1 is doubled eight times and hence contributes 1×2^8 to the final sum; the next 1 is doubled seven times and hence contributes 1×2^7 to the sum; and so on.

7.12   Convert the binary integer 101110111 to the decimal system.

Method 1

Add up the place values corresponding to the 1s.

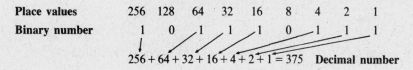

Place values	256	128	64	32	16	8	4	2	1
Binary number	1	0	1	1	1	0	1	1	1

$$256 + 64 + 32 + 16 + 4 + 2 + 1 = 375 \quad \textbf{Decimal number}$$

Method 2

Use double summing.

Binary number	1	0	1	1	1	0	1	1	1	
Doubles		2	4	10	22	46	92	186	374	
Sums	1	2	5	11	23	46	93	187	375	**Decimal equivalent**

7.13   Convert the binary number 1101.1011 to the decimal system.

Method 1

For each face value that is 1, add the corresponding power of two (Table 7-2 or 7-4):

$$1101.1011 = 2^3 + 2^2 + 2^0 + 2^{-1} + 2^{-3} + 2^{-4}$$
$$= 8 + 4 + 1 + 0.5 + 0.125 + 0.0625 = 13.6875$$

Method 2

Convert the integral part of the number, 1101, by double summing or by adding up place values.   Using double summing:

```
Integral part      1    1    0    1
                        2    6   12
                   ─────────────────
                   1    3    6   13   Decimal equivalent
```

Now convert the fractional part of the number, 0.1011, by "half summing," which is the same as double summing except that it proceeds from the right and uses $2^{-1} = 0.5$ as the multiplier:

```
                   0           1          0          1        1    Fractional part
                   0.6875      0.375      0.75       0.5
                  ────────────────────────────────────────────
Decimal equivalent 0.6875      1.375      0.75       1.5      1
```

The complete decimal equivalent is then 13.6875.

7.14   Convert the decimal integer 853 to the binary system.

Remainder Method

Use the method of Problem 7.10.

```
Decimal number   ─┐    Remainders
           2)853        1  ↑
           2)426        0
           2)213        1
           2)106        0
           2)53         1
           2)26         0
           2)13         1
           2)6          0
           2)3          1
             1
```

The desired binary number is the sequence of remainders in the reverse order, as indicated by the arrow; that is,

$$853 = 1101010101_2$$

Subtraction Method

Starting with the given decimal number, continually subtract the largest power of two until obtaining zero. The binary equivalents of those powers of two that were subtracted (some powers may be skipped) give us the required binary number.

$$
\begin{array}{rll}
\textbf{Decimal number} & 853 & \\
2^9 = & \dfrac{512}{341} & \longrightarrow \quad 1000000000 \\[4pt]
2^8 = & \dfrac{256}{85} & \longrightarrow \quad 100000000 \\[4pt]
2^6 = & \dfrac{64}{21} & \longrightarrow \quad 1000000 \\[4pt]
2^4 = & \dfrac{16}{5} & \longrightarrow \quad 10000 \\[4pt]
2^2 = & \dfrac{4}{1} & \longrightarrow \quad 100 \\[4pt]
2^0 = & \dfrac{1}{0} & \longrightarrow \quad 1 \\
& & \overline{1101010101}
\end{array}
$$

Binary place values

Equivalent binary number

Observe that 2^7, 2^5, 2^3, and 2^1 were skipped; hence their corresponding face values in the binary number are zero.

7.15   Convert the decimal number 0.6875 to the binary system.

Method 1

The remainder method works only for integers (or integral parts of numbers). However, a similar algorithm can be used to convert fractional decimal numbers (or fractional parts of decimal numbers) to the binary system. The rule is: Starting with the given (fractional) number, successively lay aside the integral part and double the fractional part. The sequence of integral parts thus generated gives the desired binary representation.

$$
\begin{array}{c|l}
\textbf{Integral} & 0 \ .6875 \quad \textbf{Decimal number} \\
\textbf{parts} & 1 \ .3750 \\
& 0 \ .7500 \\
& 1 \ .5000 \\
& 1 \ .0000
\end{array}
$$

First we doubled the given number, obtaining 1.3750; then we doubled .3750, obtaining 0.7500; etc. The process terminated with the fourth step, when a zero fractional part was obtained. The desired binary representation is 0.1011.

Method 2

The subtraction method of Problem 7.14 applies as well to fractional decimal numbers.

$$
\begin{array}{rll}
\textbf{Decimal number} & 0.6875 & \\
2^{-1} = & \dfrac{0.5}{0.1875} & \longrightarrow \quad 0.1 \\[4pt]
2^{-3} = & \dfrac{0.125}{0.0625} & \longrightarrow \quad 0.001 \\[4pt]
2^{-4} = & \dfrac{0.0625}{0.0000} & \longrightarrow \quad 0.0001 \\
& & \overline{0.1011}
\end{array}
$$

Binary place values

Equivalent binary number

7.16   Convert the decimal number 0.3 to the binary system.

Integral Part Method

$$
\begin{array}{c|l}
\textbf{Integral} & 0 \ .3 \quad \textbf{Decimal number} \\
\textbf{parts} & 0 \ .6 \\
& 1 \ .2 \\
& 0 \ .4 \\
& 0 \ .8 \\
& 1 \ .6 \\
& \ \ \ldots
\end{array}
$$

In this case, a zero fractional part is not reached. Instead, the fractional part, 6, obtained in the first step, recurs in the fifth step. This means that the block 1001 of integral parts will keep on repeating. Thus the binary representation of 0.3 is the infinite, repeating fraction

$$0.0\ 1001\ 1001\ 1001\ \cdots$$

Subtraction Method

Decimal number 0.3

$$2^{-2} = 0.25 \longrightarrow 0.01$$
$$\underline{0.05000}$$
$$2^{-5} = 0.03125 \longrightarrow 0.00001$$
$$\underline{0.018750}$$
$$2^{-6} = 0.015625 \longrightarrow 0.000001$$
$$\underline{0.003125000}$$
$$2^{-9} = 0.001953125 \longrightarrow 0.000000001$$
$$\underline{0.001171875} \qquad \underline{0.010011001}$$

Binary place values

It is clear that here, as in Problem 7.15, the subtraction method is much more difficult than the integral part method. In fact, using the subtraction method, we are not even sure that the binary representation of 0.3 will not terminate, until we notice that the difference after the second step, 0.01875, is exactly 2^{-4} times the original number, 0.3. We then know that the $(2^{-2} + 2^{-5})$ obtained in the first two steps will be followed by

$$2^{-4}(2^{-2} + 2^{-5}) = (2^{-6} + 2^{-9})$$

in the next two steps, and so on, yielding the binary number

$$0.0\ 1001\ 1001\ 1001\ \cdots$$

previously found.

7.17 Convert the binary number 1111001011.10011 into its (a) octal (base-8), (b) hexadecimal (base-16), equivalent.

(a) Partition the binary number into 3-bit groups, proceeding leftwards and rightwards from the binary point (adding zeros if necessary); and then replace each 3-bit group by its equivalent octal digit (Table 7-5).

```
001 111 001 011 . 100 110    Binary number
 1   7   1   3  .  4   6     Octal number
```

Thus 1713.46_8 is the octal equivalent.

(b) Proceed as in (a), but use 4-bit groups and the hexadecimal digits appearing in Table 7-6.

```
0011 1100 1011 . 1001 1000   Binary number
  3    C    B  .  9    8      Hexadecimal number
```

Thus $3CB.98_{16}$ is the hexadecimal equivalent.

7.18 Find the binary equivalent of (a) the octal number 25.704, (b) the hexadecimal number 3B8.D6.

Replace each octal (hexadecimal) digit by its 3-bit (4-bit) binary equivalent.

(a)
```
  2   5  . 7   0   4      Octal number
010 101 . 111 000 100    Binary number
```

Thus 10101.1110001 is the binary equivalent.

(*b*)   3   B   8 . D   6   **Hexadecimal number**
                   0011 1011 1000 . 1101 0110   **Binary number**

Thus 1110111000.1101011 is the binary equivalent.

7.19 Write each binary number in standard exponential form to obtain its mantissa and exponent: (*a*) 111.11,   (*b*) −0.00111,   (*c*) 101010,   (*d*) 11.0001 × 2^3,   (*e*) 0.11.

Write the number in exponential form with the decimal point directly in front of the first 1.   See Table 7-11.

Table 7-11

	Binary number	Standard exponential form	Mantissa	Exponent
(*a*)	111.11	0.11111×2^3	0.11111	3
(*b*)	−0.00111	-0.111×2^{-2}	−0.111	−2
(*c*)	101010	0.101010×2^6	0.101010	6
(*d*)	11.0011×2^3	0.110011×2^5	0.110011	5
(*e*)	0.11	0.11×2^0	0.11	0

7.20 Round off each binary number to 3 significant digits and write the number in standard exponential form: (*a*) 1101.1,   (*b*) 10101,   (*c*) 0.00111,   (*d*) 0.01100,   (*e*) 10.001.

Delete all digits after the third significant digit, but add 1 to the third significant digit if the next digit was a 1.

	(*a*)	(*b*)	(*c*)	(*d*)	(*e*)
Binary Number	1101.1	10101	0.00111	0.01100	10.001
Rounded Off	1110	10100	0.00111	0.0110	10.0
Standard Form	0.111×2^4	0.101×2^5	0.111×2^{-2}	0.110×2^{-1}	0.100×2^2

BINARY ARITHMETIC

7.21 Perform the following binary additions:

(*a*)   1110011 + 100111 + 1100111 + 111011   (*b*)   110.11 + 11.011 + 1011.1

Use the following addition facts:

$$0 + 0 = 0 \qquad 1 + 0 = 1 \qquad 0 + 1 = 1$$

$$1 + 1 = 0, \text{ with a carry of 1}$$

$$1 + 1 + 1 = 1, \text{ with a carry of 1}$$

(a)   Add two numbers at a time, to avoid excess carrying.

$$
\begin{array}{ll}
1110011 & \text{First number} \\
\underline{100111} & \text{Second number} \\
10011010 & \text{Sum} \\
\underline{1100111} & \text{Third number} \\
100000001 & \text{Sum} \\
\underline{111011} & \text{Fourth number} \\
100111100 & \text{Final sum}
\end{array}
$$

(b)   Write the numbers so that the binary points are vertically aligned, and add two numbers at a time:

$$
\begin{array}{ll}
110.11 & \text{First number} \\
\underline{11.011} & \text{Second number} \\
1010.001 & \text{Sum} \\
\underline{1011.1} & \text{Third number} \\
10101.101 & \text{Final sum}
\end{array}
$$

7.22   Perform the following binary multiplications:

$$(a) \quad 1111011 \times 110100 \qquad (b) \quad 110.111 \times 11.01$$

(a)   In the binary system, multiplication is nothing more than repeated addition, since we can multiply only by 0 or 1.   Here we have:

$$
\begin{array}{r}
1111011 \\
\times\ 110100 \\
\hline
0000000 \\
0000000 \\
1111011 \\
0000000 \\
1111011 \\
1111011 \\
\hline
\end{array}
$$

where the sum of the six rows gives the required product.

For notational convenience, rows of zeros are normally not entered when multiplying. Instead, we   (i) bring down any initial trailing zeros,   (ii) neglect any other zero product,   (iii) add in products one by one as they are written down.   Following this procedure, we obtain:

$$
\begin{array}{ll}
1111011 & \text{Initial zeros} \\
\underline{110100} & \\
111101100 & \text{First product} \\
\underline{1111011} & \text{Second product} \\
100110011100 & \text{Sum} \\
\underline{1111011} & \text{Third product} \\
1100011111100 & \text{Final sum (required product)}
\end{array}
$$

Note the importance of lining up the numbers in the correct columns.

(b)

$$
\begin{array}{r}
1\ 10.1\ 11 \\
\underline{1\ 1.01} \\
1\ 10\ 1\ 11 \\
110\ 11\ 1 \\
\underline{1000\ 10\ 0\ 11} \\
1101\ 11 \\
\underline{10110.01\ 0\ 11}
\end{array}
$$

As the sum of the binary places in the factors is 5, we put the binary point in the answer so that there will be 5 binary places.

7.23   Perform the following binary subtractions:

$$(a) \quad 101\,0001\,1011 - 10\,1010\,0101 \qquad (b) \quad 1101.01 - 10.1101$$

Use the following subtraction facts:

$$0 - 0 = 0 \qquad 1 - 0 = 0 \qquad 1 - 1 = 0$$

$$0 - 1 = 1, \text{ with a borrow of 1 from the next column}$$

(a)	$101\,0001\,1011$	(b)	1101.0100

```
(a)    101 0001 1011        (b)    1101.0100
     -  10 1010 0101             -   10.1101
        10 0111 0110                1010.0111
```

We note that if we need to borrow, and the next column or columns contain zeros, then we borrow from the first column that contains a 1; the intermediate columns will contain $10 - 1 = 1$ after the borrowing.

7.24   Perform the following binary divisions:

$$(a) \quad \frac{110111}{101} \qquad (b) \quad \frac{11010111}{1011}$$

Binary division is done the same way as decimal division.   Furthermore, since each digit is 0 or 1, binary division reduces to repeated subtraction of the divisor.

(a)
```
              1011
        101)110111
            101
            ---
            111
            101
            ---
            101
            101
            ---
              0
```

The quotient is 1011.

(b)
```
               10011
        1011)11010111
             1011
             ----
              10011
               1011
               ----
               10001
                1011
                ----
                 110
```

The quotient is 10011, with a remainder of 110.

7.25   Rework Problem 7.16, using binary division.

The binary representation of a decimal fraction can also be found by expressing the decimal fraction as the ratio of two binary numbers and then dividing.   Thus:

$$0.3 = \frac{3}{10} = \frac{11_2}{1010_2}$$

and

```
            0.01001
     1010)11.0000000
          10 10
          -----
          10000
           1010
           ----
           1100
```

After the second subtraction, the initial dividend, 1100, reappears. Hence the block 1001 will repeat, giving the infinite fraction

$$0.0\ 1001\ 1001\ 1001\ \cdots$$

as the required representation.

COMPLEMENTS

7.26 Find the nines and tens complements of the decimal numbers (a) 2647, (b) 80915, (c) 614370.

Subtract each digit from 9 to obtain the nines complement. Add one to the nines complement to obtain the tens complement.

	(a)	(b)	(c)
Decimal Number	2647	80915	614370
Nines Complement	7352	19084	385629
Tens Complement	7353	19085	385630

7.27 Perform the following decimal subtractions, using the addition of the tens complement:

$$\begin{array}{llll} (a) & 5316 & (b) & 94760 & (c) & 234102 \\ & -2647 & & -80915 & & -614370 \end{array}$$

Add the tens complement obtained in Problem 7.26:

$$\begin{array}{lll} (a) & 5316 & (b) & 94760 & (c) & 234102 \\ & +7353 & & +19085 & & +385630 \\ \hline & 2669 & & 13845 & & 619732 \ \textit{yielding} \ -380268 \end{array}$$

There is no overflow in (c), so the answer is the negative of the tens complement of the sum.

7.28 Find the ones and twos complements of the binary numbers (a) 110011, (b) 0111000111, (c) 10110111000.

Convert 1 to 0 and 0 to 1 to obtain the ones complement, and add one to the ones complement to obtain the twos complement.

	(a)	(b)	(C)
Binary Number	110011	0111000111	10110111000
Ones Complement	001100	1000111000	01001000111
Twos Complement	001101	1000111001	01001001000

7.29 Perform the following binary subtractions by adding the twos complement:

$$\begin{array}{llll} (a) & 111000 & (b) & 1100110011 & (c) & 10100010001 \\ & -110011 & & -0111000111 & & -10110111000 \end{array}$$

Add the twos complements obtained in Problem 7.28:

(a) 111000   (b) 1100110011   (c) 10100010001
     001101   1000111001   01001001000
     000101   0101101100   11101011001 *yielding* −00010100111

     or 101   or 101101100   or −10100111

There is no overflow in (*c*), so the answer is the negative of the twos complement of the sum.

WORDS, BYTES

7.30 Give: (*a*) two types of data stored in a computer; (*b*) the relationship between computer memory, storage locations, and bits; (*c*) two characteristics of a storage locations.

(*a*) Numerical data and character data.

(*b*) The computer memory is composed of storage locations, and each storage location, composed of two-state devices, can store a set of bits.

(*c*) Each storage location has its own address, and all bits are transmitted simultaneously.

7.31 How long is a word? a byte?

The length of a word depends on the computer, but it normally is a multiple of 8 (or 4). Larger computers contain 32-bit words or longer, while smaller computers contain 12-bit or 16-bit words. Some computers have words of variable length.

A byte is an 8-bit subunit of a word; a 32-bit word would consist of 4 bytes. (Some computers still use 6-bit bytes.)

7.32 What is the relationship, if any, between bytes and characters?

Historically, a byte consisted of the number of bits required to represent a single character. Thus, bytes were 6 bits long when 6-bit codes were used for characters. Today, mainly 8-bit codes are used for characters, and a byte is standardized to 8 bits.

7.33 What is meant by a *byte-addressable* computer?

Normally, an address is assigned only to a storage location, and therefore only to the word in that location. However, some of the larger computers allow part of a word, specifically a byte, to have its own address. These are called byte-addressable machines.

7.34 (*a*) What does it mean for a computer to have "odd parity"? (*b*) For such a computer, what should be the parity bit in each of the following bytes?

      __ 1010 1100   __ 1101 1011   __ 0101 1101   __1110 0110

(*c*) Which of the following bytes contain an error, assuming odd parity?

        1 1101 0010   1 1010 1101   0 1100 0101   0 1011 1111

(*a*) All bytes contain an odd number of 1s when the parity bit is included.

(*b*)   1 1010 1100   1 1101 1011   0 0101 1101   0 1110 0110

(*c*)   1 1010 1101   and   0 1100 0101

CHARACTER REPRESENTATION

7.35 What is the minimum number of characters recognized by a computer, and what are these characters?

> There are 48 such characters: 26 letters, 10 digits, and the 12 special characters
>
> $$+ \quad - \quad * \quad / \quad . \quad , \quad ' \quad = \quad \$ \quad (\quad)$$
>
> (The character between the parentheses is the blank character.)

7.36 In the representation of characters in a computer, what are (a) the minimum number of bits required for each character? (b) the number of bits commonly used for each character?

> (a) Since $2^5 < 48 < 2^6$, six bits suffice to represent the 48 characters but five bits are insufficient.
>
> (b) Most larger computers use 8-bit codes, thereby allowing the representation of additional special characters.

7.37 Give some similarities and some differences between EBCDIC and ASCII-8 in respect to how they represent (a) the letters of the alphabet, (b) the decimal digits.

> (a) In both systems, the representations are divided into a 4-bit zone portion and a 4-bit numeric portion. The letters as coded in ASCII-8 are divided into two groups: A through O have 1010 as their zone portion and P through Z have 1011. The letters as coded in EBCDIC are divided into three groups: A through I have 1100 as their zone portion, J through R have 1101, and S through Z have 1110.
>
> (b) Both systems have the binary representation of the digit as the numeric portion of the code; but EBCDIC has 1111 as the zone portion, whereas ASCII-8 has 0101.

NUMERIC REPRESENTATION

7.38 How does EBCDIC represent unsigned, positive, and negative integers?

> Each digit is represented by its character code, except that the zone of the last digit is used for the sign, as follows:
>
> 1111   for unsigned integer
> 1100   for positive integer
> 1101   for negative integer

7.39 How does EBCDIC represent (a) 274, (b) +274, (c) −274?

> Using the codes for the digits in Table 7-7, we obtain:
>
> (a)
>
> | 2 | 7 | 4 |
> |-------|-------|-------|
> | 1111 0010 | 1111 0111 | 1111 0100 |
>
> (b)
>
> | 2 | 7 | +4 |
> |-------|-------|-------|
> | 1111 0010 | 1111 0111 | 1100 0100 |
>
> (c)
>
> | 2 | 7 | −4 |
> |-------|-------|-------|
> | 1111 0010 | 1111 0111 | 1101 0100 |

Observe that the sign appears in the zone portion of the last digit.

7.40 Give the BCD codings for the numbers (a) 274, (b) +274, (c) −274.

The BCD (Binary-Coded Decimal) system uses a 4-bit binary code for each decimal digit, and the last 4-bit field for the sign.

(a)

2	7	4	
0010	0111	0100	1111

(b)

2	7	4	+
0010	0111	0100	1100

(c)

2	7	4	−
0010	0111	0100	1101

7.41 How is addition performed in BCD? Illustrate with 27 + 36.

BCD uses binary addition of the 4-bit codes to effect the addition of the corresponding decimal digits. Whenever the binary sum of two codes exceeds 1001 (nine), then 0001 (one) is added to the next place and 1010 (ten) is subtracted—actually, the twos complement, 0110, is added—to the given position.

```
27      0010 0111
36      0011 0110
        ─────────
        0101 1101    Sum
        0001 0110
63      0110 0011    Modified sum
```

7.42 Assuming a 32-bit word length and the sign-and-magnitude binary representation, find the storage representation of (a) 231, (b) −231.

Convert 231 to its binary representation, 11100111. With the first bit indicating the sign (0 for positive and 1 for negative) and with twenty-three leading 0s inserted to fill out the field, the integers would be represented in storage as follows:

(a)

0	0 0 0 ⋯ 0 0 1 1 1 0 0 1 1 1

(b)

1	0 0 0 ⋯ 0 0 1 1 1 0 0 1 1 1

7.43 Assuming a 32-bit word length and the twos-complement binary representation, find the storage representation of (a) 231, (b) −231.

The binary representation of 231 is, with twenty-four leading 0s (no sign bit) added, $0 \cdots 011100111$. We obtain the twos complement by converting 1 to 0 and 0 to 1, and then adding one; this yields $1 \cdots 100011001$. Hence the integers would be represented in storage as follows:

(a)

0 0 0 0 ⋯ 0 0 1 1 1 0 0 1 1 1

(b)

1 1 1 1 ⋯ 1 1 0 0 0 1 1 0 0 1

Observe that (a) is the same as (a) of Problem 7.42.

7.44 In the storage of a floating-point number, (a) how is the sign of the number represented? (b) how is the sign of the exponent represented?

(a) The first bit of the word is reserved for the sign of the number (0 for positive, 1 for negative).

(b) The sign of the exponent normally is incorporated in the field reserved for the exponent by storing the characteristic of the exponent rather than its true value.

7.45 If a 7-bit field is reserved for the exponent, find the characteristic of each of the following exponents: (a) 7, (b) 39, (c) −23, (d) 0, (e) −48, (f) 84.

The characteristic is obtained by adding $2^6 = 64$ to the true value. (a) 71. (b) 103. (c) 41. (d) 64. (e) 16. (f) The exponent 84 is too large, since $84 + 64 = 148$ is larger than $2^7 - 1 = 127$. (To attempt to store such an exponent would result in overflow.)

7.46 Suppose that a computer contains 32-bit words and stores a floating-point number by using the first bit for the sign of the number, the next 7 bits for the exponent, and the last 24 bits for the mantissa. Find the storage representations of the following binary numbers:

(a) 1111.1   (b) −1111.1   (c) 0.000011111   (d) −0.000011111

(a) Convert to standard exponential form: 0.11111×2^4. The true exponent is 4, so the characteristic is $4 + 64 = 68 = 1000100_2$. Hence the internal representation is

0	1 0 0 0 1 0 0	1 1 1 1 1 0 0 0 $\cdots$ 0 0

The first zero indicates that the number (not the exponent) is positive.

(b) The representation is the same as in (a), except that the first bit is 1.

(c) The standard exponential form is 0.11111×2^{-4}. The true exponent is −4, so the characteristic is $-4 + 64 = 60 = 0111100_2$. Hence:

0	0 1 1 1 1 0 0	1 1 1 1 1 0 0 0 $\cdots$ 0 0

(d) The representation is the same as in (c), except that the first bit is 1.

Review Questions

DECIMAL SYSTEM

7.47 Evaluate (a) 5^3, (b) 2^5, (c) 8^0, (d) 16^{-2}, (e) 10^{-4}.

7.48 Write in expanded notation: (a) 26 539, (b) 305.2468.

7.49 Write each number in standard exponential form to obtain its mantissa and exponent: (a) 24.2424, (b) 0.001212, (c) 0.666, (d) 555.444×10^2, (e) 7.89×10^{-4}.

7.50 Find the number of significant digits in each number: (a) 66.055, (b) 0.00033, (c) 5500.00, (d) 7000, (e) 0.02200.

7.51   Round off each number to two decimal places (invoke the odd-add rule):   (a) 45.4545,   (b) 6.666,   (c) 9.997,   (d) 22.225,   (e) 33.335.

7.52   Round off each number to four significant digits (invoke the odd-add rule), and then write the number in standard exponential form: (a) 7709.9,   (b) −8887770,   (c) 0.00333333,   (d) 505050,   (e) 2.2335.

7.53   In the programming language FORTRAN, the quotient of two integers is again an integer, obtained by truncation.   Find the FORTRAN values of   (a) 7/3,   (b) 6/7,   (c) −11/4,   (d) −6/7,   (e) 15/3,   (f) −24/9.

NUMBERS TO ARBITRARY BASES

7.54   Find the decimal equivalent of   (a) 20122_3,   (b) 2403_5,   (c) 1357_8,   (d) $3C7D_{16}$.

7.55   Convert the decimal number 2685 into an equivalent number to the base   (a) 5,   (b) 8,   (c) 16.

BINARY SYSTEM

7.56   Convert the following binary numbers into the decimal system: (a) 110 1101,   (b) 1010 1110,   (c) 10 1101 1011.

7.57   Convert each decimal number into the binary system: (a) 237,   (b) 359,   (c) 875.

7.58   Convert each decimal number into the binary system: (a) 22.8125,   (b) 0.4.

7.59   Convert the binary number 1011101011.10111 into its   (a) octal (base-8) equivalent,   (b) hex (base-16) equivalent.

7.60   Find the binary equivalent of   (a) 17.506_8,   (b) $2A4.C9_{16}$.

7.61   Write each binary number in standard exponential form to obtain its mantissa and exponent: (a) 11.011,   (b) −11011,   (c) 111.01×2^4,   (d) 0.11101,   (e) −0.00101.

7.62   Round off each binary number to 4 significant digits and write the number in standard exponential form: (a) 11.1011,   (b) 0.0011100,   (c) −111.11,   (d) 11.0111.

BINARY ARITHMETIC

7.63   Evaluate:

(a) 110111 + 100110 + 10101 + 111011	(c) 111011 × 11010
(b) 11.101 + 1010.11 + 110.011	(d) 1101.01 × 10.11

7.64   Evaluate:

(a) 1100 0111 0001 − 101 0101 1101	(c) 101000111 ÷ 11
(b) 11101.01 − 110.1011	(d) 10010.1011 ÷ 11.01

COMPLEMENTS

7.65 Find the nines and tens complements of the decimal numbers   (a) 3154,   (b) 60237,   (c) 82170,   (d) 345600.

7.66 Find the ones and twos complements of the binary numbers   (a) 111011,   (b) 1101111,   (c) 01100110,   (d) 1100011000.

7.67 Perform the following subtractions by adding the twos complement obtained in Problem 7.66:

$$\text{(a)}\quad 11\,1100 - 11\,1011 \qquad \text{(c)}\quad 1100\,1001 - 0110\,0110$$
$$\text{(b)}\quad 101\,0010 - 110\,1111 \qquad \text{(d)}\quad 11\,1011\,0001 - 11\,0001\,1000$$

WORDS, BYTES

7.68 State true or false.   (a) Computer memory is composed of storage locations.   (b) Computer memory is a sequential-storage medium.   (c) A storage location is a two-state device.   (d) A word is the set of bits in a storage location.   (e) Each bit in a storage location is transmitted individually.

7.69 The length of a word: (a) depends on the number of bits in a storage location,   (b) usually is divisible by 4,   (c) varies from computer to computer,   (d) all of the above.

7.70 The length of a byte is   (a) 2 bits,   (b) 4 bits,   (c) 8 bits,   (d) 16 bits.   (c)

7.71 A byte: (a) is a subunit of a word,   (b) encodes exactly one character,   (c) can be addressed in some computers,   (d) all of the above.

7.72 Suppose that a computer has even parity.   (a) What should be the parity bit in each of the following bytes?

      __ 1011 0100   __ 1011 1101   __ 1010 0010   __ 0110 1110

(b)   Which of the following bytes contain an error?

      1 1011 0111   1 0110 1101   0 1010 0011   0 1101 1111

CHARACTER REPRESENTATION

7.73 How many characters can be represented by   (a) a 6-bit code?   (b) a 7-bit code?   (c) an 8-bit code?

7.74 Normally, bytes are divided into two parts.   (a) How many bits are in each part?   (b) What are the two parts called?

7.75 ASCII, not ASCII-8, is   (a) a 4-bit code,   (b) a 6-bit code,   (c) a 7-bit code,   (d) none of the above.

7.76 State true or false.   (a) EBCDIC is mainly used by IBM computers.   (b) ASCII-8 is mainly used by IBM computers.

7.77 Write the word FORTRAN in   (a) EBCDIC,   (b) ASCII-8.

NUMERIC REPRESENTATION

7.78   How does EBCDIC represent   (*a*) 357,   (*b*) +357,   (*c*) −357?

7.79   How does BCD represent   (*a*) 357,   (*b*) +357,   (*c*) −357?

7.80   Give the 32-bit, sign-and-magnitude binary representation of   (*a*) 357,   (*b*) −357.

7.81   Give the 32-bit, twos-complement binary representation of   (*a*) 357,   (*b*) −357.

7.82   Assuming that the exponent of a floating-point number is stored in a 7-bit field, find the characteristic of each of the following exponents: (*a*) 2,   (*b*) −5,   (*c*) 27,   (*d*) −53,   (*e*) 92,   (*f*) −87.

7.83   Redo Question 7.82, assuming an 8-bit field for the exponent.

7.84   Suppose that a computer stores a floating-point number as a 32-bit word, with the first bit for the sign of the number, the next 7 bits for the exponent, and the last 24 bits for the mantissa.   Find the storage representations of the following binary numbers: (*a*) 111.0111,   (*b*) −11.10111,   (*c*) 0.0001110111,   (*d*) −0.0001110111.

Chapter 8

Flowcharts and
Programming Techniques

8.1 INTRODUCTION

A *flowchart* is a diagram consisting of labeled geometrical symbols (mostly quadrilaterals), together with arrows connecting one symbol to another. It gives a pictorial representation of a data processing procedure.

System Flowcharts

A *system flowchart* shows the path taken as data pass from one organizational unit or processing machine to another within a company. Figure 1-2, the diagram of the expanded data processing cycle, may be considered a system flowchart.

Program Flowcharts

A *program flowchart* pictures the sequence of instructions for solving a particular problem (usually by means of a computer program).

EXAMPLE 8.1 The Croesus Company plans to give a year-end 3% bonus to each of its employees. A step-by-step list of instructions for calculating the BONUS for a given employee follows:

Step 1.　Obtain employee's yearly SALARY from employee's record.

Step 2.　Calculate BONUS as:

$$BONUS = 0.03 * SALARY$$

where * means "multiply".

Step 3.　Record employee's BONUS in the bonus file.

Figure 8-1 is a program flowchart of the above instructions.

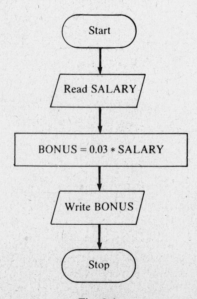

Fig. 8-1

The sequence of instructions for solving a particular problem is called an *algorithm*.   Actually, whenever an algorithm is much more complicated than that of Example 8.1, one usually displays the algorithm through a flowchart rather than through a numbered list of instructions.

When used with computer programs, flowcharts offer the following *advantages*:

(1) It is usually much easier to draw a flowchart of an algorithm and then to write the program, than to write the program directly.

(2) Flowcharts are an important aid in the development of the algorithm itself.

(3) Flowcharts are easier to understand than a program itself; hence computer programs supplied by the manufacturer normally come with their flowcharts.

(4) Flowcharts are independent of any particular programming language, so that a given flowchart can be used to translate an algorithm into more than one programming language.

This chapter is mainly devoted to the study of program flowcharts, so "flowchart" shall mean "program flowchart" unless otherwise stated or implied.   Only Section 8.8 will investigate system flowcharts.

8.2 VARIABLES, DATA-NAMES, PROGRAMMING STATEMENTS

By a *variable* in a computer program, we mean a data item whose value may change during the execution of the program.   A *data-name* (or *variable-name*) is a programmer-supplied name or label of a variable.   The rules governing these names depend upon the programming language being used.   Generally speaking, names consist of a number of alphanumeric characters, with the first character being a letter.

Normally, one chooses names so that they indicate the kind of data item they represent; e.g. BONUS might be chosen to denote the bonus of an employee in a company.   Observe that the value of BONUS may change during the execution of the program; it may be $300.00, $400.00, . . . , depending on the particular employee.   Each programming language has certain "reserved words," such as (FORTRAN's) STOP, END, DO, IF, that have specific operational meanings in the language.   These words may not be chosen as variable-names.

During the compiling of a computer program, the variables in the program are assigned specific storage locations in the memory of the computer.   We identify a variable with its storage location, e.g. we may speak of "the variable BONUS" or, equivalently, "the storage location named BONUS," or "the address BONUS."   The value of a variable at any time is the value then stored at the address of the variable.

Assignment Statements

A programming statement that assigns a value to a variable, by storing that value at the address of the variable, is called an *assignment statement*.   Recall that the previous content of the storage location is thereby obliterated.

EXAMPLE 8.2   Suppose that we want to assign the numerical value 0.08 to a variable (or memory location) called RATE.   The assignment statement is:

$$RATE = 0.08$$

Similarly, we would write the assignment statement

$$BONUS = 0.05 * SALARY$$

if the variable BONUS is to be assigned the number obtained by multiplying SALARY by 0.05, where SALARY is a variable that has already been *defined*, i.e. already has been given a value.

Many high-level languages, e.g. FORTRAN, BASIC, COBOL, use the equals sign as above, to indicate that the variable on the left is to be assigned the value of the expression on the right.   APL uses a backward arrow, ←, for this purpose, and the same sign is frequently used in assignment statements in flowcharts.   Our flowcharts will employ the equals sign.

The two statements above appear as they would in FORTRAN or PL/1. In BASIC, we would write the second statement as

$$\text{LET BONUS} = 0.05 * \text{SALARY}$$

and in COBOL it would appear as

$$\text{COMPUTE BONUS} = 0.05 * \text{SALARY}$$

or as

$$\text{MULTIPLY SALARY BY 0.05 GIVING BONUS}$$

Both statements in Example 8.2 are *arithmetic* assignment statements. The general form of such a statement is

$$\text{NAME} = arithmetic\ expression$$

in response to which the computer will (i) evaluate the arithmetic expression by replacing any variable-names by the numerical values stored at those addresses, (ii) read the value of the arithmetic expression in storage location NAME.

Table 8-1 lists the symbols used in the major languages for the five basic arithmetic operations. Thus, the algebraic expressions

$$xy \qquad \frac{x}{y} \qquad x^y$$

would appear as

$$X*Y \qquad X/Y \qquad X**Y$$

Table 8-1

Operation	Symbol
Addition	+
Subtraction	−
Multiplication	*
Division	/
Exponentiation	** (FORTRAN, COBOL) ↑ (BASIC)

EXAMPLE 8.3 (a) If three test scores are at addresses T1, T2, and T3, the assignment statement

$$\text{AVERAGE} = (T1 + T2 + T3)/3$$

instructs the computer to add the three scores and divide by 3, and store the result in AVERAGE. (b) Suppose that one wants to increase the value of HOURS by 12. This can be done by the assignment statement

$$\text{HOURS} = \text{HOURS} + 12$$

This statement may seem strange at first, since HOURS cannot equal HOURS + 12. However, the equals sign here denotes assignment. The computer first calculates HOURS + 12, using the original value in HOURS, and then stores the result back in HOURS (thereby erasing the previous value in HOURS). The net effect is that the original number in HOURS is increased by 12. (c) The assignment statement

$$\text{NEWRATE} = \text{OLDRATE}$$

instructs the computer to copy the number stored in OLDRATE into the location NEWRATE. In other words, the value of the variable OLDRATE is assigned to the variable NEWRATE. In COBOL, this type of assignment can also be accomplished by means of a "Move" statement:

MOVE OLDRATE TO NEWRATE

Input/Output Statements

These statements bring data into the computer from an outside medium or take data from the computer to an outside medium.

Read statements. Suppose that a punched card (or magnetic tape) contains an employee's number, the number of hours that he has worked, and his rate of pay. We would write

Read EMPNUMBER, HOURS, RATE

to direct that the three numbers be stored in the computer's memory in locations called EMPNUMBER, HOURS, and RATE, respectively.

Write statements. Suppose that memory locations called EMPNUMBER, GROSS, and NET contain an employee's number, gross pay, and net pay, respectively. We would write

Write EMPNUMBER, GROSS, NET

to direct that the numbers be read out onto some outside medium, such as a punched card or line printer.

The forms we have given for read and write statements are merely representative; the exact form depends on the programming language being used.

8.3 FLOWCHART SYMBOLS

The five basic symbols of a program flowchart appear in Fig. 8-2. The actual program statements are written inside the appropriate symbols. A flowchart drawn with these symbols will be understood by people in almost every part of the world. Other symbols are sometimes used, especially in system flowcharts, but these five suffice for any program flowchart.

Symbol		Meaning
 (oval)		Terminal
 (parallelogram)		Input/Output
 (small circle)		Connector
 (rectangle)		Process
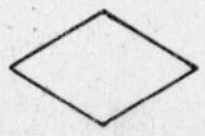 (diamond)		Decision

Fig. 8-2

Terminal symbol.   This symbol indicates the beginning or end of the program.

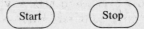

Input/output symbol.   This symbol would usually be filled with either a read or a write statement.

Connector symbol.   A pair of identically labeled connector symbols denotes that the indicated points of the flowchart are connected even though no arrow is drawn from one point to the other.   Problem 8.14 gives an example where connector symbols are used.

Process symbol.   This symbol denotes some general processing operation, usually an assignment statement or data movement instruction.

| BONUS = 0.03 * SALARY | | Move ACCOUNT to ON-HAND |

The symbol may also be used to denote a *macroinstruction*, i.e. a single instruction which normally would require an entire list of commands to implement it.

| Sort names | | Find largest account and assign the amount to BIGGEST |

Decision symbol.   This diamond-shaped box denotes a point in the program where more than one path can be taken.   The particular path that is chosen depends on the answer to a question or the result of a test.   The question (test) is inserted in the symbol, and the arrows leaving the symbol are labelled with the different results, e.g. with "yes" and "no," or with "true" and "false," or with "positive," "negative," and "zero" (see Fig. 8-3).   One frequently omits the word "Is" within the decision symbol, simply writing

COUNT ≤ 25?   Student married?   SUM = AMOUNT?

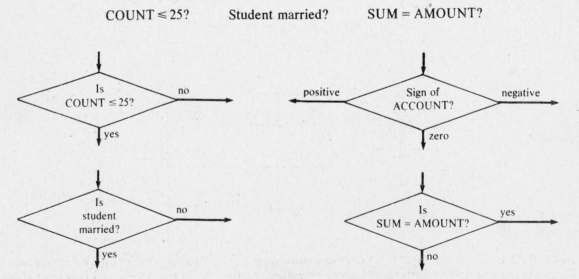

Fig. 8-3

Observe that a decision need not involve numeric data, e.g. "Is student married?".   However, if numeric data are involved, then the decision normally involves one of the six mathematical relations given in Table 8-2, or a combination of such relations using one or more of the logical connectives "and," "or," and "not."   For example, the question might be:

$$\text{Is } 30 \leq AGE \leq 40?$$

(which is equivalent to: Is $AGE \geq 30$ and $AGE \leq 40$?) or

$$\text{Is } A < 20 \text{ or } B < 15?$$

Table 8-2

Symbol	Meaning
=	Equal
≠	Not equal
<	Less than
≤	Less than or equal
>	Greater than
≥	Greater than or equal

EXAMPLE 8.4   The Mismatch Company plans to give a year-end 3% bonus to each of its employees.   However, if an employee has been working 10 or more years at the company, he is to get an additional $50.   Figure 8-4 is a flowchart of an algorithm to calculate the BONUS for a given employee.   SALARY and YEAR are variables whose values are salary and the number of years with the company.

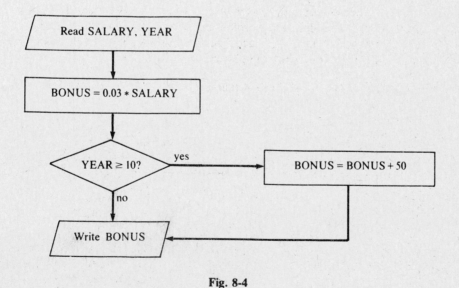

Fig. 8-4

EXAMPLE 8.5   The Square-Deal Company plans to give a year-end 3% bonus to each of its employees earning $10,000 or more per year, and a fixed $300 bonus for the other employees.   Figure 8-5 is a flowchart of an algorithm to calculate the BONUS for a given employee.   Compare Fig. 8-4.

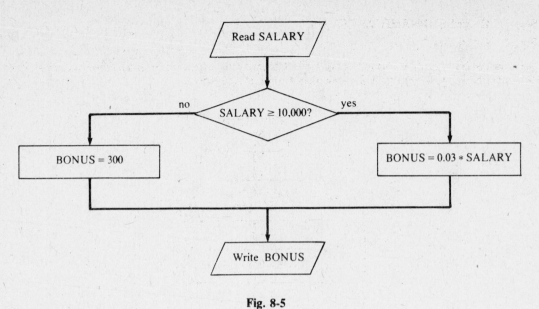

Fig. 8-5

The English word "If" appears in two general types of commands:

(1) If ... then ...   (2) If ... then ... ; else ...

In Example 8.4 one has the command

$$\text{If} \quad YEAR \geq 10 \quad \text{then} \quad BONUS = BONUS + 50$$

which is of the first type.   The flowchart translation uses a decision box, and the statement

$$BONUS = BONUS + 50$$

is either executed or omitted.   On the other hand, in Example 8.5 one has the command

$$\text{If} \quad SALARY \geq 10,000 \quad \text{then} \quad BONUS = 0.03 * SALARY; \quad \text{else} \quad BONUS = 300$$

which is of the second type.   The flowchart translation also uses a decision box, but here only one of the two statements

$$BONUS = 0.03 * SALARY \qquad BONUS = 300$$

is executed.   In other words, the first type of command implies that a statement (or block of statements) is executed or omitted, and the second type implies that one of two statements (or blocks of statements) is executed, but not both.

8.4 LOOPS AND THEIR CONTROL BY A COUNTER

Frequently one wants to repeat a process a certain number of times.   One way to accomplish this repetition is for the algorithm to transfer control of the computer from the end of the process back to its beginning.   The flowchart of such an algorithm will contain a loop; hence the term *looping* for the repetition of an algorithm or a part of an algorithm.

EXAMPLE 8.6 Suppose that the Croesus Company (Example 8.1) wants to calculate the bonus for every one of its employees, not just for a given employee.   Such an algorithm follows:

Step 1.   Obtain (the first or next) employee's name, EMPNAME and his SALARY.

Step 2.   BONUS = 0.03 * SALARY.

Step 3.   Record EMPNAME and BONUS.

Step 4.   Go to Step 1.

The flowchart of the algorithm appears in Fig. 8-6.   Observe that the arrows from the Read statement, from the BONUS statement, and from the Write statement form a closed loop.

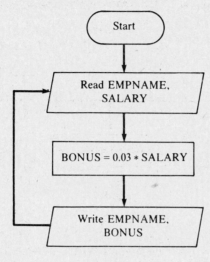

Fig. 8-6

The flowchart in Fig. 8-6 contains no provision for ceasing to repeat the process (of calculating bonuses).   Clearly, one wants to stop when all the employee records have been read and all bonuses have been recorded.   One way to "control a loop," i.e. to incorporate a stopping condition, is by using a *counter*, a variable whose value is increased by 1 for each repetition of the process.   Figure 8-7 gives a flowchart for an algorithm that is to be repeated 50 times (e.g. the loop of Fig. 8-6, if the Croesus Company has 50 employees); the counter is denoted COUNT.

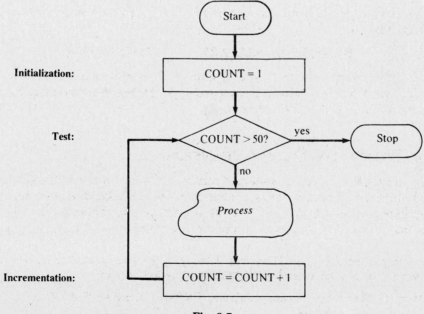

Fig. 8-7

Observe that there are three essential steps in the use of a counter to control a loop:

Initialization. The counter is set equal to one.

Test. Before executing the process, the counter is tested to see if it exceeds its maximum allowable value.

Incrementation. After the process has been executed, the counter is increased by one.

Problem 8.19 gives a valid variation of the algorithm where the test appears after the process rather than before.

8.5 CONTROL OF LOOPS BY HEADER OR TRAILER RECORDS

The algorithm flowcharted in Fig. 8-7 has one main drawback; namely, it will work properly only if there are exactly 50 records to be processed. Clearly, the number of records in a file may vary from time to time, and one would like an algorithm which is independent of that number. Such an algorithm is possible if the file is provided with a header or a trailer record (Example 3.2).

Control by a Header Record

Assuming that the header record contains (among other things) the number N of other records in the file, one can first read this number, and then use N as the end value of a counter controlling a loop that processes the file. Figure 8-8 gives such an algorithm.

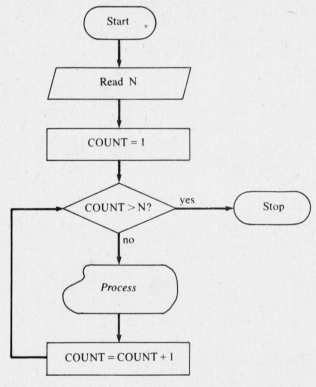

Fig. 8-8

Control by a Trailer Record

The trailer record is assumed to contain (among other things) a signal that it is the last record in the file. Thus, on reading each record, we may ask: "Is this the end of the file [abbreviated EOF]?" An algorithm based on this test is depicted in Fig. 8-9.

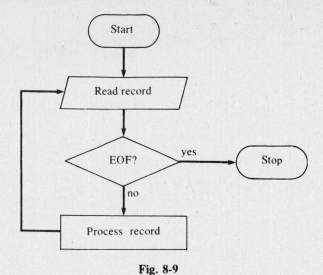

Fig. 8-9

EXAMPLE 8.7 A common way of signaling EOF is to have all 9s in some data field of the trailer record. Figure 8-10 gives an algorithm for calculating and recording the bonus of each employee in Example 8.1.

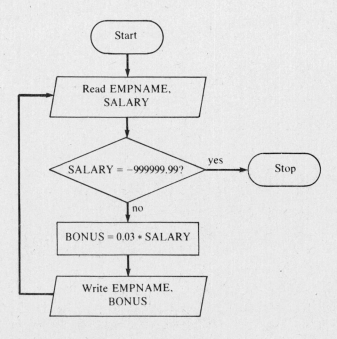

Fig. 8-10

We note that the use of a header record to control a loop requires the number N of records being processed, a number that may change very often (e.g. if patients are continually being admitted or discharged from a hospital). In such a case, it might be more advantageous to use a trailer record to control the loop, rather than recalculate the end value N each time the file is updated.

8.6 ACCUMULATORS

Frequently one wants to find the sum of certain numerical quantities that are read or calculated one at a time. This can be accomplished by first choosing a variable, say SUM, and initializing it to zero:

$$SUM = 0$$

One then executes the instruction

$$SUM = SUM + QUAN$$

as each numerical quantity, called QUAN, is obtained. The variable SUM is called an *accumulator* because it accumulates all the numerical quantities. The final value of SUM is then the required value.

EXAMPLE 8.8 Figure 8-11 is the flowchart of an algorithm for summing the first twenty integers. There we use SUM as the accumulator, and the variable K to produce the numbers 1, 2, 3, ..., 20. Observe that

$$SUM = 0 \quad \text{first assigns} \quad 0$$

to SUM. When K = 1,

$$SUM = SUM + K \quad \text{assigns} \quad 0 + 1 = 1$$

to SUM. When K = 2,

$$SUM = SUM + K \quad \text{assigns} \quad 1 + 2 = 3$$

to SUM. When K = 3,

$$SUM = SUM + K \quad \text{assigns} \quad 3 + 3 = 6$$

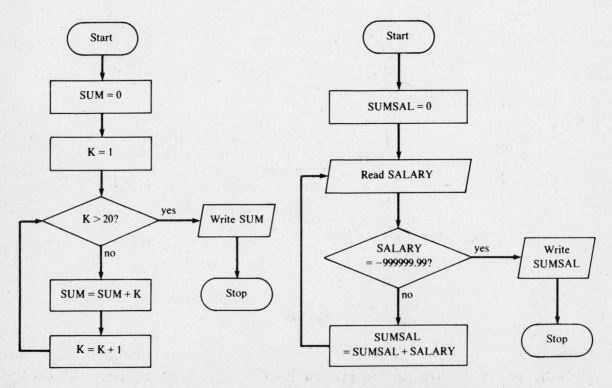

Fig. 8-11   Fig. 8-12

to SUM, and so on.   When   K = 20,   the value of SUM is 190, so

$$SUM = SUM + K \quad \text{assigns} \quad 190 + 20 = 210$$

to SUM.   This is the value of SUM when the Write statement is executed, so the output of the program is 210, which is the sum of the integers from 1 to 20.

EXAMPLE 8.9   Suppose that a company wants to find the total salary paid to its employees.   Figure 8-12 is the flowchart of an appropriate algorithm.   Observe that the accumulator SUMSAL is initialized before any record is read, and its value is printed only after all the records have been read.   The flowchart also assumes that the file has a trailer record in which -999999.99 is punched in the salary field.

8.7   TWO SPECIAL ALGORITHMS

Given a list of numerical values, say the salaries of the employees of a company, we wish to find   (*a*) the average of the salaries,   (*b*) the largest salary.   We will assume that the file of the employee records contains a trailer record, so that we may use an EOF decision box in our flowcharts.

Average Value

The idea behind this algorithm is first to find the sum of the salaries, using an accumulator, say SUM, as in Section 8.6.   Because the number N of employees is not assumed to be known in advance, the algorithm uses a counter to count the records read.   The average value, say AVG, is then SUM divided by N (final values).   Figure 8-13 is the flowchart of our algorithm; compare Fig. 8-12.

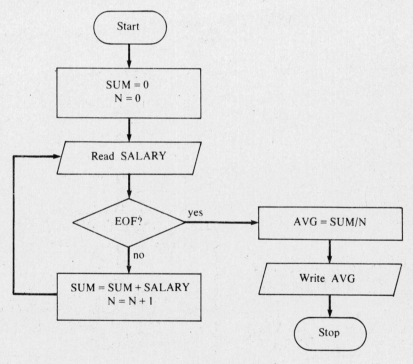

Fig. 8-13

Largest Value

In this algorithm we first set a variable, say BIGSAL, equal to the first salary.   Then we compare BIGSAL to each successive salary.   If BIGSAL exceeds or equals a salary, then we do not change BIGSAL; however, if BIGSAL is less than a salary, then we assign this larger salary to BIGSAL. The final value of BIGSAL is the largest salary. Figure 8-14 is the flowchart of the algorithm.

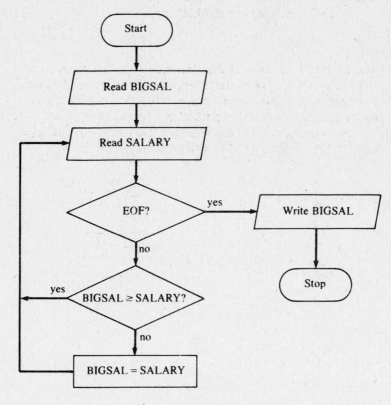

Fig. 8-14

8.8 SYSTEMS ANALYSTS AND SYSTEM DESIGN

The systems analyst in an organization or business is the person responsible for the overall design of its data processing system. The main objective of the systems analyst is to determine the most effective way of accomplishing the tasks of the organization, that is, to design a data processing system that will allow the organization to do its work in minimum time and/or at minimum cost.

Designing a data processing system involves two phases.

Study Phase

Identification. In this step one gives a clear description of the objectives of the system.

Documentation. Here one decides which files and report documents are required for the attainment of the objectives.

Evaluation. This step evaluates all possible alternative schemes and then chooses the most feasible.

Operation Phase

Design. Here one specifies in detail the new system. This includes listing the necessary files, determining which functions are manual and which require certain software or hardware, and developing new procedures and programs.

Installation. This step implements the new system by obtaining and setting up the necessary hardware, hiring appropriate personnel, and procuring programmer-supplied software (programs).

Testing. Here one ascertains whether the final system does indeed allow the goals of the organization to be more efficiently met, and whether the system can be further improved.

System Flowcharts

A system flowchart diagrams the flow of data throughout a data processing system, as well as the flow into and out of the system. The systems analyst will use such a flowchart to design and to explain a data processing system. Since the choice of input and output media and the type of operation (e.g. manual or programmed) are important considerations in the development of a data processing system, system flowcharts use symbols other than those used for program flowcharts. Figure 8-15 shows some of the symbols used in system flowcharts.

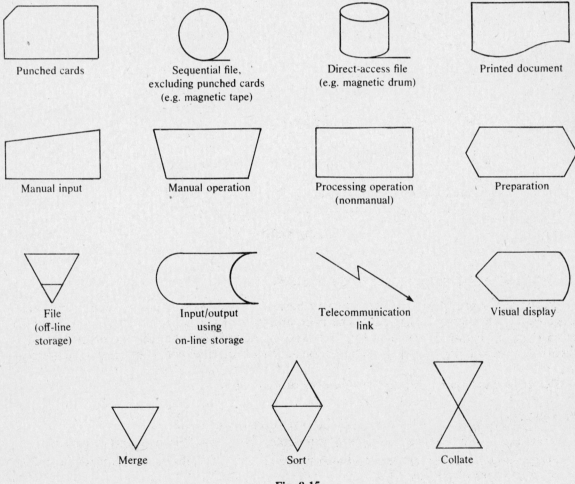

Fig. 8-15

EXAMPLE 8.10 Figure 8-16 is a system flowchart for the distribution of students' grades after final exams (essentially the same situation as treated in Example 1.3). The input consists of the final exams. These are manually graded and manually recorded on grade sheets which are sent to the registrar. At the registrar's office the students' master file is updated and then transcripts are sent to the students.

EXAMPLE 8.11 Figure 8-17 is a system flowchart for the updating of a bank's checking account records. Observe that the checks and deposits are inputted by means of punched cards and that there is a printed report showing overdrawn accounts.

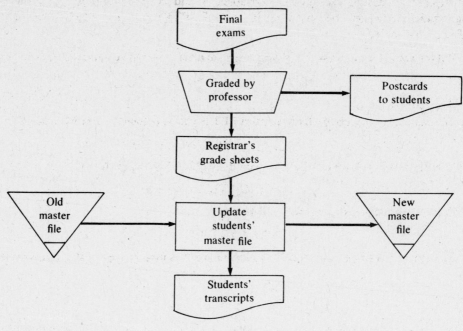

Fig. 8-16

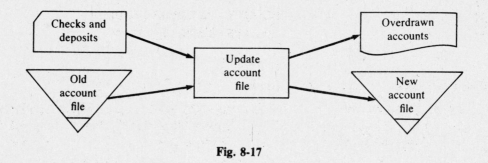

Fig. 8-17

Solved Problems

VARIABLES, NAMES, ASSIGNMENT STATEMENTS

8.1 What is a *variable* in a computer program, and what does it mean to say that a variable is *defined*?

A variable is a data item whose value may change during the execution of the program. A variable is defined if it has already been assigned a value by the program.

8.2 In reference to storage locations, what is meant by (*a*) *destructive readin*, (*b*) *non-destructive readout*?

(*a*) When data are assigned to a storage location, the data already there are destroyed.

(*b*) Data in a given storage location are *copied* (not removed) into another storage location.

8.3   It is desired to assign the sum of variables A and B to a variable C.   How would the assignment statement be written in (*a*) FORTRAN, (*b*) PL/1, (*c*) BASIC, (*d*) COBOL, (*e*) APL?

(*a*)   Put the name C on the left of the equals sign, and the arithmetic expression   A + B   on the right:

$$C = A + B$$

(*b*)   The same as in (*a*).

(*c*)   The same as in (*a*), except that the word LET is placed before the variable-name C:

$$\text{LET } C = A + B$$

(*d*)   The same as in (*a*), except that the word COMPUTE is placed before C:

$$\text{COMPUTE } C = A + B$$

COBOL also allows the equivalent statement:

$$\text{ADD A TO B GIVING C}$$

(*e*)   The same as in (*a*), except that the backward arrow is used instead of the equals sign:

$$C \leftarrow A + B$$

8.4   Write statements that will (*a*) assign 300 to a storage location called BONUS, (*b*) add 1000 to the content of ACCOUNT, (*c*) Add 0.005 to OLDRATE to obtain NEWRATE.

(*a*)   BONUS = 300

(*b*)   ACCOUNT = ACCOUNT + 1000

(*c*)   NEWRATE = OLDRATE + 0.005

8.5   Find the output of each program segment:

(*a*) SALARY = 1000	(*b*) BONUS = 300	(*c*) BONUS = 300
BONUS = 0.05 * SALARY	BONUS = BONUS + 100	BONUS = 100
Write BONUS	Write BONUS	Write BONUS

(*a*)   The second statement assigns 0.05 times 10 000, which is 500, to BONUS; hence 500 is the output.

(*b*)   The second statement adds 100 to the current value of BONUS, which is 300, and then assigns the sum, 400, back into BONUS, destroying the first value of BONUS; hence 400 is the output.

(*c*)   The second statement assigns 100 to BONUS, destroying the first value of BONUS; hence 100 is the output.

8.6   Suppose that BONUS1 contains 300 and BONUS2 contains 400, and that we want to interchange the values in BONUS1 and BONUS2.   (*a*) Why won't the following statements accomplish the interchange?

$$\text{BONUS2} = \text{BONUS1}$$

$$\text{BONUS1} = \text{BONUS2}$$

(*b*) How may one perform the interchange?

(*a*)   The first statement assigns 300, the value in BONUS1, to BONUS2, destroying the 400 in BONUS2.   Hence BONUS1 and BONUS2 will both contain 300 after the first statement.   The second statement will not change the value of BONUS1, since it is the same as BONUS2.

(*b*)   To perform the interchange, one must temporarily preserve the original value of BONUS2 in another storage location.   Thus:

$$TEMP = BONUS2$$
$$BONUS2 = BONUS1$$
$$BONUS1 = TEMP$$

The first statement assigns 400 to TEMP. The second statement changes the value of BONUS2 to 300.   The third statement changes the value of BONUS1 to 400, the value stored in TEMP.

8.7   Table 8-1 lists five arithmetic operations.   In the absence of parentheses, the computer evaluates an arithmetic expression using the following convention:

> *First precedence*:   Exponentiation (**)
> *Second precedence*:   Multiplication (*) and division (/)
> *Third precedence*:   Addition (+) and subtraction (−)

That is, the computer scans a parenthesis-free arithmetic expression from left to right three times.   The first time, it performs each exponentiation; the second time, each multiplication and division; and the third time, each addition and subtraction.   Since the computer scans from left to right, if two operations have the same precedence, then the left one is executed first.   (Normally, unary plus and minus are treated on the same level as addition and subtraction, e.g. −3**2 means −(3**2), not (−3)**2.)   Find the value of each expression:

(a) $8 + 4*7/2 - 6/3$ (c) $8 + 4*3**2 - 20$

(b) $(8 + 4)*7/2 - 6/3$ (d) $8 + (4*3)**2 - 20$

(a)   First, $4*7 = 28$, $28/2 = 14$ and $6/3 = 2$,   giving

$$8 + 14 - 2$$

Then, $8 + 14 = 22$ and $22 - 2 = 20$.   Hence, 20 is the value of the expression.

(b)   The computer first evaluates inside the parentheses, giving $8 + 4 = 12$.   Then, $12*7 = 84$, $84/2 = 42$ and $6/3 = 2$,   giving $42 - 2$.   Hence

$$42 - 2 = 40$$

is the value of the expression.

(c)   First, $3**2 = 9$.   Secondly, $4*9 = 36$,   giving

$$8 + 36 - 20$$

Then, $8 + 36 = 44$ and, finally, $44 - 20 = 24$,   which is the value of the expression.

(d)   The computer first evaluates inside the parentheses, giving $4*3 = 12$.   Then, $12**2 = 144$, giving

$$8 + 144 - 20$$

Then, $8 + 144 = 152$ and, finally, $152 - 20 = 132$,   which is the value of the expression.

PROGRAM FLOWCHARTS

8.8   Name and describe the five basic symbols of a (program) flowchart.

Terminal symbol (oval), *input/output symbol* (parallelogram), *connector symbol* (small circle), *process symbol* (rectangle), *decision symbol* (diamond).

8.9   What is a *macroinstruction*?   Give some examples.

A macroinstruction is a single instruction which normally would require a number of instructions to implement it.   For example:

| Calculate average | | Merge files |

8.10 Determine the appropriate flowchart symbol in which each of the following instructions or questions should be placed:

(*a*)   Move FILE1 to FILE2   (*d*)   Add B to C giving A
(*b*)   Read A, B, C   (*e*)   Start
(*c*)   Is A = 0?   (*f*)   Is B less than C?

(*a*)   Rectangle, since it is a process (assignment).

(*b*)   Parallelogram, since it is an input instruction.

(*c*)   Diamond, since it asks a question.

(*d*)   Rectangle, since it is a process (calculation).

(*e*)   Oval.

(*f*)   Diamond, since it asks a question.

8.11 Determine the minimum number of arrows connected to a diamond in a flowchart.

There must be at least one arrow going to the diamond, and at least two arrows leaving the diamond; hence there are at least three arrows connected to a diamond.

8.12 Consider the flowchart in Fig. 8-18. Find the output if the input is (*a*)   A = 5, B = 10; (*b*)   A = 10, B = 5.

(*a*)   Since A is less than B, BONUS is not increased in value, and 300 is outputted.

(*b*)   Since A is greater than B, BONUS = BONUS + 100 is executed, which increases the value of BONUS by 100.   Hence, 400 is outputted.

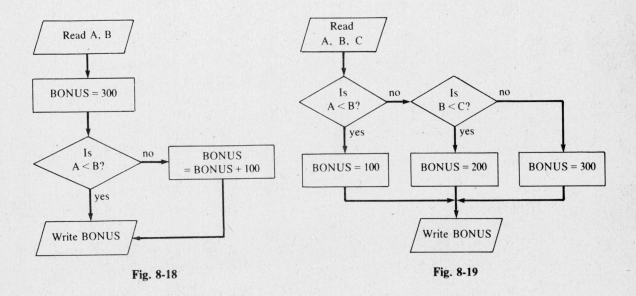

Fig. 8-18   Fig. 8-19

8.13 Consider the flowchart in Fig. 8-19. Find the output if the input is (*a*)   A = 5,   B = 10 C = 15; (*b*)   A = 15,   B = 5,   C = 10; (*c*)   A = 15,   B = 10,   C = 5.

(*a*)   Since A is less than B, BONUS = 100 is executed, and 100 is outputted.

(*b*)   A is greater than B, but B is less than C; so BONUS = 200 is executed, and 200 is outputted.

(*c*)   A is greater than B, and B is greater than C; so BONUS = 300   is executed, and 300 is outputted.

The flowchart in Fig. 8-20 uses connector symbols labeled A, B, or C. Two or more of the symbols can have the same label, but only one of the like-labeled symbols can have an arrow exiting. Find the output if the input is (a) X = 15, Y = 20; (b) X = 5, Y = 5; (c) X = 1, Y = 4; (d) X = 15, Y = 2.

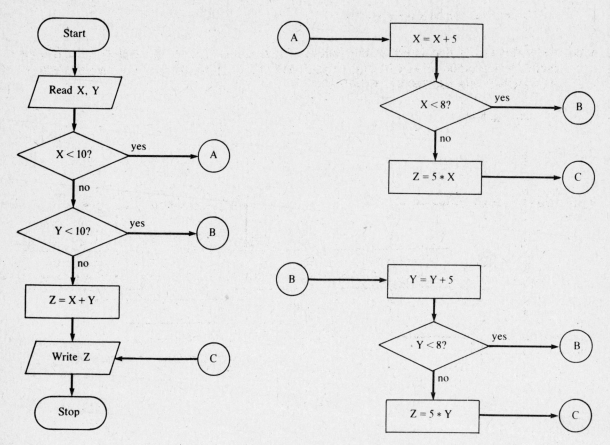

Fig. 8-20

(a) The answer is "no" to "X < 10?" and to "Y < 10?"; hence

$$Z = X + Y$$

is executed, and $15 + 20 = 35$ is the output.

(b) The answer is "yes" to "X < 10?"; so control is transferred to "X = X + 5" by way of connector symbols labeled A. This increases the value of X to 10; hence the answer is "no" to "X < 8?". Thus

$$Z = 5*X = 5*10 = 50$$

is executed. Control is transferred to "Write Z" by way of connector symbols labeled C, so that 50 is the output.

(c) The answer is "yes" to "X < 10?"; hence "X = X + 5" is executed and the value of X is increased to 6. The answer is "yes" to "X < 8?"; hence "Y = Y + 5" is executed, and the value of Y is increased to 9. The answer is "no" to "Y < 8?"; so

$$Z = 5*Y = 5*9 = 45$$

is executed, and 45 is the output.

(d) The answer is "no" to "X < 10?", but is "yes" to "Y < 10?"; hence "Y = Y + 5" is executed, and the value of Y is increased to 7. The answer is "yes" to "Y < 8?"; so control is transferred back to "Y = Y + 5", and the value of Y is increased to 12. Now the answer is "no" to "Y < 8?"; so

$$Z = 5*Y = 5*12 = 60$$

is executed, and 60 is the output.

8.15 Draw flowcharts that interpret the following statements. (a) If ACCOUNT is 10,000 or more, then add 500 to ACCOUNT. (b) If ACCOUNT is 10,000 or more, then add 500 to ACCOUNT; else add 300 to ACCOUNT

See Fig. 8-21.

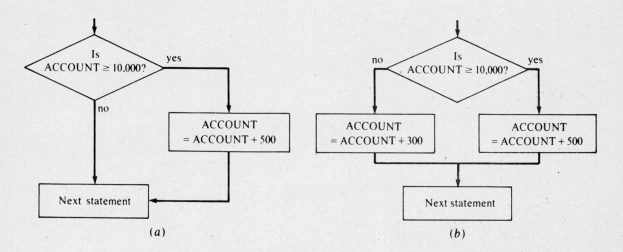

Fig. 8-21

LOOPS

8.16 Draw a flowchart of an algorithm that calculates:

(a)
$$SUM = \frac{1}{1} + \frac{1}{3} + \frac{1}{5} + \cdots + \frac{1}{25}$$

(b)
$$SUM = \frac{1}{1} + \frac{1}{3} + \frac{1}{5} + \cdots + \frac{1}{N}$$

where one first reads N.

(a) First set SUM = 0, where SUM is an accumulator, and then successively add 1/K to SUM, for K = 1, 3, 5, ..., 25. Figure 8-22(a) is the flowchart. Observe that we first set K = 1 and each time increase K by 2, since the sum involves only odd numbers. We stop after K exceeds 25.

(b) The algorithm is the same as in (a), except that we first read N and stop after K exceeds N. Figure 8-22(b) is the flowchart.

8.17 Suppose that $5000 is deposited in a savings account in 1980 for fifteen years, and suppose that the bank pays 9 percent interest, compounded annually. Draw a flowchart which outputs the YEAR and AMOUNT in the account from 1980 until 1995, when the fifteen years is over.

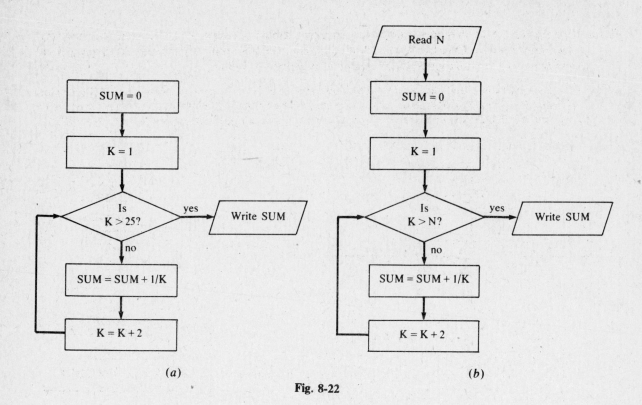

Fig. 8-22

Each year, AMOUNT is increased by 9 percent, so one uses the assignment statement

$$AMOUNT = AMOUNT + 0.09*AMOUNT$$

or the arithmetically equivalent statement $AMOUNT = 1.09*AMOUNT$.   We stop the program as soon as YEAR exceeds 1995.   Figure 8-23 gives the required flowchart.

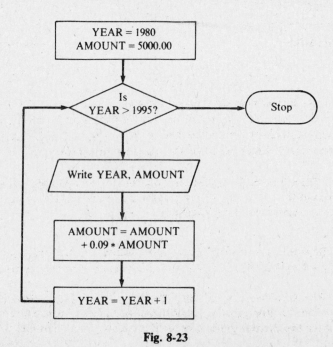

Fig. 8-23

8.18 In a certain file, each record contains a nonzero number, and there is a trailer record containing the number zero.   Give the flowchart of an algorithm which counts the number POS of positive numbers and the number NEG of negative numbers in the file.

See Fig. 8-24. Initially we set POS = 0 and NEG = 0. There is a three-way sign test of NUMBER: if NUMBER is positive, we increase POS by 1; if NUMBER is negative, we increase NEG by 1; but if NUMBER is zero, then we have read the entire file and we write the values of POS and NEG.

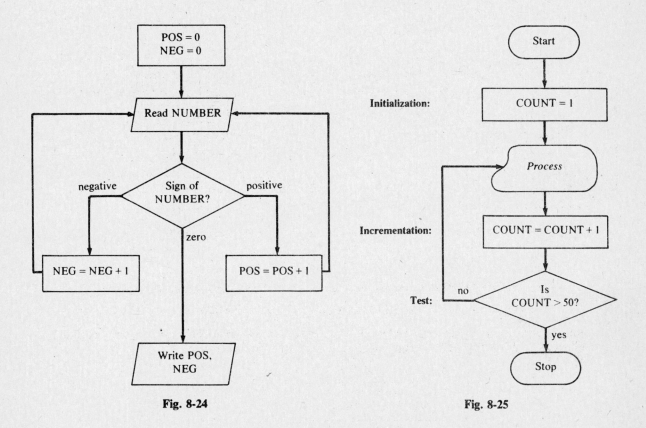

Fig. 8-24   Fig. 8-25

8.19 Figure 8-7 is a flowchart which shows how to repeat a process 50 times, using a counter, COUNT. The Test step takes place after the Initialization step, but before the process. Draw an equivalent flowchart where the Test step takes place after the Incrementation step (and after the process).   Which form of the algorithm is preferable?

See Fig. 8-25.   There is no basis for preferring one form of the algorithm over the other; both result in exactly 50 repetitions of the process.   However, there are special cases of loops where there would be a difference.   See, for example, Problem 9.10(*b*).

8.20 Consider the equation $y = x^3 - 8x^2 + 5x - 4$. Draw a flowchart which calculates y for values of x from -4 to 4 in steps of 0.2, and prints each x and its corresponding y.

First assign -4 to X, calculate Y, and then print X and Y.   Next, increase X by 0.2 and repeat the process.   Continue until X exceeds 4.   The test can take place either before the process step, as in Fig. 8-26(*a*), or after the incrementation, as in Fig. 8-26(*b*); both flowcharts accomplish the same thing.

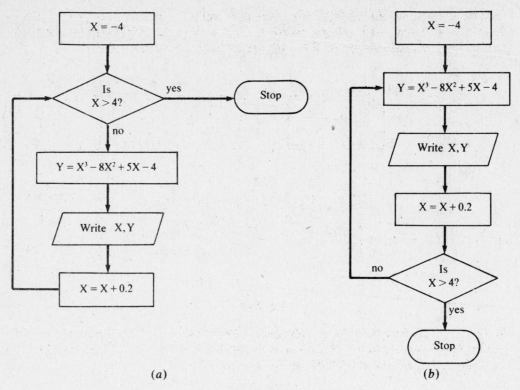

Fig. 8-26

SYSTEM DESIGN, SYSTEM FLOWCHARTS

8.21 What is the main objective of the systems analyst?

The systems analyst is the person responsible for the overall design of a data processing system and for making the system as efficient an instrument as possible for the attainment of the organization's goals.

8.22 (a) Briefly describe the three steps in the study phase of the design of a data processing system. (b) Name the next phase and the steps composing it.

(a) *Identification*: states the objective(s) of the system. *Documentation*: describes the required files and report documents. *Evaluation*: chooses the best system plan from among alternatives.

(b) The *operation phase*, consisting of *design, installation*, and *testing*.

8.23 In which step in the design of a new data processing system does one (a) train personnel? (b) study different systems that perform the same function? (c) design the new computer (system) programs? (d) check the cost effectiveness of the new system? (e) describe required files? (f) acquire new hardware?

(a) installation, (b) evaluation, (c) design, (d) testing, (e) documentation, (f) installation.

8.24 Why do system flowcharts utilize many more symbols than program flowcharts?

A system flowchart must specify many things that are presumed or immaterial in a program flowchart; for example, the type of input/output medium, the type of file storage (random-access or sequential), and the type of process (manual or software program).

8.25 Indicate, employing the appropriate system flowchart symbol, (*a*) manual input, (*b*) punched-card input, (*c*) manual sorting, (*d*) sorting by software program, (*e*) sequential file, (*f*) random-access file, (*g*) preparation, (*h*) printed output.

See Fig. 8-27.

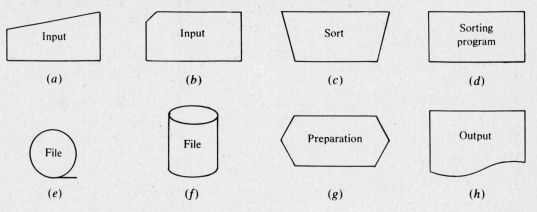

Fig. 8-27

8.26 The May Kit Company requires new employees to fill out a printed personnel form. The data are punched on cards, sorted, and then incorporated in the company's master file. Draw a system flowchart for the above procedure.

See Fig. 8-28.

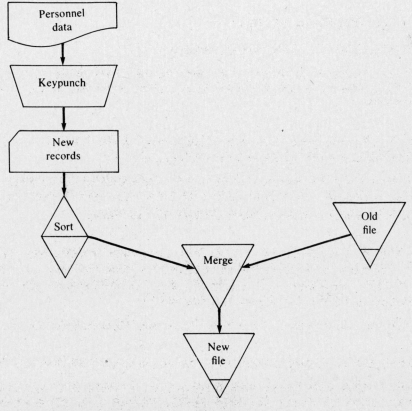

Fig. 8-28

8.27 Ace Appliance Stores Inc. has four local stores. Each day, daily sales transactions are sent by telecommunication to the main office. These reports are collated and put into a transaction file that is compared to the current inventory file. This results in a delivery report, an inventory shortage report, and an updated inventory file. Draw the system flowchart of the above.

See Fig. 8-29.

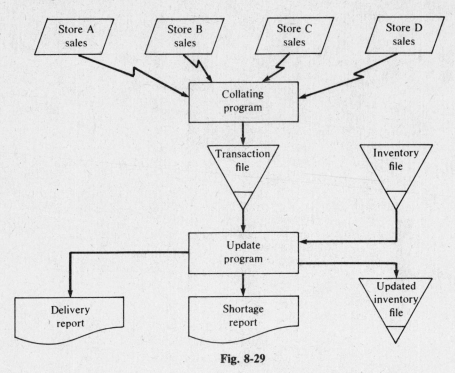

Fig. 8-29

Review Questions

VARIABLES

8.28 A variable in a computer program: (*a*) can be assigned a nonnumerical value, (*b*) is supplied a name, (*c*) is a data item whose value may change, (*d*) all of the above.

8.29 A variable-name in a computer program: (*a*) is supplied by the manufacturer, (*b*) is supplied by the programmer, (*c*) may be any word, (*d*) none of the above.

8.30 A variable is defined in a computer program (*a*) in the first program statement; (*b*) by a loop; (*c*) once a value has been assigned to it; (*d*) once it has been tested as positive, negative, or zero.

8.31 What are *reserved words*?

8.32 What are (*a*) destructive readin, (*b*) nondestructive readout?

ASSIGNMENT STATEMENTS

8.33 The product of A and B is to be assigned to a variable, PRODUCT. How would such an assignment be written in (*a*) BASIC, (*b*) FORTRAN, (*c*) PL/1, (*d*) COBOL, (*e*) APL?

CHAP. 8]   FLOWCHARTS AND PROGRAMMING TECHNIQUES   179

8.34 Write statements that will (a) assign 11500 to the variable SALARY, (b) subtract 800 from the value of SALARY, (c) increase SALARY by the amount in RESERVE, (d) decrease SALARY by 8 percent.

8.35 Find the output of each program segment:

(a) COST = 700   (b) DISCOUNT = 70   (c) DISCOUNT = 70
     DISCOUNT = 0.10 * COST   DISCOUNT = 20   DISCOUNT = DISCOUNT − 20
     Write DISCOUNT   Write DISCOUNT   Write DISCOUNT

8.36 Find the output of each program segment:

(a) A = 20   (b) A = 20   (c) A = 20
     B = 30   B = 30   B = 30
     A = A + B   B = A + B   A = B
     B = A + B   A = A + B   B = A
     Write A, B   Write A, B   Write A, B

ARITHMETIC EXPRESSIONS

8.37 Write the following in computer notation, using the operation symbols in Table 8-1:

(a) $5a + 3b$ (c) $(a + b)(x + y)$ (e) $\dfrac{a + b}{c}$

(b) $a^2 + b^3$ (d) $a + \dfrac{b}{c}$ (f) $a + \dfrac{b}{c + d^2}$

8.38 Find the value of each expression:

(a) $6 + 20/2 * 5 - 3$ (c) $6 + 20/(2 * 5) - 3$

(b) $(6 + 20)/2 * (5 - 3)$ (d) $(6 + 20/2) * 5 - 3$

8.39 Find the value of each expression:

(a) $8 + 2 * 4 + 2 ** 3 - 1$ (c) $8 + (2 * 4) + 2 ** (3 - 1)$

(b) $(8 + 2) * 4 + 2 ** 3 - 1$ (d) $8 + 2 * (4 + 2) ** 3 - 1$

PROGRAM FLOWCHARTS

8.40 Give the shape of the program flowchart symbol for (a) Decision, (b) Input, (c) Connector, (d) Terminal, (e) Output, (f) Process.

8.41 Which of the following are macroinstructions? (a) Increase SALARY by 500. (b) Interchange X and Y. (c) Read A, B, C. (d) Find largest value of SALES. (e) Decrease SCORE by XYZ. (f) Compute AVERAGE value of SALES.

8.42 Give the shape of the flowchart symbol within which each of the following would be written. (a) Write X, Y, Z. (b) Is TEST < 80? (c) Stop. (d) Move SALES3 to SALES5. (e) Compute TEST = SCORE + 0.10 * SCORE. (f) Is SALES greater than 5000?

8.43 Consider Fig. 8-30(a). Find the output if the input is (a) A = 5, B = 10; (b) A = 20, B = 10.

8.44 Rework Question 8.43 for the flowchart of Fig. 8-30(b).

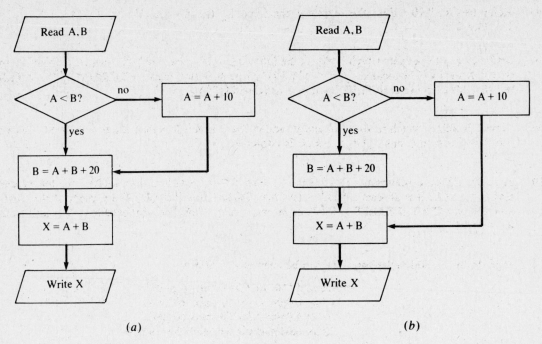

Fig. 8-30

8.45   Consider the flowchart in Fig. 8-31(*a*).   Find the output if the input is   (*a*)   A = 5,   B = 10,   C = 20;   (*b*)   A = 15,   B = 10,   C = 20;   (*c*)   A = 30,   B = 10,   C = 20.

8.46   Redo Question 8.45 using the flowchart in Fig. 8-31(*b*).

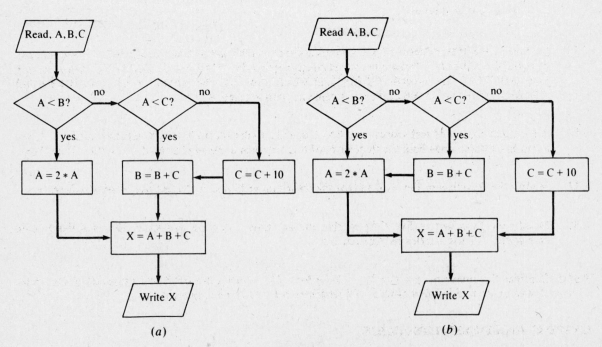

Fig. 8-31

8.47   Refer to Fig. 8-20. Find the output if the input is (a) X = 15, Y = 4; (b) X = 1, Y = 1; (c) X = 15, Y = 5.

8.48   Draw flowchart segments which interpret the following statements. In both segments, show where the next statement will be located. (a) If TEST is less than 80, then increase TEST by 5. (b) If TEST is less than 80, then increase TEST by 5; else increase TEST by 7%.

8.49   Draw a flowchart which reads A, B, and C, and writes A if A is less than B and less than C, but writes B if A is less than C only. Otherwise, C is outputted.

8.50   The BONUS on a salesman's SALES is (i) zero if SALES is less than $2000; (ii) ten percent of SALES if SALES is at least $2000 but less than $5000; (iii) $500 plus five percent of the excess of SALES over $5000, if SALES is $5000 or more. Draw a flowchart that calculates BONUS from the input SALES.

8.51   Suppose the monthly telephone bill is to be computed as follows:

> Minimum $7.50 for first 80 message units
> *plus* 0.06/unit for the next 60 units
> *plus* 0.05/unit for the next 60 units
> *plus* 0.04/unit for any units beyond 200

Draw a flowchart which calculates the monthly BILL, with input MESSAGE, the number of message units.

LOOPS

8.52   Draw a flowchart of an algorithm that calculates
(a) $SUM = 1/2 + 2/3 + 3/4 + \cdots + 49/50$
(b) $SUM = 1/2 + 2/3 + 3/4 + \cdots + (N-1)/N$
where one first reads N.

8.53   Suppose that $5000 is deposited in a savings account in 1980 and that the bank pays 9 percent interest, compounded annually. Draw a flowchart which outputs the YEAR and the AMOUNT in the account, until AMOUNT first exceeds $15,000, and which also finds the number N of years it takes for AMOUNT to reach $15,000 or more. (Compare with Problem 8.17.)

8.54   A file contains a set of test scores from 0 to 100, and a trailer record bearing a negative number. Draw a flowchart which finds both the number N of test scores and the number K of test scores 90 or above.

8.55   Modify the flowchart in Fig. 8-14 so that the algorithm finds the largest and the smallest salary.

8.56   Modify the flowchart in Fig. 8-14 so that the algorithm finds the salaries of the two highest-paid employees. (Their salaries may be equal.)

8.57   Consider the equation $y = x^4 + 2x^3 - 13x^2 - 14x + 24$. Draw a flowchart that calculates y for values of x from −5 to 5 in steps of 0.25, and writes each x and its corresponding y.

SYSTEMS AND SYSTEM FLOWCHARTS

8.58   The systems analyst normally: (a) writes the computer programs, (b) conceives optimal data processing systems, (c) has a major or minor in psychology, (d) all of the above.

8.59 Name two things an organization may want to minimize while pursuing its goals.

8.60 The system flowchart: (a) is an important tool in the design of a data processing system, (b) uses many more symbols than program flowcharts, (c) shows the flow of data from the source documents to the final reports, (d) all of the above.

8.61 Describe the types of operation indicated by the following system flowchart symbols:

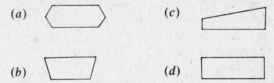

8.62 Draw the system flowchart symbol for (a) printed input, (b) punched-card input, (c) sequential file, (d) random-access file, (e) punched-card output, (f) printed output.

8.63 Weekly time cards are submitted by the employees. The data are recorded on punched cards, which are then sorted. A payroll program uses these cards together with the master payroll file to output the weekly paychecks for the employees, and a weekly payroll report for the employer. Draw the system flowchart.

8.64 A customer requests space on a particular airplane flight. The salesperson sends the request by telecommunication to the central reservations headquarters, where a reservations program checks the request against the master reservations file. Either the "NO SPACE" signal is given to the salesperson, or the "SPACE AVAILABLE" signal is given to the salesperson and the reservations file is updated. In the latter case, the salesperson writes the flight ticket for the customer. Draw the system flowchart.

8.65 A customer places a sales order with a salesperson. The customer receives a copy of the sales order and a copy is sent to the billing office. The billing office sends a shipping order to the warehouse, where the shipping order is checked against the inventory file. If the item is not in stock, a cancellation order is sent to the customer and to the billing office, which then sends a repayment to the customer. On the other hand, if the item is in stock, a shipping order is sent to the customer and to the delivery department. When the merchandise is delivered, the customer signs a receipt, of which one copy is given to the customer and one copy is sent to the billing office. Draw a system flowchart.

Chapter 9

Data Structures

9.1 INTRODUCTION

This chapter is devoted to ways of assembling data, or *data structures*. So far, we have discussed the hierarchical relationship between files, records, and data items. That is, a *file* is a collection of related *records*, and each record is a collection of related *data items* called *fields*. Furthermore, we noted that an integrated collection of files is called a *data base*. Now we shall discuss some other data structures; namely, *tables*, *arrays*, and *lists*. We begin by giving a more detailed description of the structure of a record.

9.2 RECORD STRUCTURE; TREES

A record is a collection of related data items. If a data item has two or more parts, it is called a *group item*; otherwise it is called an *elementary item*.

EXAMPLE 9.1 Figure 9-1(*a*) shows a student record punched on an 80-column card. The record consists of four items: (i) student number, punched in columns 1–6; (ii) name, punched in columns 11–40; (iii) birthday, punched in columns 43–48; (iv) major, punched in columns 51–65.

The student name is a group item divided into three parts: last name in columns 11–25, last name in columns 26–39, and middle initial in column 40. Also, birthday is a group item divided into three parts: month in columns 43–44, day in columns 45–46, and year in columns 47–48. Altogether the record contains 8 elementary items.

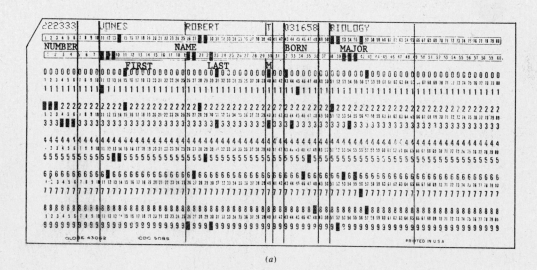

(*a*)

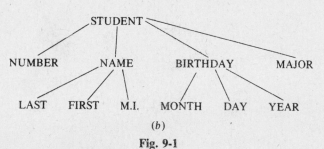

(*b*)

Fig. 9-1

183

One way of picturing the structure of this record is by the tree diagram in Fig. 9-1(*b*). Observe that there is a line drawn from group item X to item Y if Y is a subitem of X. (The entire record, STUDENT, is not considered a group item.) The elementary items correspond to the ends of the diagram.

Formally, a *tree* consists of *nodes* (points) and *branches* (lines) such that (1) each branch corresponds to two nodes, (2) any pair of nodes is joined by a unique path of branches. We assume that our trees are *rooted*, i.e. one node in each tree is distinguished as the *root*. (Any node may be chosen as the root.) This gives rise to a direction on each branch, away from the root. More precisely, a branch joining nodes X and Y is directed from X to Y or from Y to X according as the path joining the root R and Y does or does not pass through X. Those nodes at the ends of the tree are called *leaves*. In the tree in Fig. 9-1(*b*), STUDENT is the root, and the leaves are the eight elementary items. By convention, the tree is drawn with the root at the top and the leaves toward the bottom (an "uprooted" tree). Problem 9.4 shows that trees can also be used to describe the structure of arithmetic expressions.

A tree may be described by assigning its nodes to numbered *levels*: the root is put in level 1; nodes joined by a branch to the root are put in level 2; and so on. Figure 9-2 shows the level structure of the tree of Fig. 9-1(*b*).

```
01  STUDENT
      02  NUMBER
      02  NAME
            03  LAST
            03  FIRST
            03  M.I.
      02  BIRTHDAY
            03  MONTH
            03  DAY
            03  YEAR
      02  MAJOR
```

Fig. 9-2

9.3 TABLES

Certain types of data can be presented by means of a table. The simplest type of table is a collection of paired entries such that no two pairs have the same first entry. The first entry in each pair is called the *argument*, and the second entry is called the *value* (of the table for that argument). For example, Table 9-1 is a table giving the probability of throwing one of the numbers

Table 9-1

Number	Probability
2	1/36
3	2/36
4	3/36
5	4/36
6	5/36
7	6/36
8	5/36
9	4/36
10	3/36
11	2/36
12	1/36

2, 3, 4, ..., 12 with a pair of fair dice.   Mathematically speaking, such a one-argument table is a *function* (of a single variable).

Tables may also have two arguments.   For example, Table 9-2 gives the number of students in a college according to age and class status.   Observe that one argument, age, is listed on the left of the table, and the other argument, class status, is listed on the top of the table.

Table 9-2

Age \ Class	Freshman	Sophomore	Junior	Senior	Special
16 and under	22	2	0	0	8
17	65	18	0	0	3
18	244	52	11	0	0
19	11	197	41	6	3
20	0	12	135	44	6
21	0	4	15	142	3
22	0	0	7	19	8
23 and over	8	13	11	22	58

9.4   ARRAYS

Let A be a collection of N elements displayed in a row, i.e. side by side, or in a column, i.e. one beneath another.   Then A is called a *linear array* with N elements.   One writes A(1) for the first element in the array, A(2) for the second element in the array, and so on.   The integer K in A(K) is called a *subscript*, even though it appears between parentheses after the name of the array.

EXAMPLE 9.2   Consider the array of eight students in Fig. 9-3.   If we let STUDENT denote the array, then

$$\text{STUDENT(1)} \quad \text{denotes} \quad \text{Richard Ash}$$
$$\text{STUDENT(2)} \quad \text{denotes} \quad \text{Linda Bloom}$$
$$\text{STUDENT(3)} \quad \text{denotes} \quad \text{Saul Chandler}$$

....

Student
Ash, Richard
Bloom, Linda
Chandler, Saul
Davis, Donald
Edwards, Mary
Finney, Alfred
Goodwin, Audrey
Hamilton, Frank

Fig. 9-3

If, in a computer program, a variable-name is to denote an array rather than an individual data item, one must inform the computer of this fact by some special statement. Each programming language has its own syntax for this; Table 9-3 gives the appropriate forms for the array of Example 9.2. In this book, statements of the form

> Dimension STUDENT(8)

will be used in flowcharts; we shall also write

> Read STUDENT

to indicate that the 8 names are to be read into STUDENT, and

> Write STUDENT

to indicate that the 8 names in STUDENT are to be outputted.

Table 9-3

Language	Statement
FORTRAN	DIMENSION STUDENT(8)
BASIC	DIM STUDENT(8)
PL/1	DECLARE STUDENT(8)
COBOL	STUDENT OCCURS 8 TIMES

9.5 DO LOOPS

Before we use arrays in flowcharts, it is convenient to introduce a special type of loop that is headed by a special macroinstruction. We write the statement

$$\text{Do } K = 1 \text{ to } N$$

before a list of instructions, called the *body* of the loop, as in Fig. 9-4. We call the resultant loop a *DO*

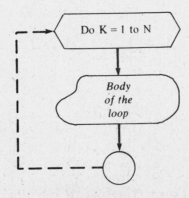

Fig. 9-4

loop. This terminology comes from FORTRAN, although many programming languages have this type of loop. For example,

PL/1	*BASIC*	*FORTRAN*
DO K = 1 to N;	FOR K = 1 to N	DO n K = 1, N
[*body of loop*]	[*body of loop*]	[*body of loop*]
END;	NEXT K	n CONTINUE

The precise meaning of the above loops is given by the flowchart in Fig. 9-5(*a*) or in Fig. 9-5(*b*), depending on which language and which compiler is used. in brief, the loops instruct the computer to execute the body of the loop first with K = 1, then with K = 2, ..., and finally with K = N. The variable K is called the *index*, the number 1 the *initial value*, and N the *end value* of the loop. In a more general type of DO loop, the initial value need not be 1 and the index need not increase in steps of 1; see Problem 9.10.

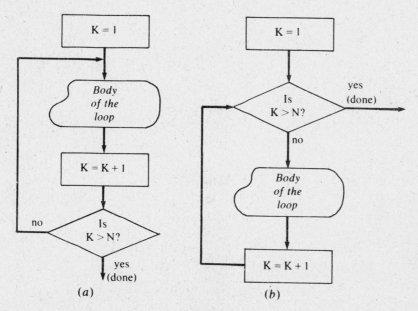

Fig. 9-5

The index itself can be one of the variables in the body of a DO loop. This fact is especially important when one or more of the other variables are arrays.

EXAMPLE 9.3 A company has 80 employees. The flowchart in Fig. 9-6 gives an algorithm that finds the average salary and the number of employees earning above the average salary. Observe that the salaries are read into an array, SALARY. Next, the average salary, AVG, is calculated. Then each salary, SALARY(K), is compared with AVG to obtain the number NUM of salaries greater than AVG.

9.6 MULTIDIMENSIONAL ARRAYS

The linear arrays discussed in Section 9.4 have exactly one subscript. Most computers can handle arrays with two and three subscripts, and some of the larger computers allow as many as seven subscripts. The number of subscripts is called the *dimension* of the array, so that linear arrays are one-dimensional arrays.

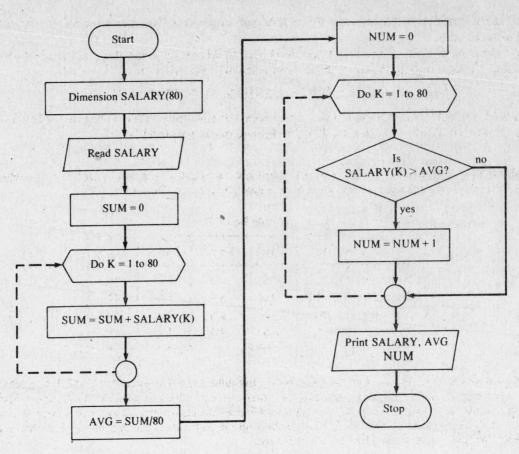

Fig. 9-6

Matrices

Frequently, data are arranged as a rectangular array. For example, a chain of three stores, each store having four departments, might display its weekly sales (in hundreds of dollars) as follows:

	Dept. 1	Dept. 2	Dept. 3	Dept. 4
Store 1	21	8	22	41
Store 2	31	11	26	36
Store 3	15	19	23	29

The horizontal lines of numbers are called the *rows* of the array; the vertical lines of numbers, the *columns*. Thus, the array has three rows and four columns, and we call it a *3 by 4* (written 3×4) *array*. Observe that the array has $3*4 = 12$ entries. Each entry is identified by two integers, the first labeling its row and the second labeling its column. Suppose that we let SALES denote the entire array of numbers. Then $SALES(2,3) = 26$, the entry in the second row (store 2) and third column (department 3). SALES is an example of a two-dimensional array, also called a *matrix array* or simply a *matrix*.

Formally, a two-dimensional $M \times N$ array is a collection of $M*N$ entries such that each entry is identified by a pair of integers, J and K, where $1 \leqslant J \leqslant M$ and $1 \leqslant K \leqslant N$. The first subscript, J, is called the *row*, and the second subscript, K, the *column*, of the entry. Similarly, a three-dimensional $M \times R \times S$ array is a collection of $M*R*S$ entries such that each entry is identified by three integers J, K, L (the subscripts), where

$$1 \leqslant J \leqslant M \qquad 1 \leqslant K \leqslant R \qquad 1 \leqslant L \leqslant S$$

The first subscript is called the *row*, the second subscript the *column*, and the third subscript the *page*, of the entry.

As with linear arrays, a special statement is used to inform the computer that a variable-name is to denote a multidimensional array rather than a scalar.   We will write

Dimension NAME(120), TEST(120, 3), SCHOOL(4, 25, 15)

when we want NAME to denote a linear array with 120 elements, TEST to denote a 120×3 matrix array, and SCHOOL to denote a $4 \times 25 \times 15$ (three-dimensional) array.

EXAMPLE 9.4   Four employees work a week (5 days) and put in hours as shown in Table 9-4.   An algorithm which calculates the week's pay of each employee is given by the flowchart in Fig. 9-7.

Table 9-4

	Day 1	Day 2	Day 3	Day 4	Day 5
Worker 1	8.0	7.0	8.0	6.5	9.0
Worker 2	8.0	8.0	8.5	7.0	9.0
Worker 3	8.0	8.0	8.0	8.0	7.5
Worker 4	8.0	8.0	8.0	7.5	9.0

A 4×5 matrix, HOURS, stores the tabulated data.   In addition, linear arrays EMPNAME, RATE, SUM, and PAY are used to store the employees' names, their hourly rates of pay, the total hours each has worked, and the pay of each.   The flowchart in Fig. 9-7 gives the algorithm.   Observe that there are two DO loops, one inside the other.   The inner DO loop sums up the elements in the Kth row of HOURS to obtain SUM(K), the total hours worked by the Kth employee.

9.7   LINKED LISTS

There is often some logical order or relationship between one record and another in a file or in a data base.   This relationship can be indicated by means of a list organization wherein each record has an extra field, called a *pointer* or *link*, which gives the address of the record that logically follows.   Figure 9-8 schematizes such a *linked list*.   Observe that one needs only the address of the first record in order to follow one's way through the entire list.   A special character is employed as the pointer of the last record in the list.

EXAMPLE 9.5   A hospital ward contains ten beds, of which eight are occupied as shown in Table 9-5.   Here the pointer gives the address (bed number) of the patient whose name alphabetically follows that of the given patient.   We also use the variable FIRSTNAME to store the address of the first patient in the list. Thus   FIRSTNAME = 6,   since patient Brown occupies bed 6.   Also, Brown's pointer is 1, since Davis, the next name, occupies bed 1; Davis's pointer is 8, since Evans, the next name, occupies bed 8; and so on.   We use the special character * (asterisk) for the pointer of the last name, Wallace.

The empty beds are separately linked; FIRSTEMP stores the address of the first empty bed.

EXAMPLE 9.6   A brokerage firm keeps a file of its brokers and a file of its customers.   One way to indicate which customers belong to which brokers would be for each customer record to have a field which gives the name of his/her broker.   Observe that one would have to search through all the customer records in order to find all the customers belonging to a given broker.

Another way to organize the files is through linked lists.   The customers of a given broker are linked alphabetically, and the broker's record has a pointer giving the address of the first customer in his list.   This is indicated in Fig. 9-9, where, say, broker Chandler has three customers, Brown, Murphy, and Zim-

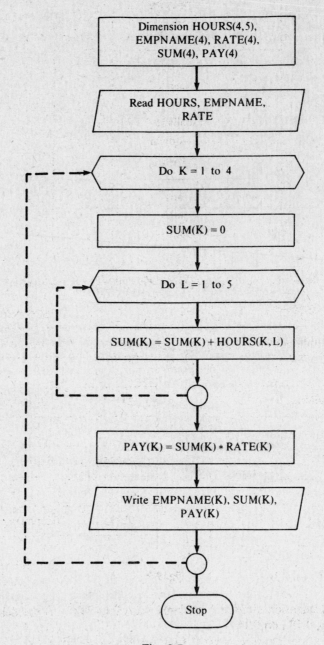

Fig. 9-7

Fig. 9-8

Table 9-5

FIRSTNAME = 6 FIRSTEMP = 7		
Bed	Name of Patient	Pointer
1	Davis	8
2	Lane	9
3	————	*
4	Wallace	*
5	Goodman	10
6	Brown	1
7	————	3
8	Evans	5
9	Smith	4
10	Jones	2

merman. With these linked lists, one need only locate the broker's record to get all his/her customers.

BROKER FILE

Address	Broker Information	Pointer
123	Chandler, . . .	2478

CUSTOMER FILE

Address	Customer Information	Pointer
2315	Murphy, . . .	2623
2478	Brown, . . .	2315
2623	Zimmerman, . . .	*

Fig. 9-9

The linked-list organization simplifies not only searching but also the deletion or addition of a record. See Problems 9.13 and 9.14.

We have been considering *single-linked lists* (or *forward-linked lists*). There are two other types of linked lists:

Double-linked list. Here each record between the first and last records has two pointers, one pointer giving the address of the succeeding record and the other pointer giving the address of the preceding record. The scheme is given in Fig. 9-10.

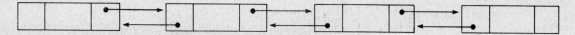

Fig. 9-10

Ring-linked list. Here the pointer of the last record gives the address of the first record, as indicated in Fig. 9-11.

Fig. 9-11

Solved Problems

RECORD STRUCTURE; TREES

9.1 Figure 9-12 shows an employee record form. (a) Draw the appropriate tree diagram. (b) Which of the data items are group items? (c) Which of the data items are elementary items?

```
01  Employee
    02  Personal
        03  Name
                04   First
                04   Last
                04   Middle
        03  ID number
        03  Marital status
        03  Dependents
    02  Financial
        03  Hours
                04   Regular
                04   Overtime
        03  Rate
        03  Insurance
                04   Health
                04   Life
```

Fig. 9-12

(a) See Fig. 9-13.

(b) The group items are those data items which are subdivided into other items, i.e. those nodes in the tree which are neither leaves nor the root. Thus, Personal, Name, Financial, Hours, and Insurance are group items.

(c) The elementary items are those data items which are not subdivided, i.e. those nodes which are leaves. Thus, First, Last, Middle, ID number, Marital status, Dependents, Regular, Overtime, Rate, Health, and Life are the elementary items.

9.2 Let N be a node in a tree, but not a leaf. Then N is the root of a unique subtree whose nodes are N and all nodes that follow N (in the orientation imposed by the root of the entire tree). (a) Draw the subtrees of the tree of Fig. 9-13 corresponding to the nodes (i) Name and (ii) Financial. (b) Which elementary items are referenced by (i) Name and (ii) Financial?

(a) The subtrees appear in Fig. 9-14.

(b) The elementary items referenced by a node (group item) are the leaves of the unique oriented subtree rooted in the given node. Hence (i) First, Last, Middle; (ii) Regular, Overtime, Rate, Health, Life.

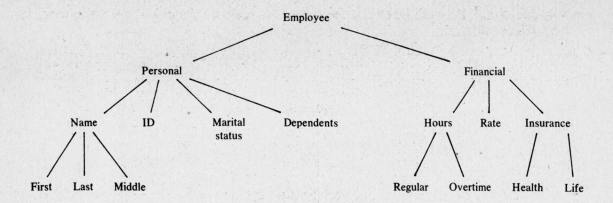

Fig. 9-13

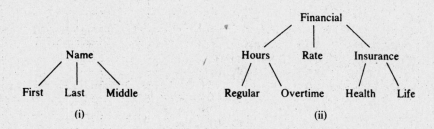

(i)   (ii)

Fig. 9-14

9.3   Consider the following tree structure: 01 Automobiles, 02 Domestic, 03 Ford, 03 General Motors, 04 Buick, 04 Chevrolet, 05 Chevette, 05 Nova, 04 Oldsmobile, 02 Foreign, 03 Volkswagen, 04 Beetle, 04 Rabbit, 03 Honda, 03 Datsun. (Observe that we do not have to write the items underneath one another so long as the items are assigned level numbers and the order of listing is observed.) (a) Draw the appropriate tree diagram. (b) Which subtree is referenced by General Motors?

See Fig. 9-15; we have encircled the subtree referenced by General Motors.

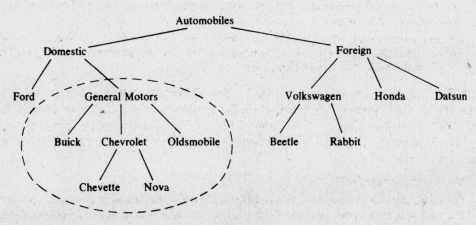

Fig. 9-15

9.4   The assignment statements $X = A + B$ and $Y = A * (B + C)$ are represented by trees as shown in Fig. 9-16.

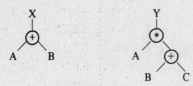

Fig. 9-16

By convention, each tree is drawn in such a way that the order of the leaves from left to right is the order of the corresponding terms on the right side of the assignment statement.   One can similarly represent any arithmetic expression involving binary operations such as addition, subtraction, multiplication, and division.   Draw a tree representing

$$Z = (A - B)/(C * D + E)$$

See Fig. 9-17 that Z is the root, and the variables A, B, C, D, and E in the arithmetic expression are the leaves.   We emphasize that the binary operations are read from left to right, e.g. $A - B$, not $B - A$, and $C * D$, not $D * C$.   This is, of course, of no importance with regard to the multiplication and the addition, but it is critical with regard to the subtraction and the division.

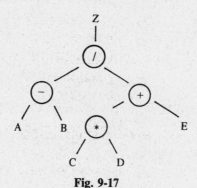

Fig. 9-17

TABLES

9.5   From Table 9-2, find the number of   (a) 19-year-old freshmen,   (b) 21-year-old seniors, (c) 15-year-old juniors,   (d) 28-year-old sophomores.

This is a two-argument table.   First find the age on the left side of the table; then move rightwards to the column labeled by the class status.

(a)   11

(b)   142

(c)   0 (there are no juniors 16 and under)

(d)   The table does not give this information, since all students 23 and older are put in the same group.

9.6   Table 9-6 evaluates the trigonometric functions sine (sin), cosine (cos), and tangent (tan), for certain angles.   Find   (a) sin(19°),   (b) tan(17°),   (c) cos(20°),   (d) sin(36°).

First find the row containing the angle, and then find the column in which the function appears.   (a) 0.3256;   (b) 0.3057;   (c) 0.9397;   (d) the angle does not appear in the table.

Table 9-6

Angle	sin	cos	tan
11°	0.1908	0.9816	0.1944
12°	0.2079	0.9782	0.2126
13°	0.2250	0.9744	0.2309
14°	0.2419	0.9703	0.2493
15°	0.2588	0.9659	0.2680
16°	0.2756	0.9613	0.2868
17°	0.2924	0.9563	0.3057
18°	0.3090	0.9511	0.3249
19°	0.3256	0.9455	0.3443
20°	0.3420	0.9397	0.3640
21°	0.3584	0.9336	0.3839
22°	0.3746	0.9272	0.4040

ARRAYS, DO LOOPS

9.7 Consider the array STUDENT in Fig. 9-3. Find STUDENT(7), STUDENT(4), and STUDENT(6).

STUDENT(K) denotes the Kth student in the list of names.   Hence:

STUDENT(7) denotes Audrey Goodwin

STUDENT(4) denotes Donald Davis

STUDENT(6) denotes Alfred Finney

9.8 Find the numbers of elements in arrays SALES, DEPT, COST, according to the following dimension statement:

Dimension SALES(5, 8, 6), DEPT(8, 7), COST(20)

SALES has $5*8*6 = 240$ elements; DEPT has $8*7 = 56$ elements; COST has 20 elements.

9.9 Table 9-2 is a two-argument table giving the number of students according to age and class status.   How might these data be stored in a computer?

This table may be stored as a matrix array,

Dimension AGE(8), CLASS(5), STUDENTS(8, 5)

where the age groups are coded from 1 to 8 and the class statuses from 1 to 5.   The numbers of students are put in an 8×5 array of which the row subscript is the age label and the column subscript is the class status label.

9.10 The precise meaning of a DO loop headed by the statement

Do K = INT to END by INC

is given by one of the flowcharts in Fig. 9-18.   Determine how many times, and for what values of the index K, the computer will execute a DO loop headed by

(*a*)   Do K = 3 to 17 by 4   (*b*)   Do K = 6 to 3 by 2

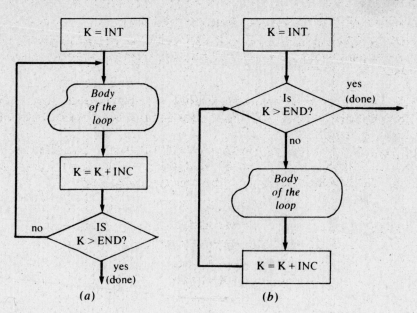

Fig. 9-18

(a) Four times, for

$$K = 3 \qquad K = 3 + 4 = 7 \qquad K = 7 + 4 = 11 \qquad K = 11 + 4 = 15$$

[unless otherwise instructed; see Problem 9.11(b)].

(b) This is the case where the initial value, INT, exceeds the end value, END. The computer executes the loop either once or not at all, depending on whether the interpretation of the DO loop is Fig. 9-18(a) or 9-18(b). This in turn depends on the programming language and compiler being employed. Thus, FORTRAN IV will execute the loop once, for K = 6, but PL/1 and FORTRAN 77 will not execute the loop at all.

9.11 Find the output for each flowchart in Fig. 9-19.

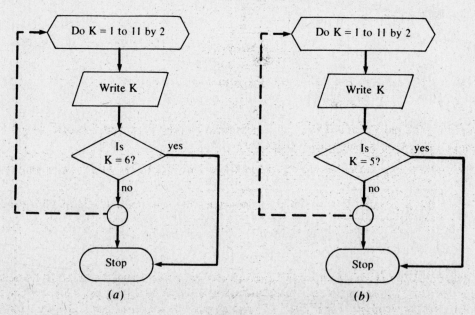

Fig. 9-19

(a) The output consists of the values of K: 1, 3, 5, 7, 9, and 11.

(b) Here the DO loop is abandoned when K = 5, so that the output consists of 1, 3, and 5. This is an example which shows that a loop need not be executed as many times as indicated by the Do statement.

9.12 Let WAGE be a linear array giving the salaries of N employees. Give an algorithm that finds the largest salary and who earns it, i.e. that finds the subscript L, assumed unique, such that WAGE(L) is largest.

First set L = 1 and set MAX = WAGE(1). Then compare MAX to each WAGE(K). If MAX is less than WAGE(K), reset L = K and reset MAX = WAGE(K). The flowchart of the algorithm appears in Fig. 9-20.

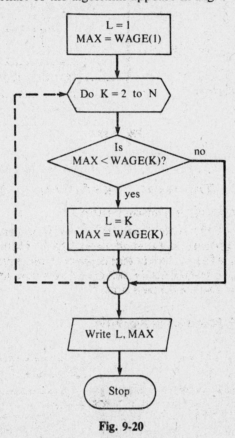

Fig. 9-20

LINKED LISTS

9.13 Refer to Example 9.5 and Table 9-5. If patient Goodman in bed 5 is discharged from the hospital, how should Table 9-5 be updated?

We wish to bypass Goodman in the linked list, as indicated by the curved arrow below:

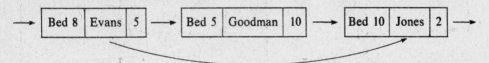

So Evans's pointer should be changed from 5 to 10. Now bed 5 must be linked to the other empty beds. This may be accomplished without conducting a search by making bed 5 the *first* empty bed on the list. Hence we reset FIRSTEMP = 5 and change the pointer of bed 5 to 7, the "old" value of FIRSTEMP. Thus Table 9-5 is updated as Table 9-7. Italic type in Table 9-7 indicates a changed value.

Table 9-7

Bed	Name of Patient	Pointer
FIRSTNAME = 6 FIRSTEMP = 5		
1	Davis	8
2	Lane	9
3	———	*
4	Wallace	*
5	———	7
6	Brown	1
7	———	3
8	Evans	10
9	Smith	4
10	Jones	2

9.14   Suppose that patient Ryan is added to the linked list in Table 9-5 (instead of patient Goodman being deleted, as in Problem 9.13).   How should Table 9-5 be updated?

First of all, we assign Ryan to bed 7, the first empty bed on the list (FIRSTEMP = 7).   Next we reset   FIRSTEMP = 3,   the pointer of bed 7, since bed 3 was the next, and is now the first, empty bed on the list.   Finally, we want to insert Ryan in the linked list between Lane and Smith, as follows:

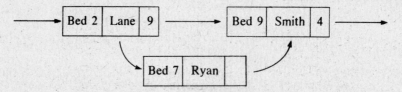

Hence we change the pointer of Lane to 7, Ryan's bed, and the pointer of Ryan to 9, Smith's bed.   Thus Table 9-5 is updated as Table 9-8, where italic type indicates changed values.

Table 9-8

Bed	Name of Patient	Pointer
FIRSTNAME = 6 FIRSTEMP = 3		
1	Davis	8
2	Lane	7
3	———	*
4	Wallace	*
5	Goodman	10
6	Brown	1
7	Ryan	9
8	Evans	5
9	Smith	4
10	Jones	2

Review Questions

RECORD STRUCTURE; TREES

9.15 In a record, a data item that is subdivided into two or more parts is called a *(a)* _____, whereas an item that is not subdivided is called a *(b)* _____.

9.16 Each store in a chain sends in a weekly record of its sales according to the following structure: 01 Store, 02 Hardware, 02 Clothing, 03 Men, 03 Women, 03 Children, 04 Boys, 04 Girls, 02 Drugs, 03 Prescription, 03 Nonprescription, 02 Stationery. *(a)* Draw the appropriate tree diagram. *(b)* How many group items are there? *(c)* How many elementary items are there? *(d)* Which elementary items are referenced by *(i)* Clothing, *(ii)* Drugs.

9.17 Draw tree diagrams corresponding to:

$$(a) \quad x = a\left(b + \frac{c-d}{e+f}\right) \qquad (b) \quad Y = A + B/C * (D+E) - F$$

TABLES

9.18 From Table 9-2, find the number of *(a)* 17-year-old special students, *(b)* 21-year-old freshmen, *(c)* 18-year-old juniors, *(d)* 16-year-old seniors, *(e)* 22-year-old sophomores, *(f)* 23-year-old juniors.

9.19 Using Table 9-6, find *(a)* $\tan(21°)$, *(b)* $\sin(15°)$, *(c)* $\cos(18°)$, *(d)* $\tan(11°)$, *(e)* $\cos(25°)$.

ARRAYS, DO LOOPS

9.20 Consider the array STUDENT in Fig. 9-3. *(a)* Find STUDENT(5), STUDENT(8), and STUDENT(11). *(b)* How may one denote Linda Bloom, Audrey Goodwin, and Richard Ash?

9.21 Find the numbers of elements in arrays STUDENT, TEST, and GRADE, according to the following dimension statement:

Dimension STUDENT(5, 4, 18), TEST(360, 4), GRADE(320)

9.22 How many times, and for which values of the index, will the DO loops whose headings follow be cycled?

(a) Do K = 3 to 24 by 5   *(c)* Do L = 8 to 4 by 3

(b) Do K = 6 to 17   *(d)* Do M = 2 to 200 by 3

9.23 Find the output for each flowchart in Fig. 9-21.

9.24 Draw a flowchart, containing a DO loop, that calculates:

(a) SUM = $1/2 + 2/3 + 3/4 + \cdots + 49/50$ [compare Question 8.52(*a*)]

(b) SUM = $1/1 + 1/3 + 1/5 + 1/7 + \cdots + 1/25$ [compare Problem 8.16(*a*)]

9.25 In what manner would one declare GRADE to be a linear array with 320 elements, in *(a)* FORTRAN, *(b)* BASIC, *(c)* COBOL, *(d)* PL/1?

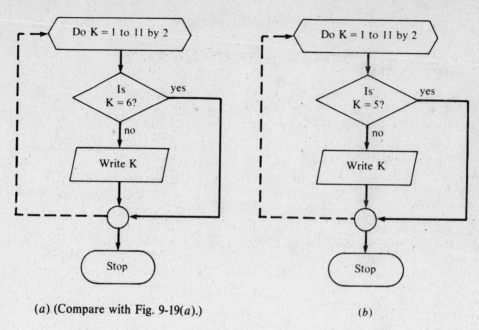

(a) (Compare with Fig. 9-19(a).)   (b)

Fig. 9-21

9.26 The weekly sales (in hundreds of dollars) of a chain of three stores, each store having four departments, is given in Table 9-9.

Table 9-9

	Dept. 1	Dept. 2	Dept. 3	Dept. 4
Store 1	21	8	22	41
Store 2	31	11	26	36
Store 3	15	19	23	29

Draw a flowchart which inputs the data as a 3×4 array, SALES, and which outputs the total weekly sales of each store and of the chain.

LINKED LISTS

9.27 Figure 9-3 gives a list of 8 students. Assuming that the address of each student is the student's position in the array, add a pointer to the array so that the men and women are linked separately. (Let FIRSTMAN and FIRSTWOMAN store the address of the first man and first woman, respectively.)

9.28 How should Table 9-5 be updated if Brown is discharged?

9.29 How should Fig. 9-9 be updated if Chandler gains two new customers, Applebaum (address 3147) and Winard (address 3233)?

9.30 How should Table 9-7 be updated if patient Zimmerman is added to the list?

Answers to Review Questions

CHAPTER 1

1.20 punched-card data processing, electronic data processing

1.21 electronic data processing

1.22 (b), (d)

1.23 (a), (b), (c)

1.24 true

1.25 (a) record, (b) data base, (c) file

1.26 input, processing, output

1.27 origination, distribution, storage

1.28 processing and storage

1.29 source documents

1.30 report documents

1.31 (a) M 91, E 85, A 86
(b) M 91, E 83, A 85
(c) M 92, E 88, A 88

1.32 (a) S $192.50, K $206.25
(b) S $192.50, K $209.38
(c) S $195.63, K $214.38

1.33 (a), (d)

1.34 (a), (b)

1.35 (a) $83.60, (b) $44.00
(c) $444.00, (d) $99.90
(e) $283.05

1.36 (1) (b), (2) (f), (3) (a)
(4) (c), (5) (d), (6) (e)
(7) (h), (8) (i), (9) (g)

1.37 (a) classifying, (b) calculating
(c) recording, (d) sorting
(e) summarizing, (f) merging

1.38 key

1.40 (a) classifying, (b) sorting
(c) merging

CHAPTER 2

2.21 (b)

2.22 (c)

2.23 (b)

2.24 (c)

2.25 $a = 12$, $b = 8$
$c = 2$

2.26 (c)

2.27 (a), (c), (e)

2.28 (a), (d)

2.29 (b), (c)

2.30 (b)

2.31 (b)

2.32 (d)

2.33 (a)

2.34 (b)

2.35 (c)

2.36 (d)

2.37 (b)

2.38 (c)

2.39 (d)

2.40 (e)

2.41 true

2.42 (d)

2.43 (d)

2.44 (a) FORTRAN
(b) COBOL

2.45 (d)

2.46 (c)

2.47 (b)

2.48 (d)

2.49 (b)

2.50 (d)

CHAPTER 3

3.34 character

3.35 digits and letters of the alphabet; 36 (unless there are lowercase letters)

3.36 (d)

3.37 (a)

3.38 (a) master, (b) detail, (c) summary

3.39 (a) sequential, (b) random-access
(c) sequential, (d) random-access

3.40 (a) once, (b) once, (c) once

3.41 (b)

3.42 (a) 12, (b) the top three rows (12-row, 11-row, and 0-row)
(c) the bottom ten rows (0-row through 9-row)
(d) 12-edge, (e) 9-edge

3.43 (a) one (in the corresponding digit row)
(b) two (one zone-punch row and one digit-punch row)

3.44 (a) detail
(b) 5, 20, 6, 5, 7
(c) 02226, TOM MIX, 040924
03432, 0044510
(d) April 9, 1924; $445.10

3.45 (a) 050459, (b) 012374, (c) 100382

3.46 (a) June 28, 1973; (b) Nov. 22, 1933
(c) Mar. 5, 1970
(d) error (there is no 14th month)

3.47 (a) 000567, (b) 001234
(c) 022555, (d) field too small

3.48 (a) 00033344, (b) 00666677
(c) 00044400, (d) field too small

3.49 (a) $9,999.99, (b) $999,999.99
(c) $99,999,999.99

3.50 (b)

3.51 (a) SAILBOAT, (b) USED TABLE
(c) NEW CHAIRS, (d) field too small

3.52	(*b*)
3.53	(*d*)
3.54	(*d*)
3.55	(*a*)
3.56	(*c*)
3.57	(*d*)
3.58	(*b*)
3.59	N

3.60	true
3.61	(*d*)
3.62	(*d*)
3.63	(*b*)
3.64	(*a*)
3.65	(*a*), (*c*), and (*e*) are sequential
	(*b*), (*d*) and (*f*) are direct-access

CHAPTER 4

4.26 (*a*) cards are cheaper, EAM are cheaper, EAM are less sophisticated
(*b*) slow processing, manual intervention, large storage areas

4.27 (*a*) F, (*b*) T, (*c*) T, (*d*) T

4.28 (*c*)

4.29 (*a*) in reading station
(*b*) depress DUP key

4.30 (*d*)

4.31 (*c*)

4.32 (*d*)

4.33 (*d*)

4.34 verifier

4.35 needle checking, sight checking

4.36 (*a*) reproducer, (*b*) gang punching (*c*) master card, (*d*) detail card

4.37 (*b*)

4.38 (*b*)

4.39 (*a*)

4.40 key

4.41 (*a*) 65 min, (*b*) 62 min

4.42 (*a*) 6, (*b*) 12

4.43 See Fig. A-1.

4.44 See Fig. A-2. The cards are still not sorted.

4.45 Sort the 12-row letters, A through I, according to their digit punch, with letters J through R in pocket 11 and letters S through Z in pocket 0, as in Fig. A-3. Then 11-row letters, J through R, are sorted. Lastly, 0-row letters, S through Z, are sorted.

4.46 80

4.47 two, *primary feed* and *secondary feed*

4.48 sequence checking, selecting, matching

4.49 (*a*) See Fig. A-4(*a*).
(*b*) See Fig. A-4(*b*).

4.50 (*a*) F, (*b*) T, (*c*) T, (*d*) T, (*e*) T

	62	51
53	42	41
43	52	61
3	**2**	**1**

(*a*) After First Sort

	53	43
62	52	42
61	51	41
6	**5**	**4**

(*b*) After Second Sort

Fig. A-1

	51	41
62	53	43
61	52	42
6	**5**	**4**

(*a*) After First Sort

	62	61
53	52	51
43	42	41
3	**2**	**1**

(*b*) After Second Sort

Fig. A-2

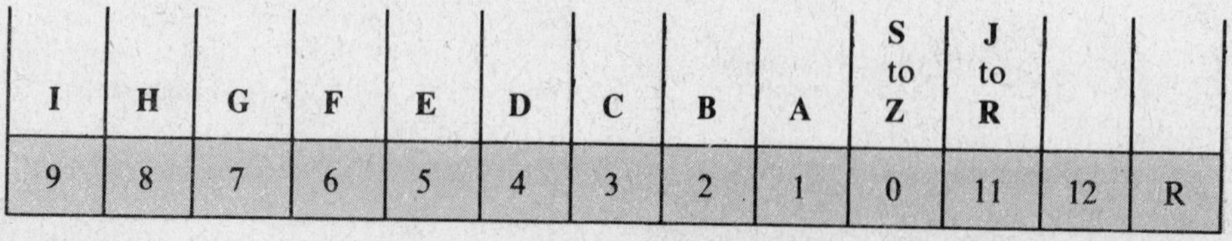

I	H	G	F	E	D	C	B	A	S to Z	J to R		
9	8	7	6	5	4	3	2	1	0	11	12	R

Fig. A-3

39			
35			40
33			38
31			36
29	34	34	32
27	30	30	26
25	28	28	22
21	24	24	20

(a)

39	34		
35	34		40
33	30		38
31	30		36
29	28		32
27	28		26
25	24		22
21	24		20

(b)

Fig. A-4

4.51 accounting machine

4.52 (a) addition, subtraction

(b) addition, subtraction, multiplication, division

4.53 reader, calculator, printer

4.54 (c)

4.55 (c)

4.56 (a) summary punching, (b) reproducer

4.57 (1) (a), (2) (c), (3) (b)

CHAPTER 5

5.34 (1) (b), (2) (c), (3) (d), (4) (a)

5.35 hybrid computer

5.36 analog computer

5.37 (d)

5.38 general-purpose digital computer

5.39 (d)

5.40 computer program

5.41 (1) (b), (2) (c), (3) (a)

5.42 (1) (e), (2) (a), (3) (d), (4) (b), (5) (c)

5.43 mass storage unit

5.44 (1) (b), (2) (c), (3) (a)

5.45 (a) 2000 characters/sec, (b) 400 times

5.46 ten times as much

5.47 (d)

5.48 (c)

5.49 (a), (c)

5.50 (c)

5.51 (1) (b), (2) (c), (3) (a)

5.52 (c)

5.53 ROM

5.54 4096

5.55 (d)

5.56 (1) (c), (2) (a), (3) (b)

5.57 (c)

5.58 (a) F, (b) T, (c) F

5.59 (a) F, (b) F, (c) F

CHAPTER 6

6.44 (1) (c), (2) (a), (3) (b)

6.45 (1) (c), (2) (b), (3) (d), (4) (a)

6.46 (d)

6.47 (d)

6.48 (b)

6.49 (1) (b), (2) (a), (3) (c)

6.50 (d)

6.51 (1) (c), (2) (a), (3) (d), (4) (b)

6.52 (b)

6.53 (b)

6.54 (1) (a), (2) (c), (3) (b)

6.55 (d)

6.56 (1) (b), (2) (a), (3) (d), (4) (c)

6.57 (c)

6.58 (1) (b), (2) (c), (3) (a)

6.59 (b)

6.60 (1) (b), (2) (c), (3) (a)

6.61 (1) (c), (2) (a), (3) (b)

6.62 (d)

6.63 (a)

6.64 (1) (a), (2) (c), (3) (b)

6.65 (c)

6.66 (b)

6.67 (a), (c)

6.68 (1) (c), (2) (a), (3) (d), (4) (e), (5) (b)

6.69 (c)

6.70 (a)

6.71 (1) (b), (2) (a), (3) (d), (4) (c)

6.72 (1) (a), (2) (d), (3) (b)

(4) (c), (5) (b), (6) (a)

CHAPTER 7

7.47 (a) 125, (b) 32, (c) 1, (d) 1/256, (e) 1/10000

7.48 (a) $2 \times 10^4 + 6 \times 10^3 + 5 \times 10^2 + 3 \times 10 + 9$

(b) $3 \times 10^2 + 0 \times 10 + 5 + 2 \times 10^{-1} + 4 \times 10^{-2} + 6 \times 10^{-3} + 8 \times 10^{-4}$

7.49 (a) 0.242424×10^2, (b) 0.1212×10^{-2}, (c) 0.666×10^0, (d) 0.555444×10^5, (e) 0.789×10^{-3}

7.50 (*a*) 5, (*b*) 2, (*c*) 6, (*d*) ambiguous (1, 2, 3, or 4), (*e*) 4

7.51 (*a*) 45.45, (*b*) 6.67, (*c*) 10.00, (*d*) 22.22, (*e*) 33.34

7.52 (*a*) 0.7710×10^4, (*b*) -0.8888×10^7, (*c*) 0.3333×10^{-2}
(*d*) 0.5050×10^6, (*e*) 0.2234×10^1

7.53 (*a*) 2, (*b*) 0, (*c*) -2, (*d*) 0, (*e*) 5, (*f*) -2

7.54 (*a*) 179, (*b*) 353, (*c*) 751, (*d*) 15485

7.55 (*a*) 41220_5, (*b*) 5175_8, (*c*) $A7D_{16}$

7.56 (*a*) 109, (*b*) 174, (*c*) 731

7.57 (*a*) 1110 1101, (*b*) 1 0110 0111, (*c*) 11 0110 1011

7.58 (*a*) 10110.1101, (*b*) 0.0 1100 1100 1100 $\cdots$

7.59 (*a*) 1353.56, (*b*) 2EB.B8

7.60 (*a*) 1 111.101 000 11, (*b*) 10 1010 0100.1100 1001

7.61 (*a*) 0.11011×2^2, (*b*) -0.11011×2^5, (*c*) 0.1101×2^6
(*d*) 0.11101×2^0, (*e*) -0.101×2^{-2}

7.62 (*a*) 0.1111×2^2, (*b*) 0.1110×1^{-2},
(*c*) -0.1000×2^4, (*d*) 0.1110×2^2

7.63 (*a*) 1010 1101, (*b*) 10100.110, (*c*) 101 1111 1110, (*d*) 10 0100.0111

7.64 (*a*) 111 0001 0100, (*b*) 10110.1001, (*c*) 110 1101, (*d*) 101.11

7.65 (*a*) 6845, 6846; (*b*) 39762, 39763
(*c*) 17829, 17830; (*d*) 654399, 654400

7.66 (*a*) 000100, 000101; (*b*) 0010000, 0010001;
(*c*) 10011001, 10011010;
(*d*) 0011100111, 0011101000

7.67 (*a*) 1, (*b*) -11101, (*c*) 110 0011, (*d*) 1001 1001

7.68 (*a*) T, (*b*) F, (*c*) F, (*d*) T, (*e*) F

7.69 (*d*)

7.70 (*c*)

7.71 (*d*)

7.72 (*a*) 0, 0, 1, 1; (*b*) first and fourth

7.73 (*a*) $2^6 = 64$, (*b*) $2^7 = 128$, (*c*) $2^8 = 256$

7.74 (*a*) 4 and 4, (*b*) zone and numeric

7.75 (*c*)

7.76 (*a*) T, (*b*) F

7.77 (*a*)

1100 0110	1101 0110	1101 1001	1110 0011	1101 1001	1100 0001	1101 0101

or C6 D6 D9 E3 D9 C1 D5, in hex

(*b*)

1010 0110	1010 1111	1011 0010	1011 0100	1011 0010	1010 0001	1010 1110

or A6 AF B2 B4 B2 A1 AE, in hex

7.78 (*a*)

1111 0011	1111 0101	1111 0111

(*b*)

1111 0011	1111 0101	1100 0111

(*c*)

1111 0011	1111 0101	1101 0111

7.79 (*a*)

0011	0101	0111	1111

, (*b*)

0011	0101	0111	1100

(*c*)

0011	0101	0111	1101

7.80 (*a*) 0000 $\cdots$ 000101100101, (*b*) 1000 $\cdots$ 000101100101

7.81 (*a*) 0000 $\cdots$ 000101100101, (*b*) 1111 $\cdots$ 111010011011

7.82 (a) 66, (b) 59, (c) 91, (d) 11, (e) (overflow), (f) (overflow)

7.83 (a) 130, (b) 123, (c) 155, (d) 75, (e) 220, (f) 41

7.84 (a) | 0 | 1000011 | 111011100···00 | , (b) | 1 | 1000010 | 111011100···00 |

(c) | 0 | 0111101 | 111011100···00 | , (d) | 1 | 0111101 | 111011100···00 |

CHAPTER 8

8.28 (d)

8.29 (b)

8.30 (c)

8.31 Words with operational meaning in the programming language; they cannot be chosen as variable-names.

8.32 (a) Previous content of a storage location is erased when new data are entered.

(b) The content of a storage location is unchanged even after the content has been assigned to another location.

8.33 (a) LET PRODUCT = A∗B   (c) PRODUCT = A∗B   (e) PRODUCT ← A∗B

    (b) PRODUCT = A∗B   (d) COMPUTE PRODUCT = A∗B

8.34 (a) SALARY = 11500   (c) SALARY = SALARY + RESERVE

    (b) SALARY = SALARY − 800   (d) SALARY = SALARY − 0.08 ∗ SALARY

                                or SALARY = 0.92 ∗ SALARY

8.35 (a) 70, (b) 20, (c) 50

8.36 (a) 50, 80; (b) 70, 50; (c) 30, 30

8.37 (a) 5∗A + 3∗B   (c) (A + B)∗(X + Y)   (e) (A + B)/C

    (b) A∗∗2 + B∗∗3   (d) A + B/C   (f) A + B/(C + D∗∗2)

8.38 (a) 53, (b) 26, (c) 5, (d) 77

8.39 (a) 23, (b) 47, (c) 20, (d) 439

8.40 (a) diamond, (b) parallelogram, (c) small circle, (d) oval
(e) parallelogram, (f) rectangle

8.41 (b), (d), (f)

8.42 (a) parallelogram, (b) diamond, (c) oval, (d) rectangle
(e) rectangle, (f) diamond

8.43 (a) 40, (b) 90

8.44 (a) 40, (b) 40

8.45 (a) 40, (b) 65, (c) 100

8.46 (a) 40, (b) 80, (c) 70

8.47 (a) 45, (b) 55, (c) 50

8.48 See Fig. A-5.

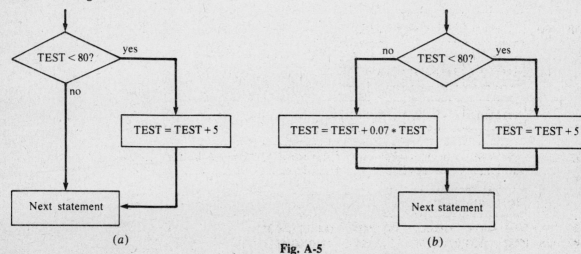

(a)   **Fig. A-5**   (b)

8.49   See Fig. A-6.   **8.50**   See Fig. A-7.   **8.51**   See Fig. A-8.

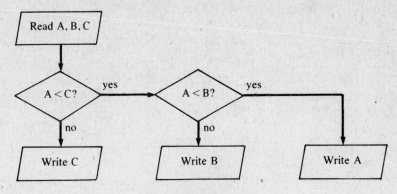

Fig. A-6

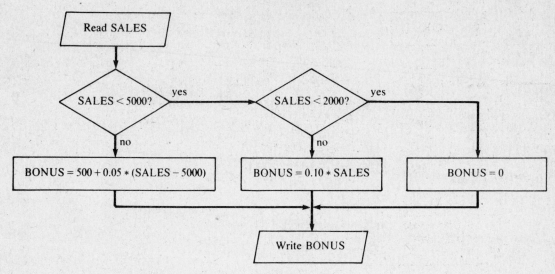

Fig. A-7

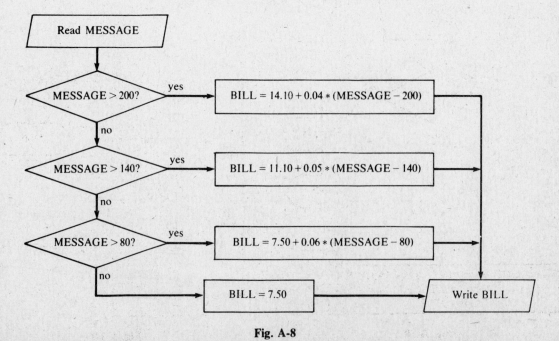

Fig. A-8

8.52 See Fig. A-9.

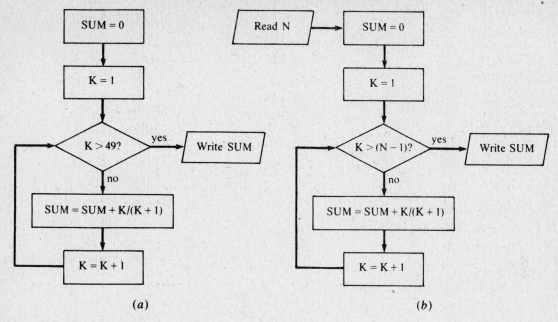

Fig. A-9

8.53 See Fig. A-10.   **8.54** See Fig. A-11.

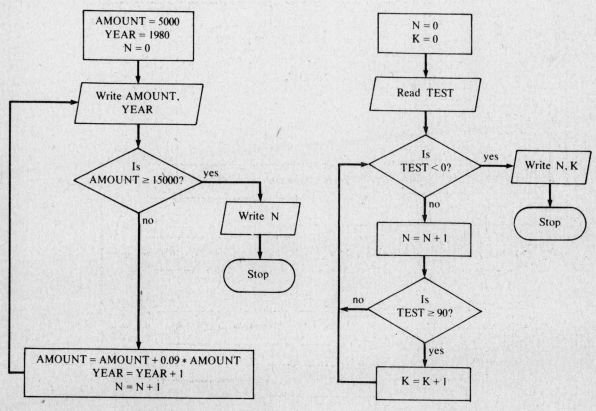

Fig. A-10   **Fig. A-11**

8.55   See Fig. A-12.

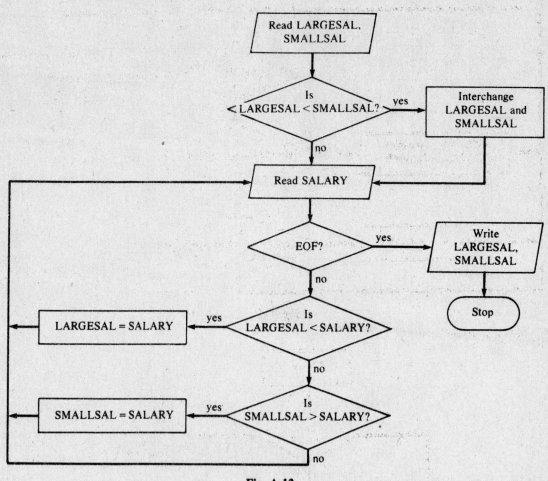

Fig. A-12

8.56 See Fig. A-13.

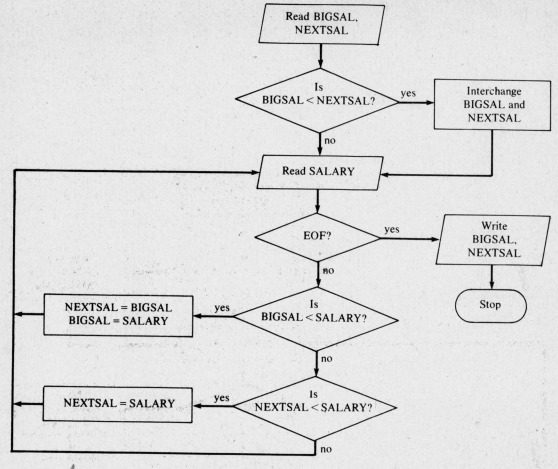

Fig. A-13

8.57 See Fig. A-14.

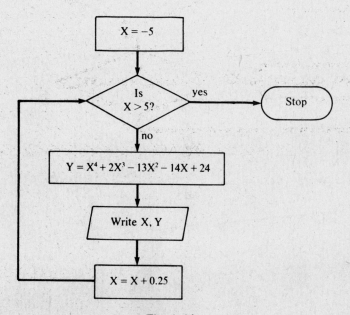

Fig. A-14

8.58 (*b*)
8.59 time, costs
8.60 (*d*)
8.61 (*a*) preparation, (*b*) manual operation, (*c*) manual input, (*d*) nonmanual operation
8.62 (*a*) and (*f*) (*b*) and (*e*) (*c*) (*d*)

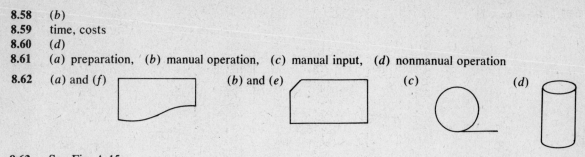

8.63 See Fig. A-15.
8.64 See Fig. A-16.

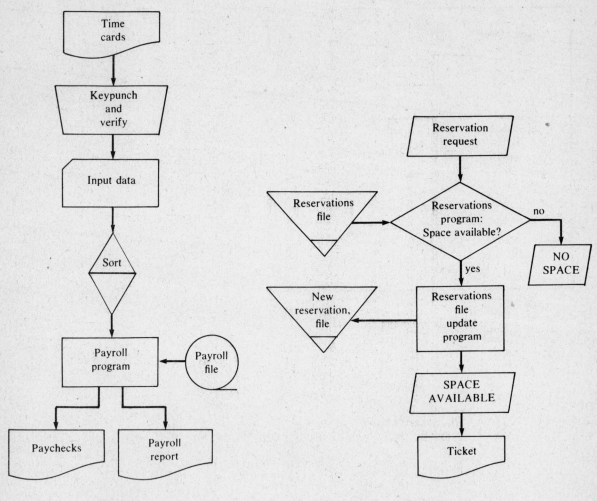

Fig. A-15

Fig. A-16

8.65   See Fig. A-17

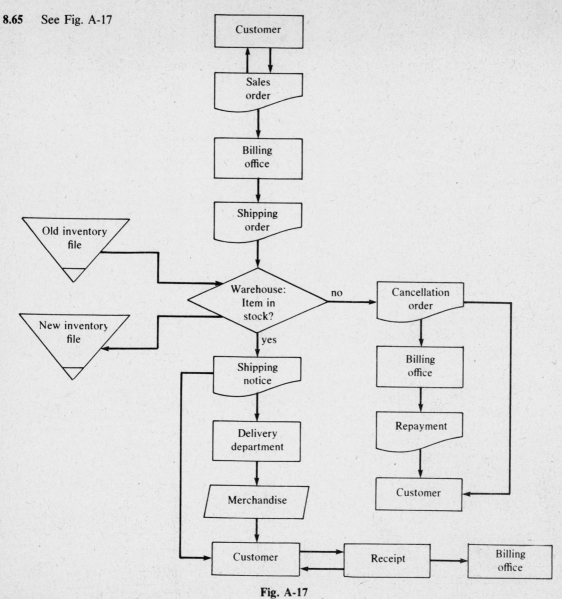

Fig. A-17

CHAPTER 9
9.15   (a) group item,   (b) elementary item
9.16   (a) See Fig. A-18.   (b) 3.   (c) 8.   (d) (i) Men, Women, Boys, Girls;   (ii) Prescription, Non-prescription.

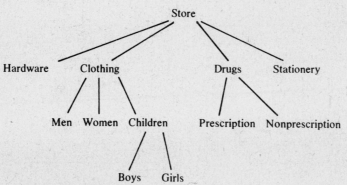

Fig. A-18

9.17   See Fig. A-19.

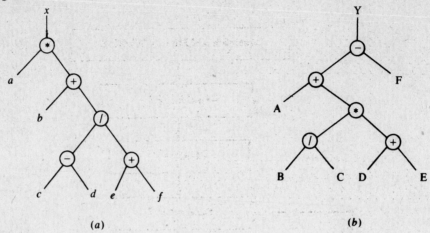

Fig. A-19

9.18   (*a*) 3,   (*b*) 0,   (*c*) 11,   (*d*) 0,   (*e*) 0,   (*f*) data lacking
9.19   (*a*) 0.3839,   (*b*) 0.2588,   (*c*) 0.9511,   (*d*) 0.1944,   (*e*) data lacking
9.20   (*a*) Mary Edwards and Frank Hamilton.   There is no STUDENT(11), since STUDENT has only 8
          elements.

          (*b*) STUDENT(2), STUDENT(7), STUDENT(1)
9.21   360, 1440, 320
9.22   (*a*) five: $K = 3, 8, 13, 18, 23$ (*c*) none, or once for $L = 8$
          (*b*) twelve; $K = 6, 7, 8, 9, \dots, 17$ (*d*) sixty-seven; $K = 2, 3, 5, 11, \dots, 200$
9.23   (*a*) 1, 3, 5, 7, 9, 11;   (*b*) 1, 3, 7, 9, 11
9.24   See Fig. A-20.
9.25   (*a*) DIMENSION GRADE(320)
          (*b*) DIM GRADE(320)
          (*c*) GRADE OCCURS 320 TIMES
          (*d*) DECLARE GRADE(320)

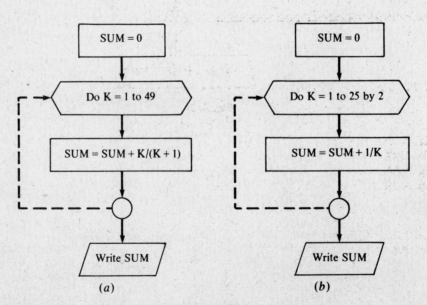

Fig. A-20

9.26 See Fig. A-21. Observe that the flowchart is independent of the particular data each week.

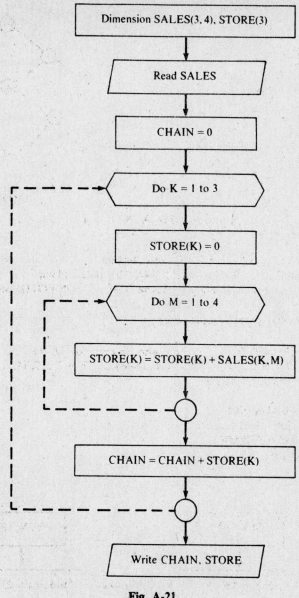

Fig. A-21

9.27 See Fig. A-22.
9.28 See Fig. A-23.
9.29 See Fig. A-24.
9.30 See Fig. A-25.

	FIRSTMAN = 1 FIRSTWOMAN = 2	
	Student	Pointer
1	Ash, Richard	3
2	Bloom, Linda	5
3	Chandler, Saul	4
4	Davis, Donald	6
5	Edwards, Mary	7
6	Finney, Alfred	8
7	Goodwin, Audrey	*
8	Hamilton, Frank	*

Fig. A-22

	FIRSTNAME = *1* FIRSTEMP = 6	
Bed	Name of Patient	Pointer
1	Davis	8
2	Lane	9
3	———	*
4	Wallace	*
5	Goodman	10
6	———	7
7	———	3
8	Evans	5
9	Smith	4
10	Jones	2

Fig. A-23

BROKER FILE

Address	Broker Information	Pointer
123	Chandler,...	*3147*

CUSTOMER FILE

Address	Customer Information	Pointer
2315	Murphy,...	*3233*
2478	Brown,...	2315
2623	Zimmerman,...	*
3147	Applebaum,...	2478
3233	Winard,...	2623

Fig. A-24

	FIRSTNAME = 6 FIRSTEMP = 7	
Bed	Name of Patient	Pointer
1	Davis	8
2	Lane	9
3	———	*
4	Wallace	*5*
5	Zimmerman	*
6	Brown	1
7	———	3
8	Evans	10
9	Smith	4
10	Jones	2

Fig. A-25

Index